Published by Creative Design & Marketing Ltd
www.creativem.co.nz

Photography by Richard Brimer

Printed in China through Colorcraft Ltd, Hong Kong

ISBN 978-0-473-25788-0

Cover image: Carlos Pene, shearer, Andrew (Butch) Smith's woolshed, Central Hawke's Bay

CONTENTS

YOU MATTER

"You matter because you are you. You matter to the last moment of your life, and we will do all we can, not only to help you die peacefully, but also to live until you die."

Dame Cicely Saunders (1918 – 2005)
Founder of the Hospice movement.

'Living every moment' is the philosophy of Cranford Hospice and Hospice New Zealand. In essence, this means helping people to live every moment of their lives, in whatever way is important to them and for however long that may be.

For many, this will mean being made comfortable enough to remain in their own homes surrounded by their loved ones. For others, it may mean a few days or weeks of respite care at Cranford Hospice, allowing their caregivers to have a much-needed rest.

Living every moment might involve ticking something off a bucket list, planning a holiday, visiting a new grandchild or even marrying the love of their lives.

Every year with your support, Cranford Hospice helps around 600 people and their families to 'live every moment.' Our care extends beyond the physical needs of a person to their social, emotional, spiritual and practical needs, and to those of their family.

Cranford Hospice is truly grateful to Creative Marketing for initiating and managing this project and to Richard Brimer for his stunning photography. Their passion and vision has made the production of this book possible.

Finally, by purchasing this book, you are helping Cranford Hospice to continue the care. From the bottom of our hearts, we thank you for your support.

Warm wishes,

Helen Blaxland
General Manager
Cranford Hospice

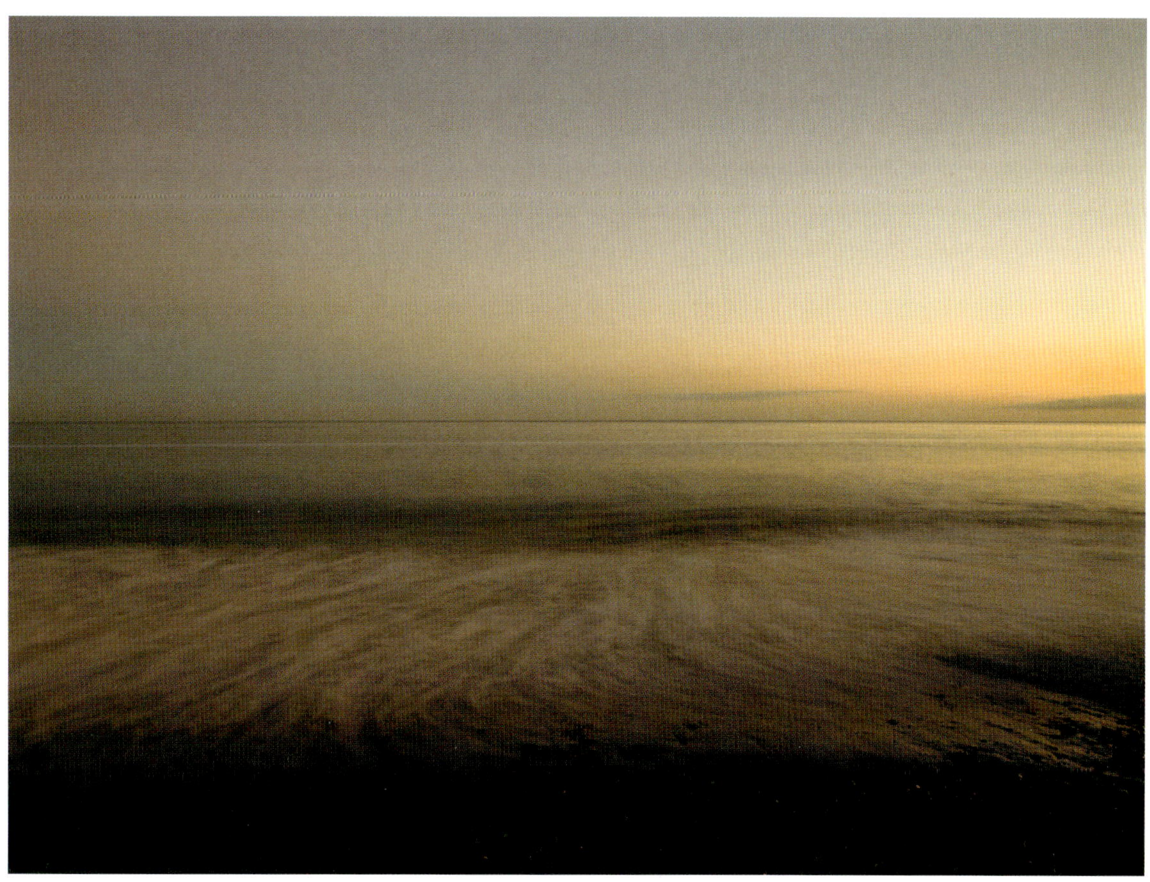

RICHARD BRIMER

Richard is one of Hawke's Bay's most well respected commercial and fine art photographers, travelling for commissions both nationally and internationally. His work has appeared in numerous publications and he is the author of nine books.

Richard's passion for photography and documenting a way of life is obvious and has resulted in his work being widely exhibited. A study on the thoughts and feelings of Hawke's Bay people titled "Portrait and Opinion" was a major exhibition at the Hastings City Art Gallery to commemorate the millennium. In 2010, a body of work titled 'Personals' – a collection of portraits taken of people from all walks of life was exhibited at the Hastings City Art Gallery and the New Zealand Portrait Gallery in Wellington.

As a third generation Hastings boy, Richard was brought up in Hastings and educated at Frimley School, Heretaunga Intermediate and St John's College. He has seen Hawke's Bay go from a sleepy rural backwater where the main employment was either at Watties or the freezing works, to an international tourist destination with huge investment in the wine industry and world class restaurants. "I remember when the local café scene consisted of The Hawke's Bay Farmers' Tearooms, The Dominion Restaurant and Caferama in Hastings; fine dining was the Travelodge or Mayfair Hotels; kids played at Fantasyland and the nightlife centred around the Valhalla nightclub."

Richard is passionate about Hawke's Bay and always gets that 'back home' feeling when driving into Te Awanga – his home of 30 years. "I love Hawke's Bay - to me it has the perfect balance of rural, uncluttered landscapes married with great cafés and restaurants, minimal traffic and good people!"

Richard's relationship with Cranford Hospice goes back twenty years with the death of his mother Valerie, after which he offered his photography services to the hospice. For the past ten years, Richard has supported the hospice by photographing the catalogue for the annual Cranford Hospice Charity Wine Auction.

This year, with the passing of his son Joseph, it seemed appropriate to produce a book about Hawke's Bay – an area Joseph loved. "I hope this book shows the real Hawke's Bay – our province's rich tapestries, something Joseph was passionate about." It was Joseph's wish to spend his final days at home in Te Awanga, and this was made possible with the care and support of Cranford Hospice. "Cranford supported our whole family through this difficult time, not only caring for Joseph, but providing unconditional support to myself, my wife Sue and our daughters Alice and Anna. I dedicate my work in this book to the memory of my son Joseph."

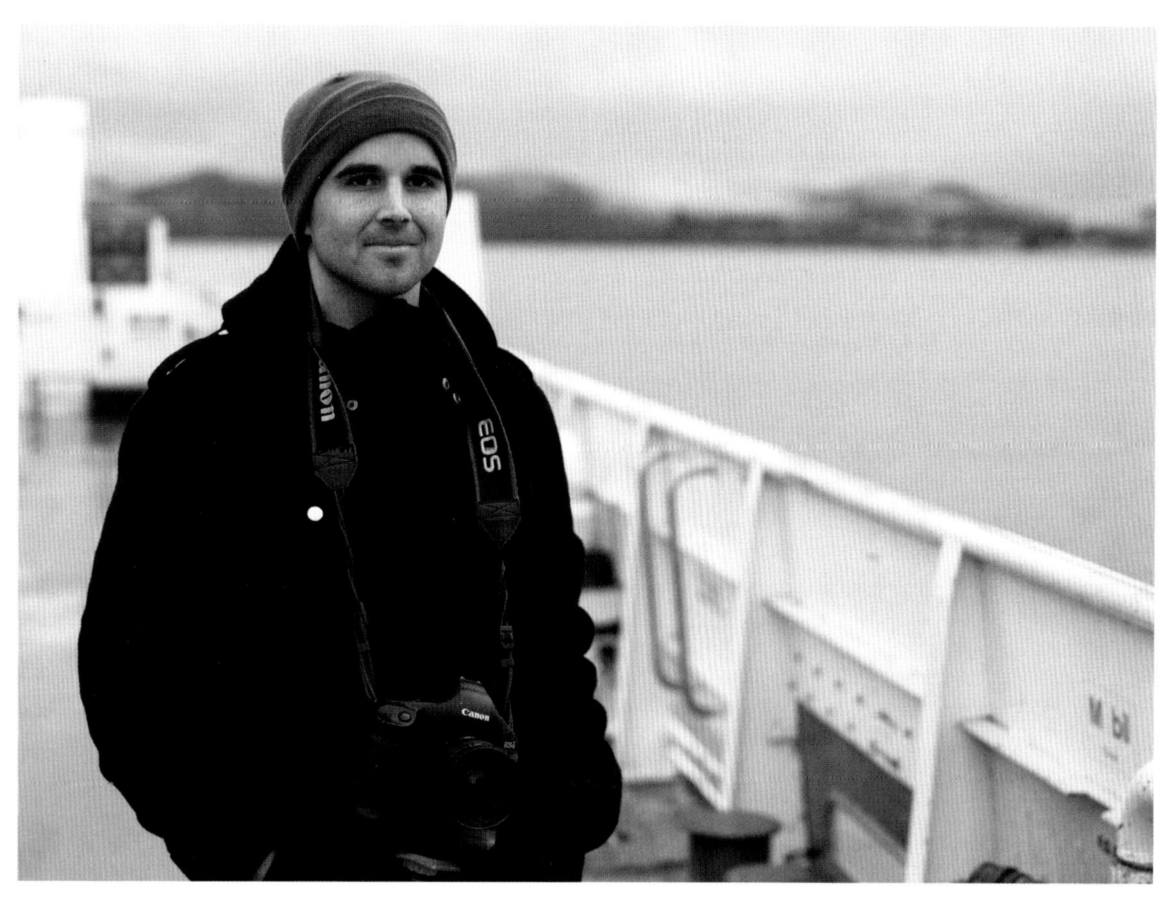

Joseph McGruddy Brimer
20 October 1987 - 12 January 2013

HAWKE'S BAY – PORTRAIT OF A PROVINCE

PULL up a chair and join us on an exciting journey through our region.

This amazing tapestry of land, sea, sky, architecture and people is known as Hawke's Bay, but to the locals, it's just called 'home'.

More than 150,000 people call Hawke's Bay home, of which around a quarter are Māori. As the indigenous population, Māori enjoy the status of being 'tangata whenua' (or 'people of the land'). Boasting an amazingly diverse landscape, Hawke's Bay stretches from the Wairoa District in the north to Central Hawke's Bay in the south, with the majority of residents living and working in the two main urban areas of Napier and Hastings.

So, what comes to mind when you think of Hawke's Bay? Is it the vast array of fresh fruit and vegetables grown on the fertile plains? The endless rows of well-tended grapevines? The miles of stunning coastline, punctuated by unspoilt beaches? Or perhaps it's the secluded lakes and rivers, the rugged mountains, rolling farmland or dense forest trails? For many, it's the memory of long hot summers with grass burnt yellow by the blistering sun, tanned kids playing barefoot and even the occasional tractor cruising the city streets!

Agriculture and horticulture form the backbone of the Hawke's Bay economy, but the region is also a hive of industry and innovation. Progressive new businesses and cottage industries are springing up as entrepreneurs and disillusioned city-dwellers flock to the region to enjoy a better lifestyle.

Hawke's Bay has also grown into a major tourist destination with its food and wine attracting international acclaim. Award-winning wines, cosmopolitan cuisine and some of the best coffee in the world can be found everywhere from humble cafés to winery restaurants and sharp urban eateries.

Attractions such as Splash Planet, the iWay cycle trails, Cape Kidnappers and Marine Parade are frequented by locals and visitors, young and old. World renowned Spanish Mission and Art Deco architecture attract thousands of tourists every year, while events such as farmers' markets, sporting fixtures and winery concerts keep them coming back for more.

This amazingly diverse province may only be 14,000 square kilometres in size, but with so much to offer, it certainly punches above its weight. Hawke's Bay cleverly combines big-city sophistication with small-town charm and a relaxed, chilled-out lifestyle second to none.

It's a heady combination and utterly addictive, both to visitors and to those of us lucky enough to call Hawke's Bay 'home'.

HE AHA TE MEA NUI O TE AO?
HE TANGATA! HE TANGATA! HE TANGATA!

WHAT IS THE MOST IMPORTANT THING IN THE WORLD?
IT IS PEOPLE! IT IS PEOPLE! IT IS PEOPLE!

 French chocolatier, Anissa Talbi Dobson, Te Awanga

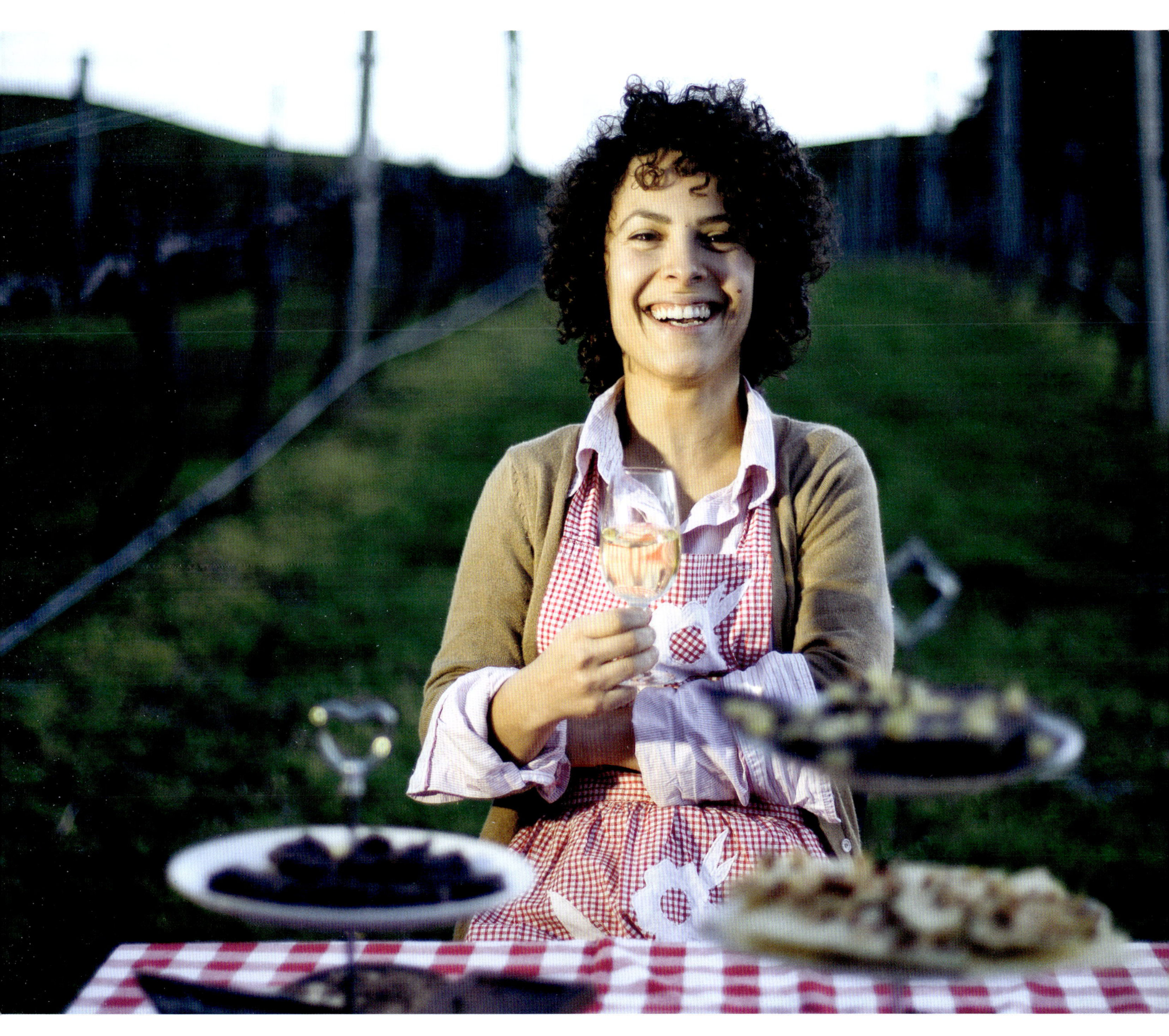

PORTRAIT OF OUR PEOPLE

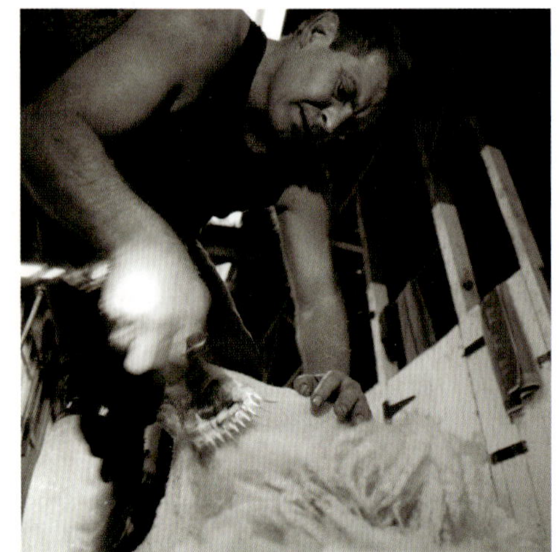

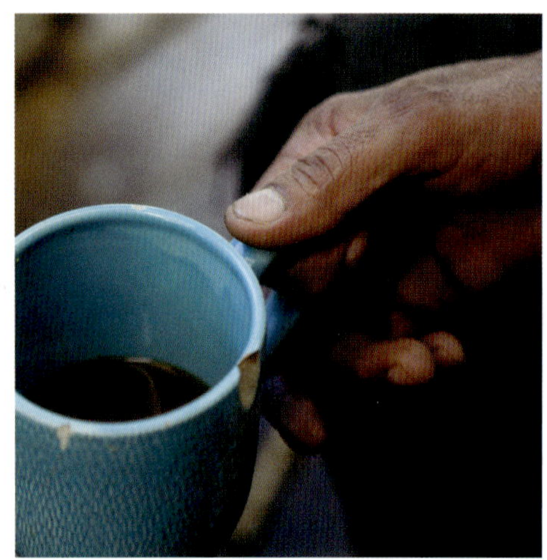

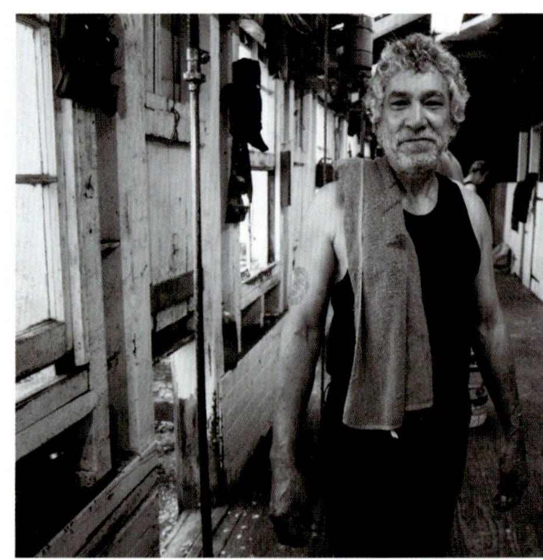

 Shearing gang, Andrew (Butch) Smith's woolshed, Central Hawke's Bay

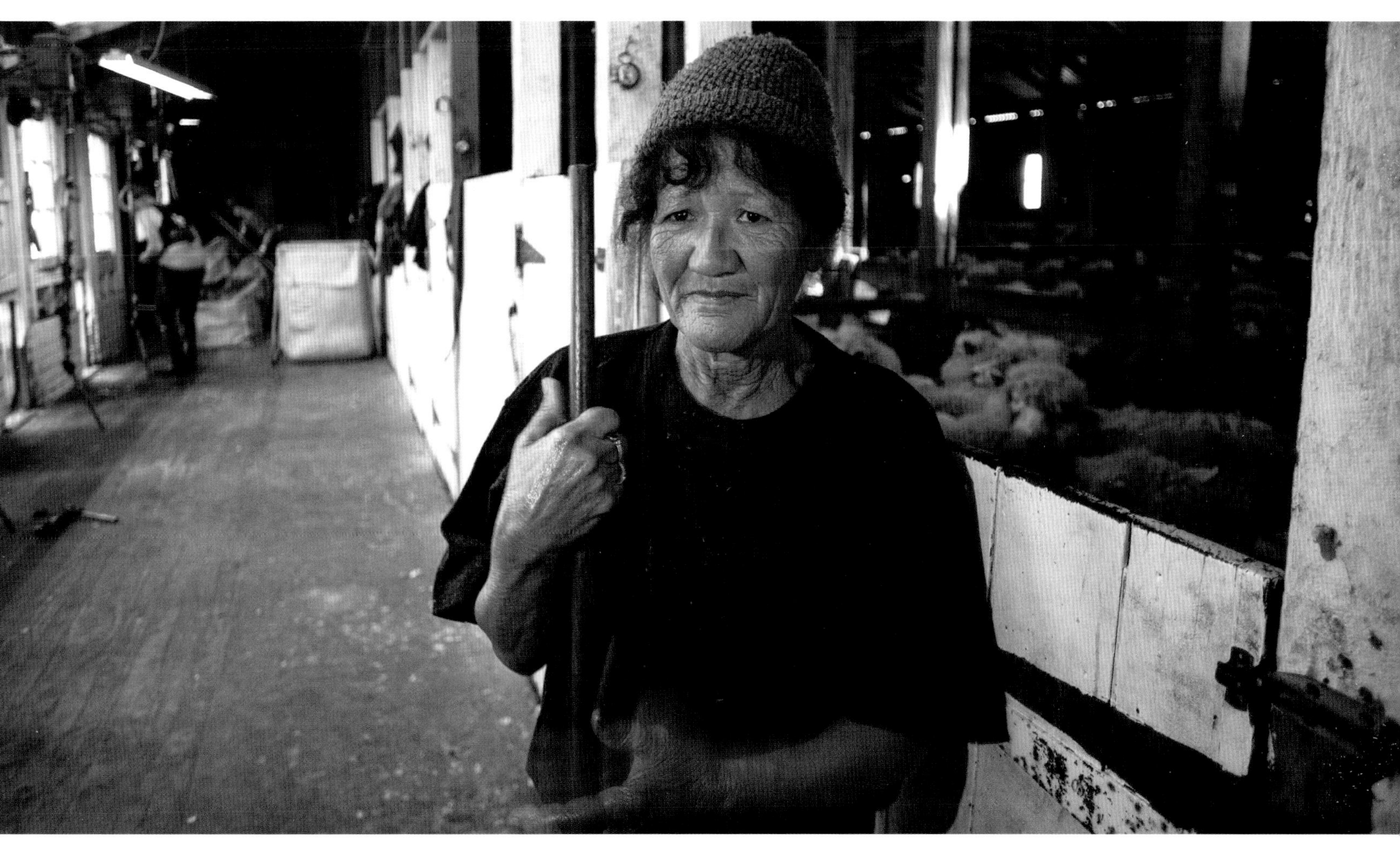

Mere Waikato, rousie (woolhandler), Andrew (Butch) Smith's woolshed, Central Hawke's Bay

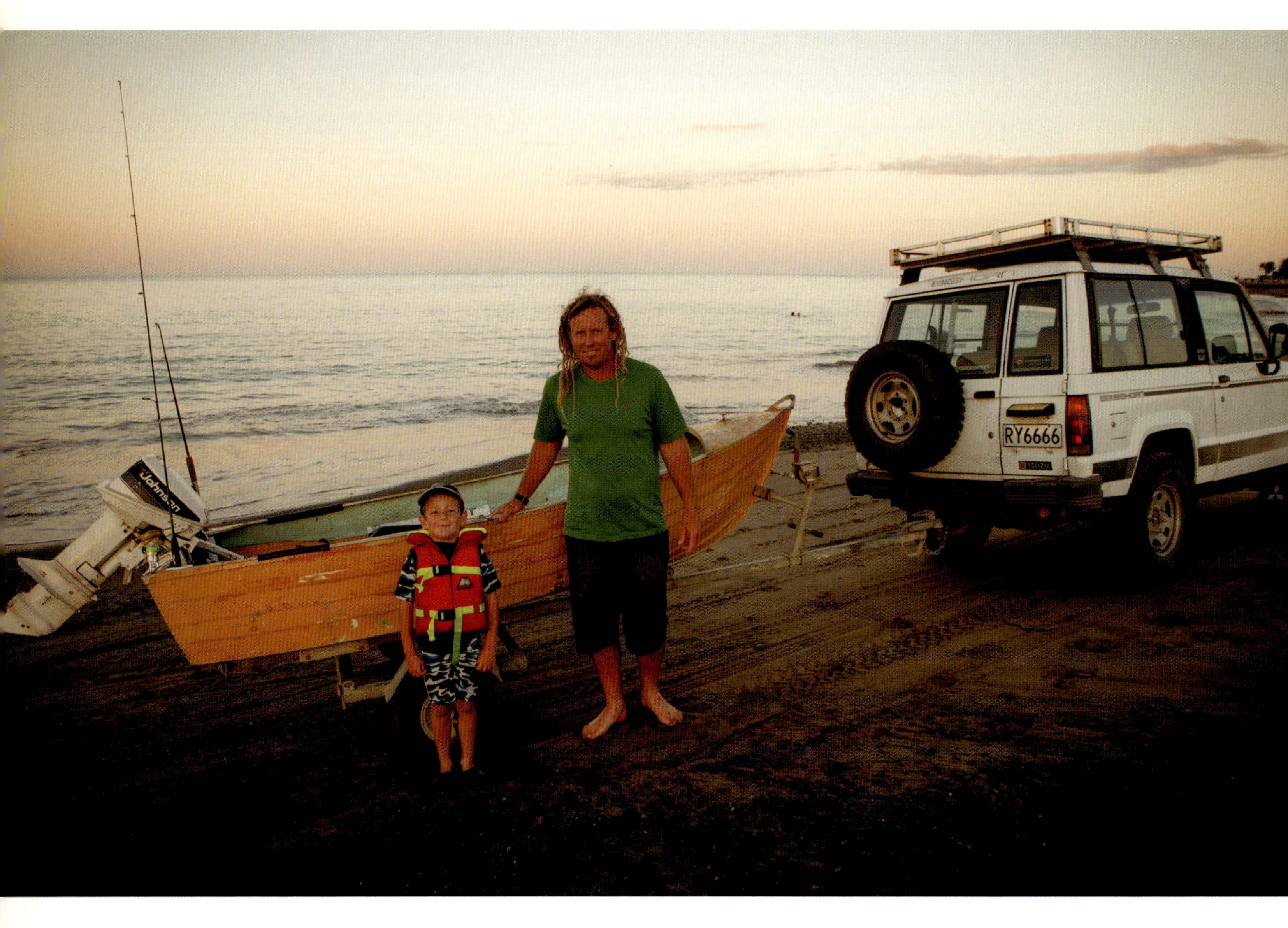

 Simon Hinton helping George Chote at the end of a day's fishing, Te Awanga

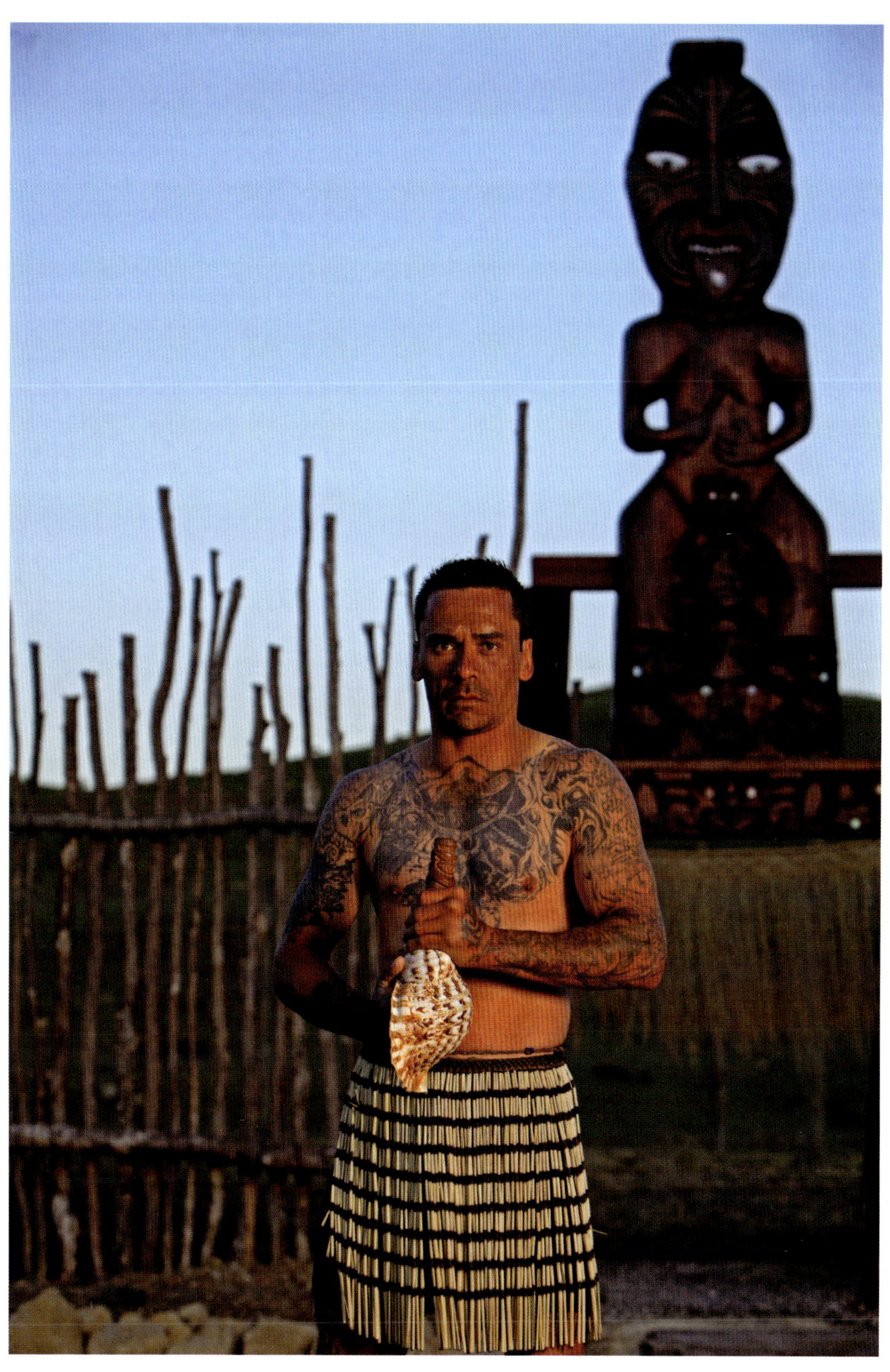

Murray August, Waimarama Māori Tours

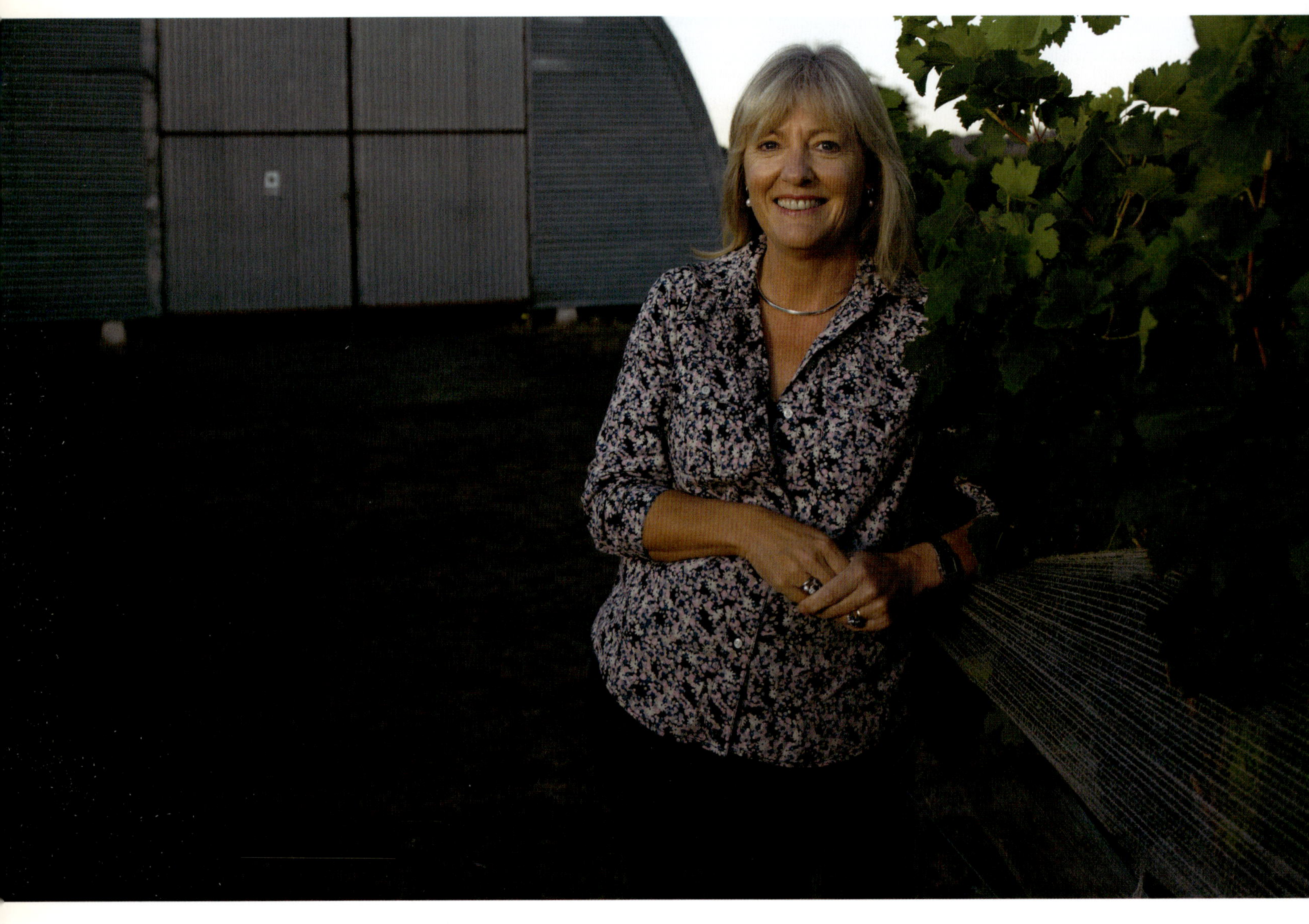

 Kate Radburnd, Winemaker and Managing Director, Pask winery, Hastings

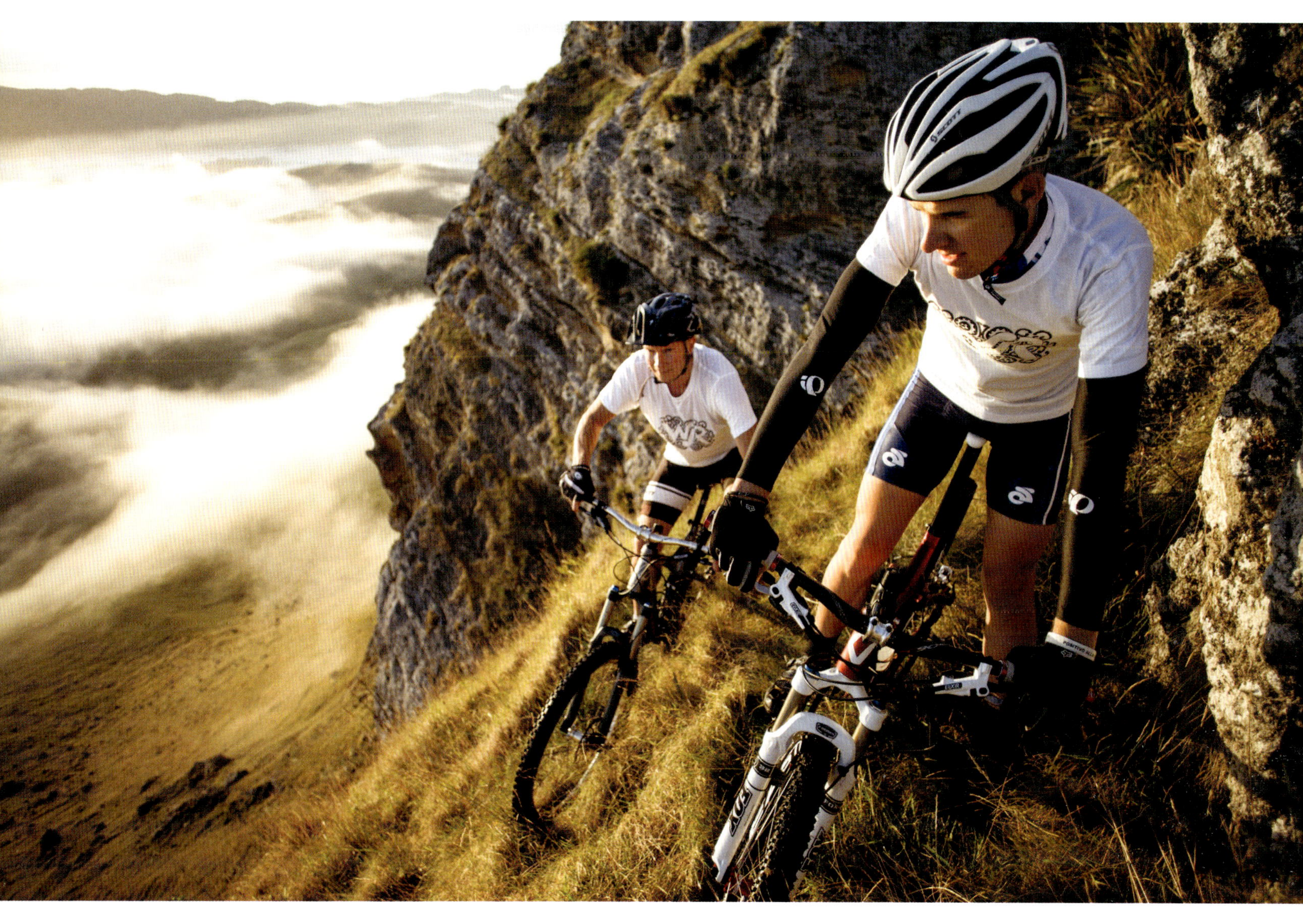

Ashton Ireland and Josh Page, Te Mata Peak, Havelock North

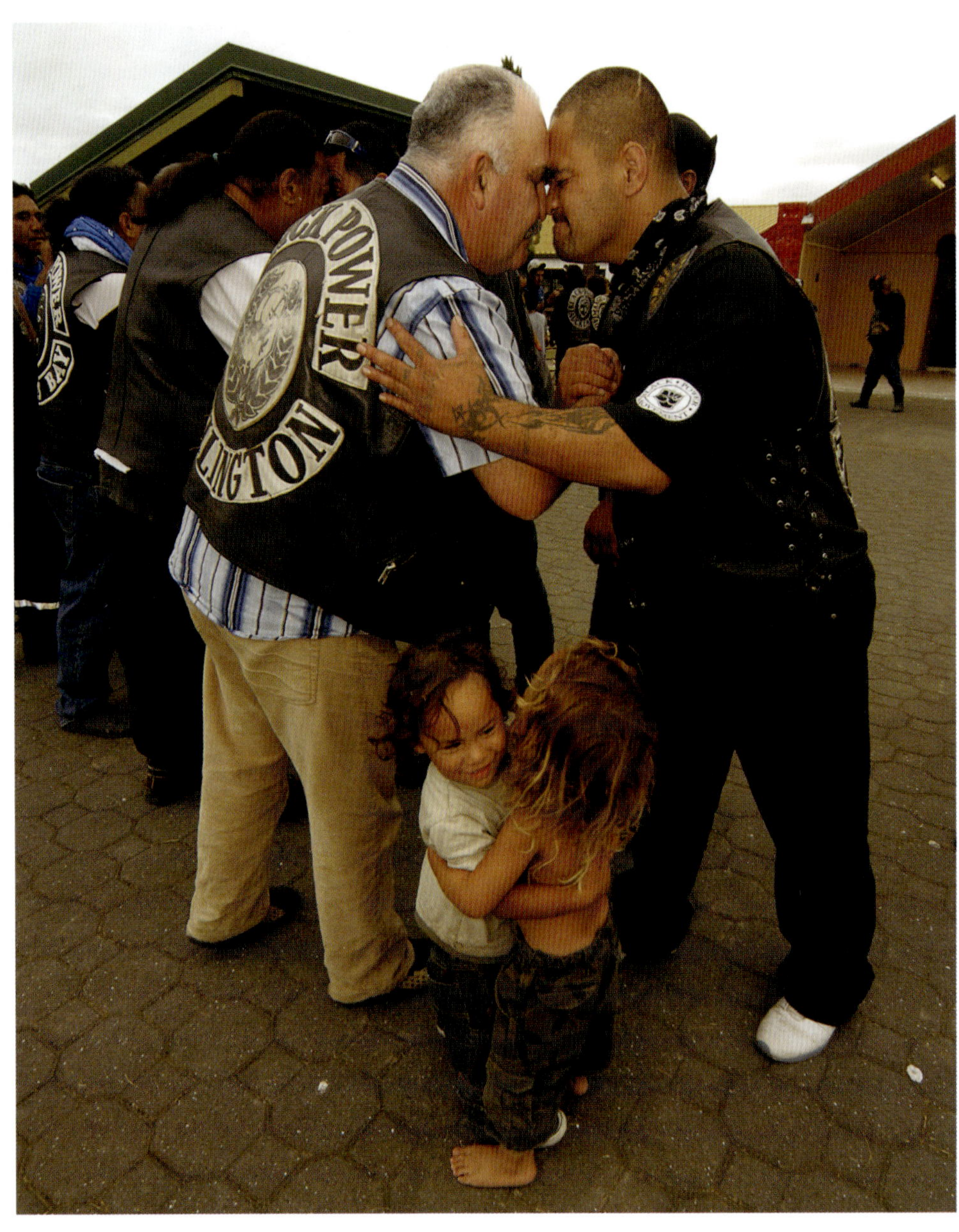

 Whakawhanaungatanga: families connecting and reconnecting, Black Power 35th anniversary, Hamuera Marae, Moteo

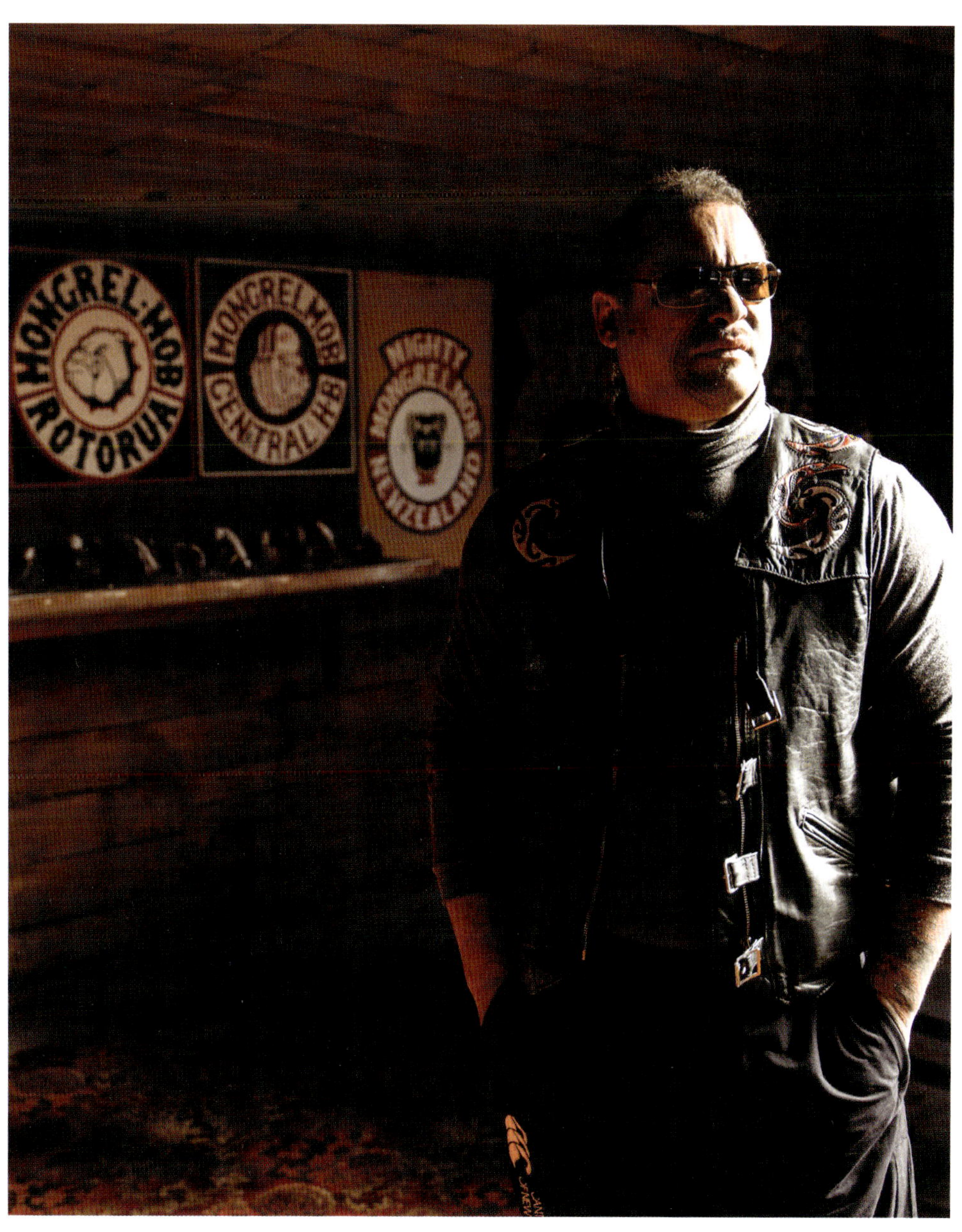

Whānau Development Coordinator, Rex Timu, Mongrel Mob headquarters, Camberley, Hastings

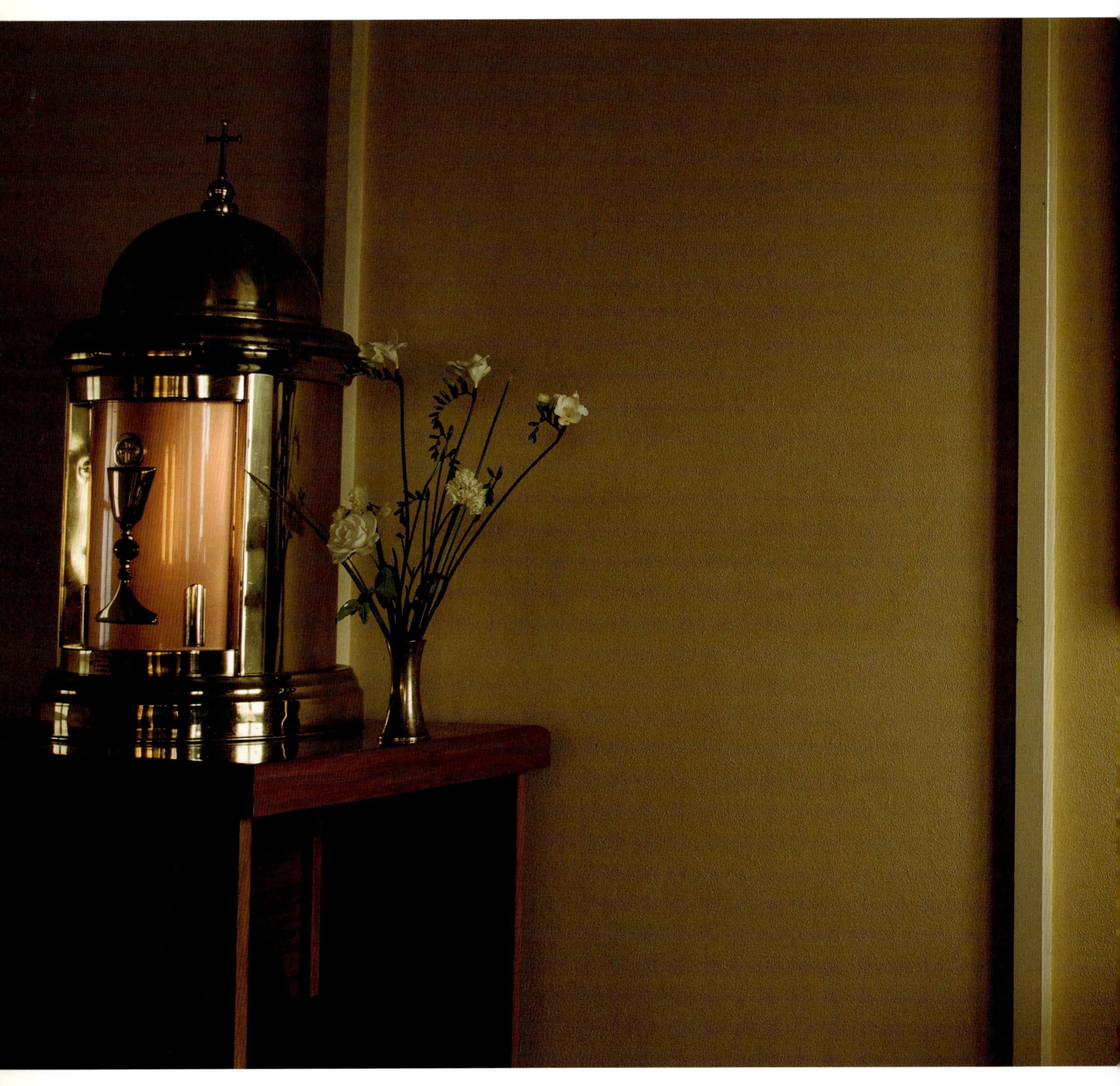

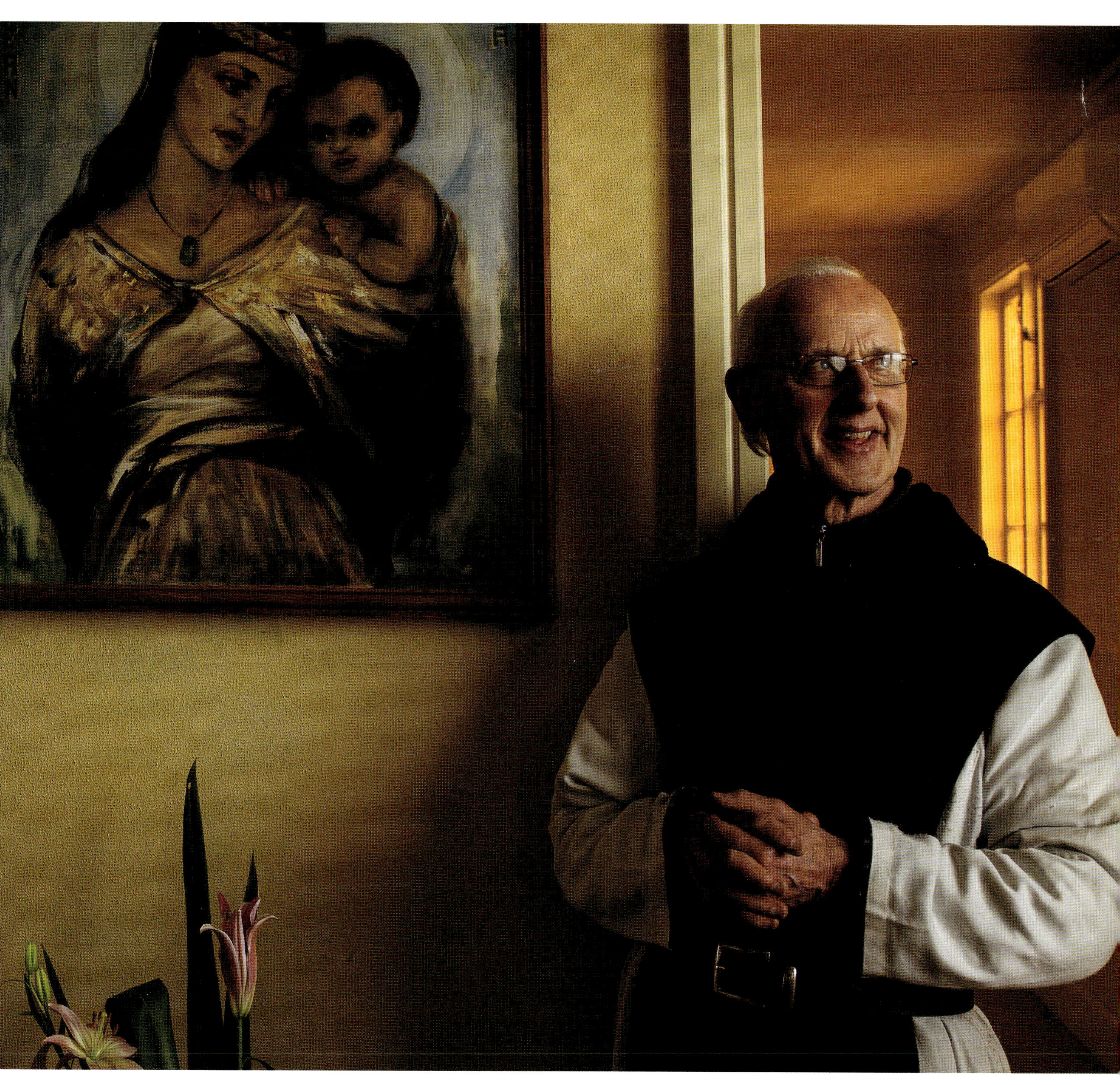

Father Niko Verkley, Southern Star Abbey, Kopua, Takapau, Central Hawke's Bay

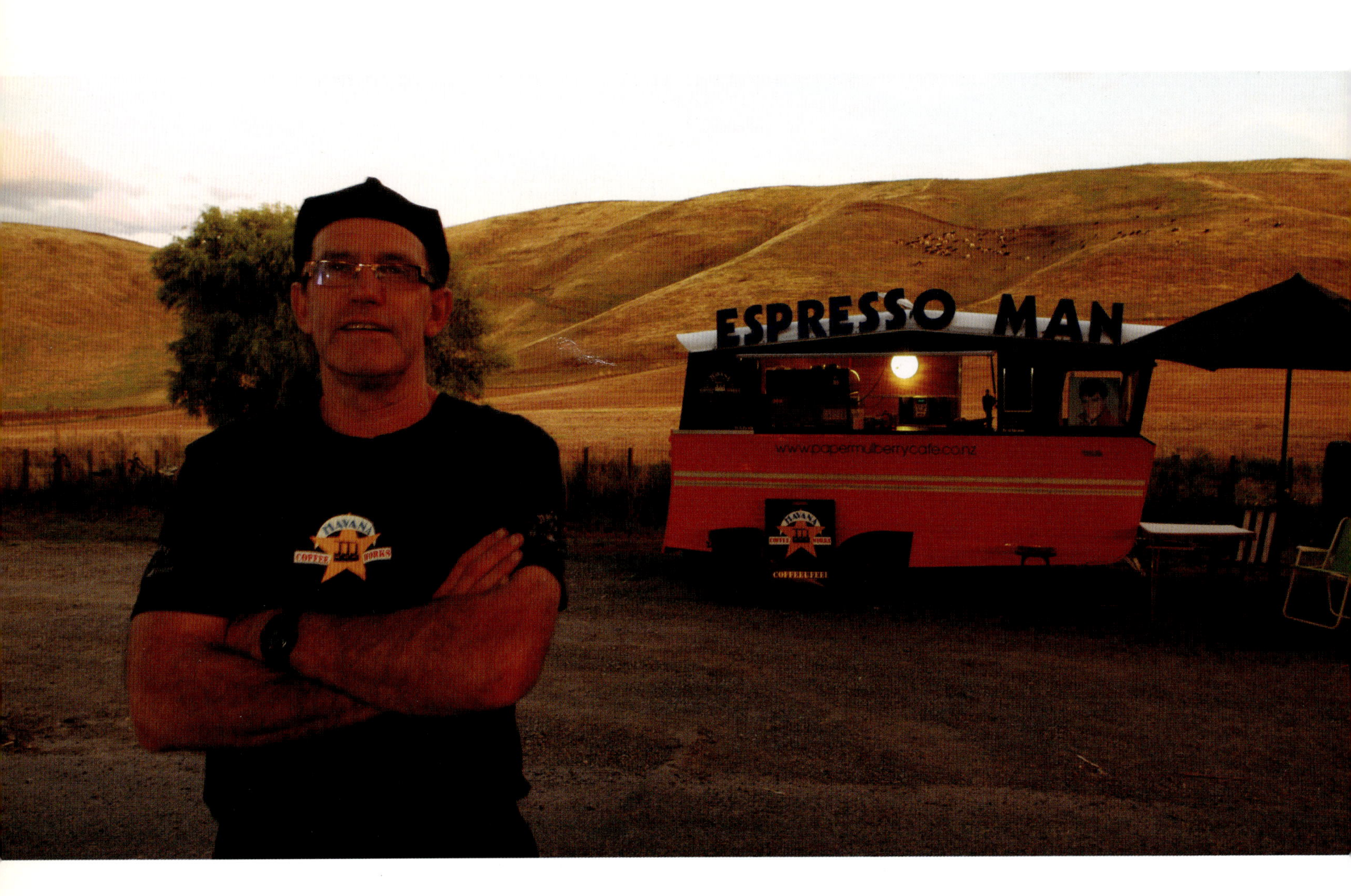

 Dave Robertson, the 'Espresso Man', Central Hawke's Bay

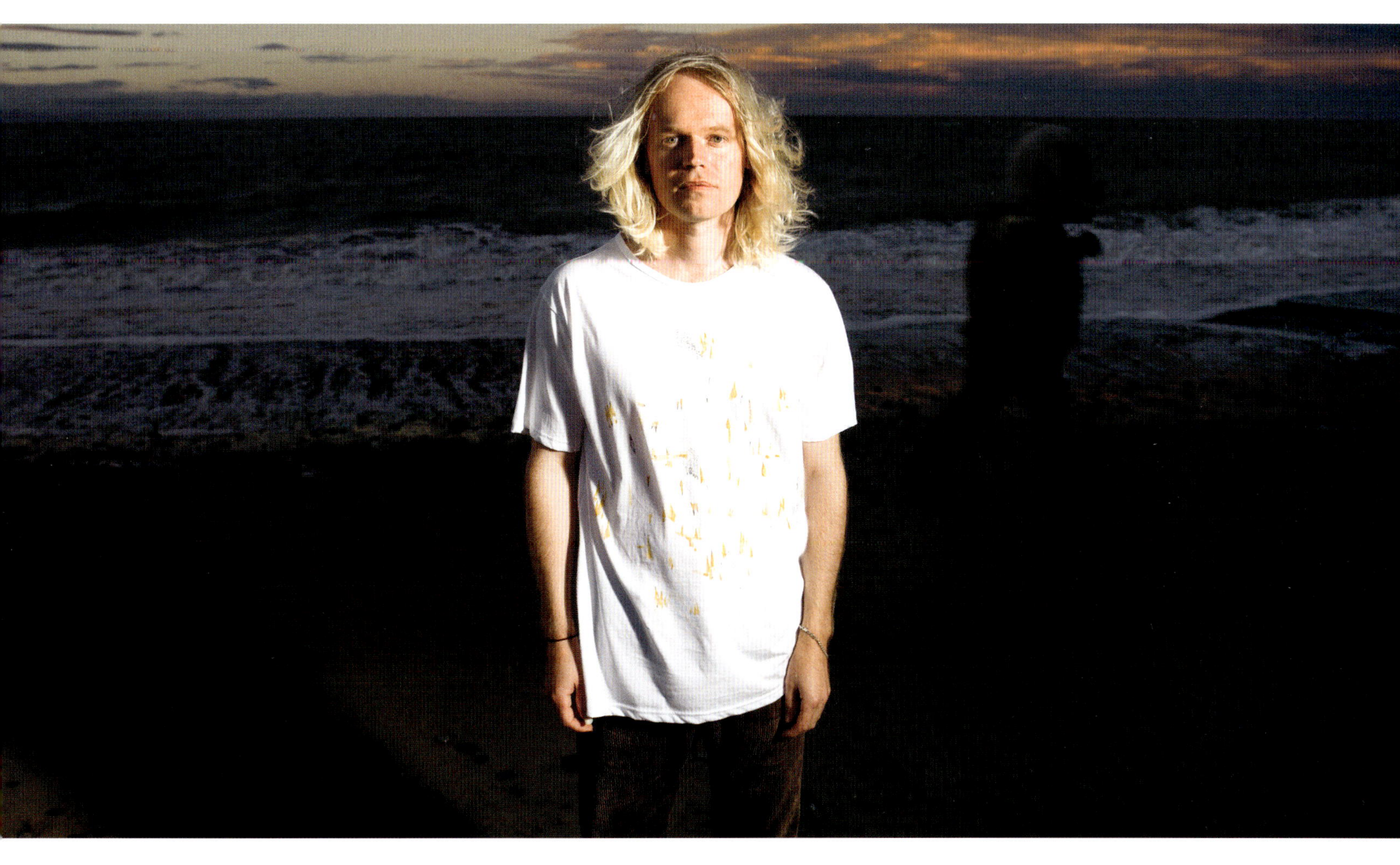

Connan Hosford, a.k.a musician Connan Mockasin, Te Awanga

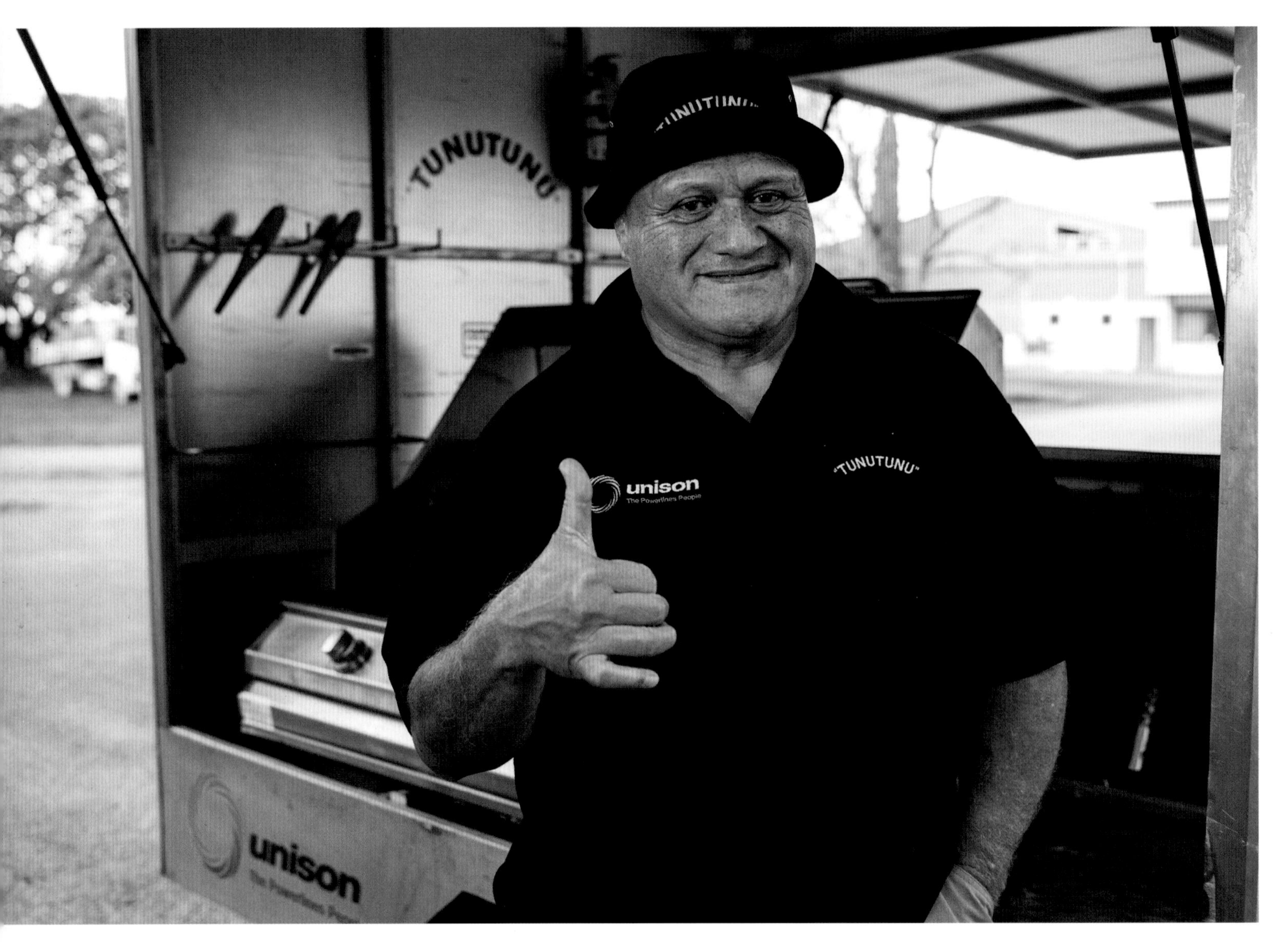

 Hastings District Councillor Henare O'Keefe with his custom-built mobile barbecue, 'Tunutunu'

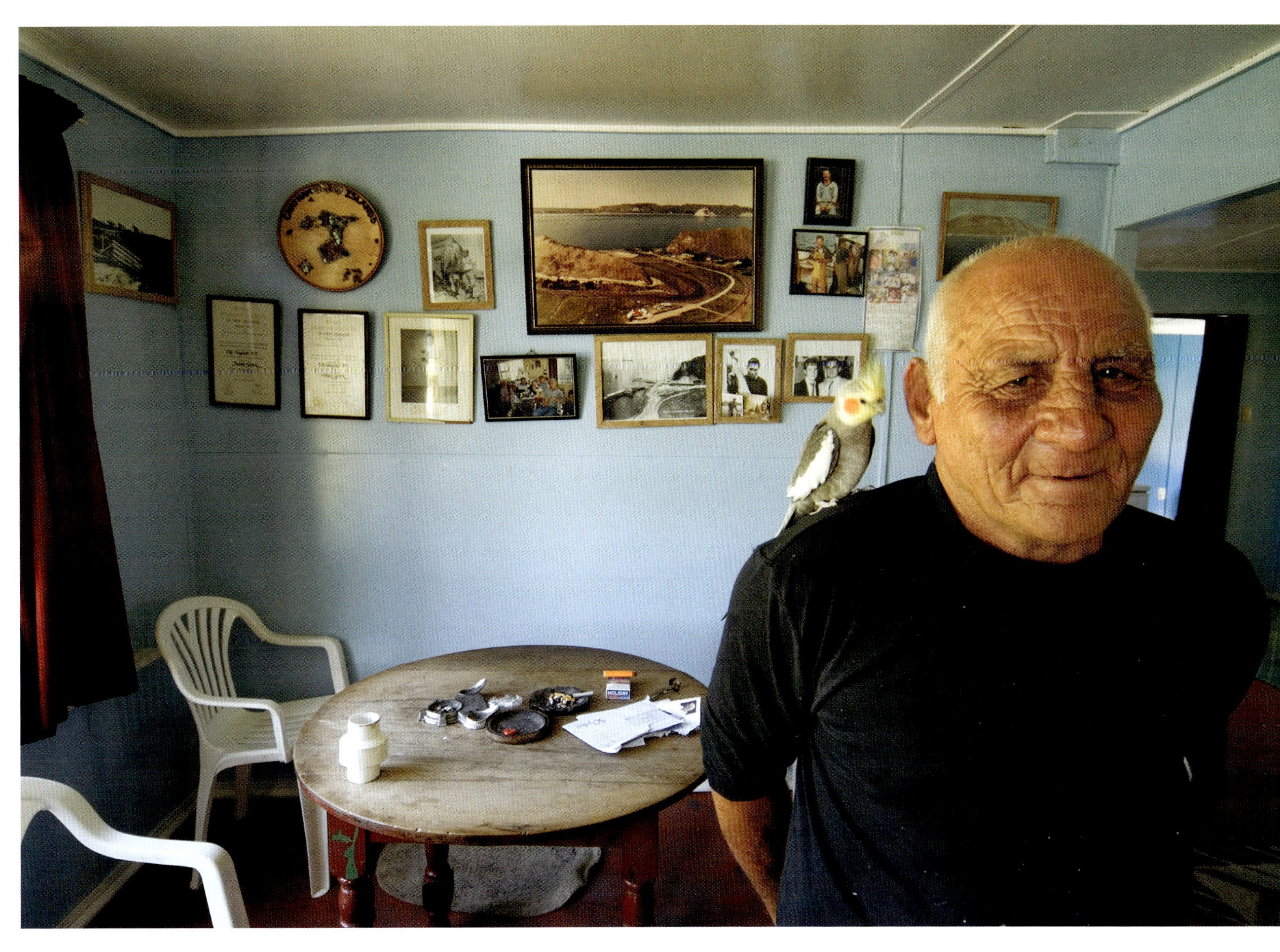

Crayfisherman James Spark and friend, Mahia Peninsula, Northern Hawke's Bay

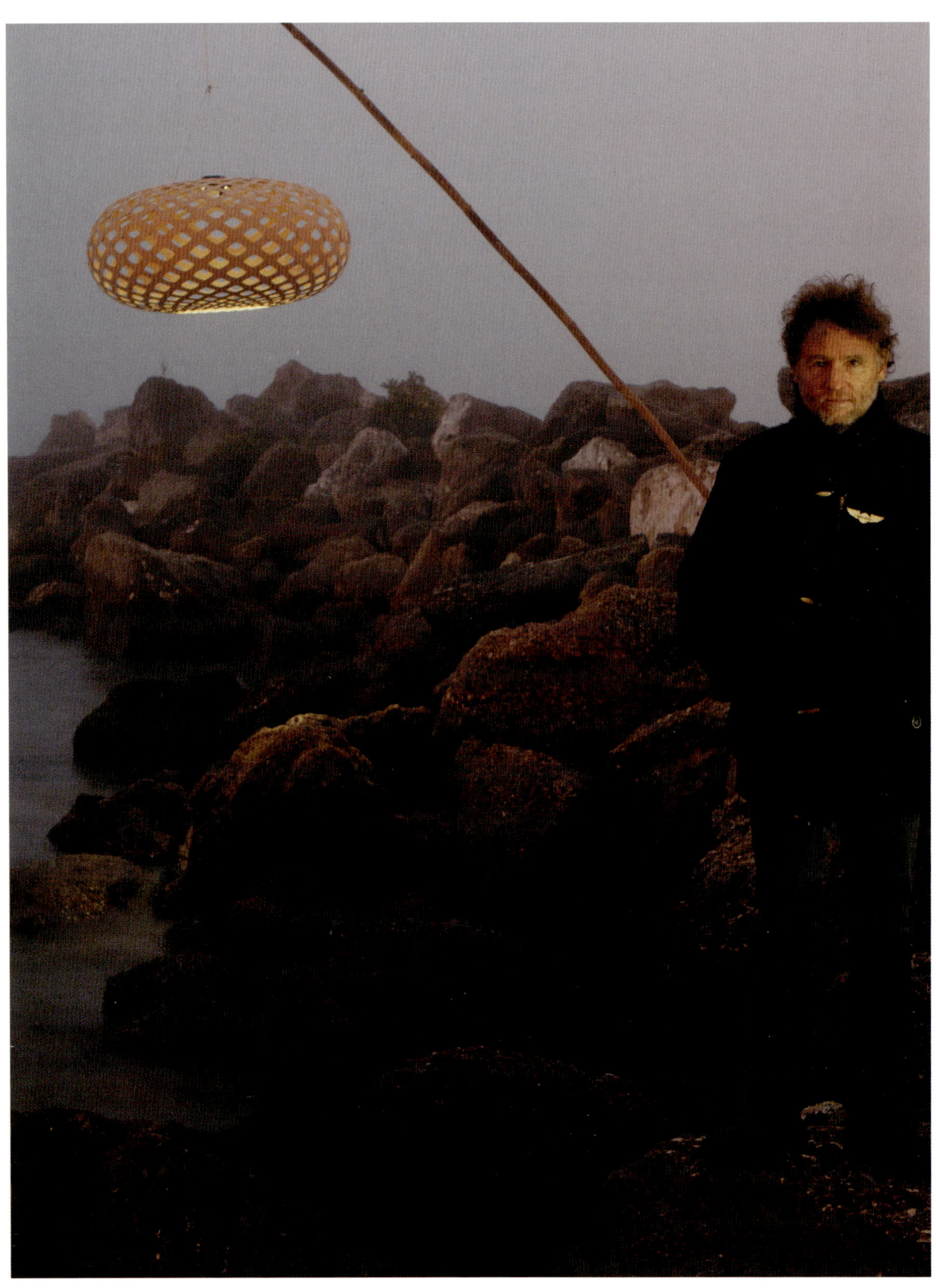

 Internationally-renowned designer, David Trubridge

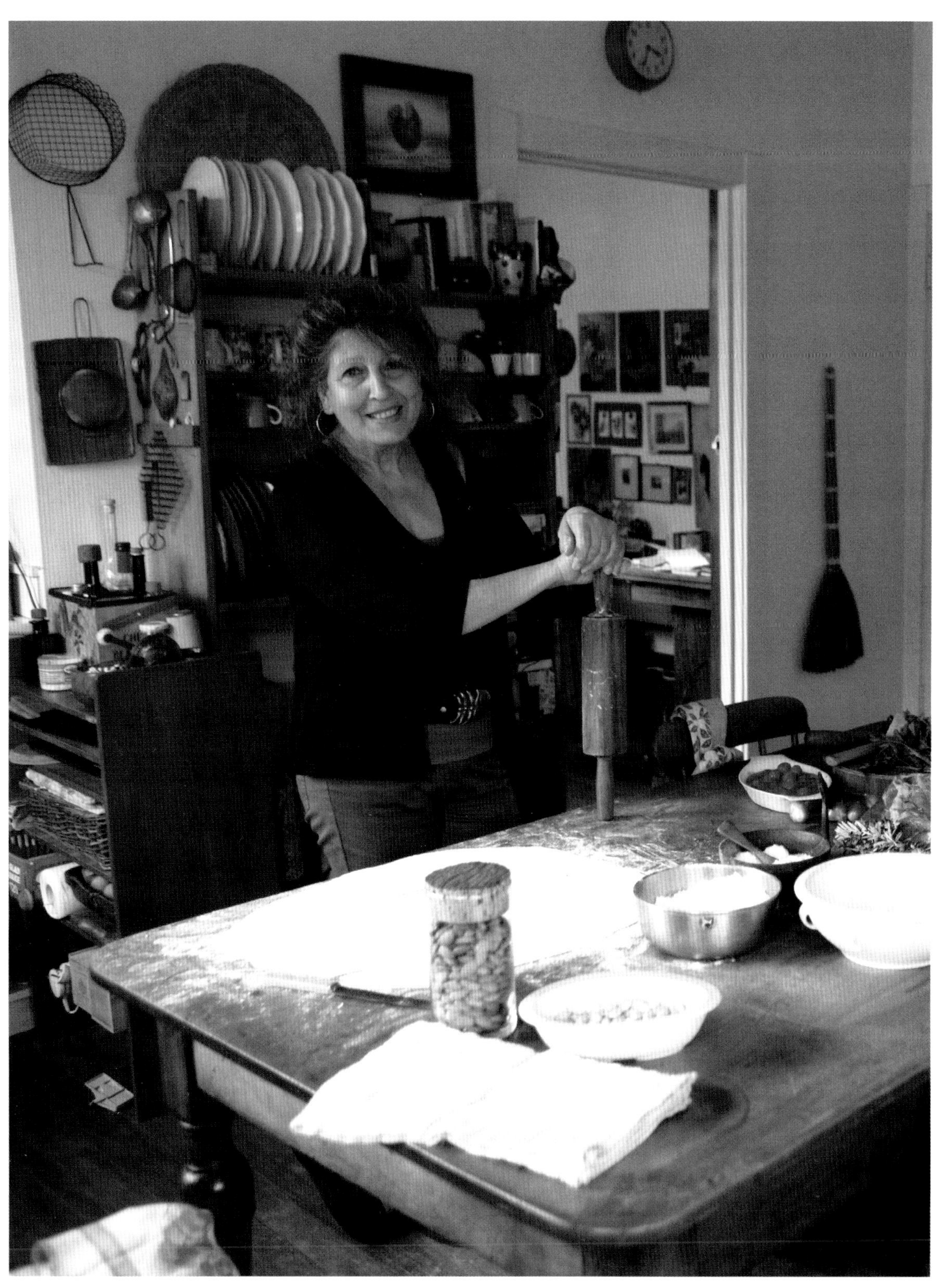

Italian artisan chef, Raffaella Turner, Havelock North

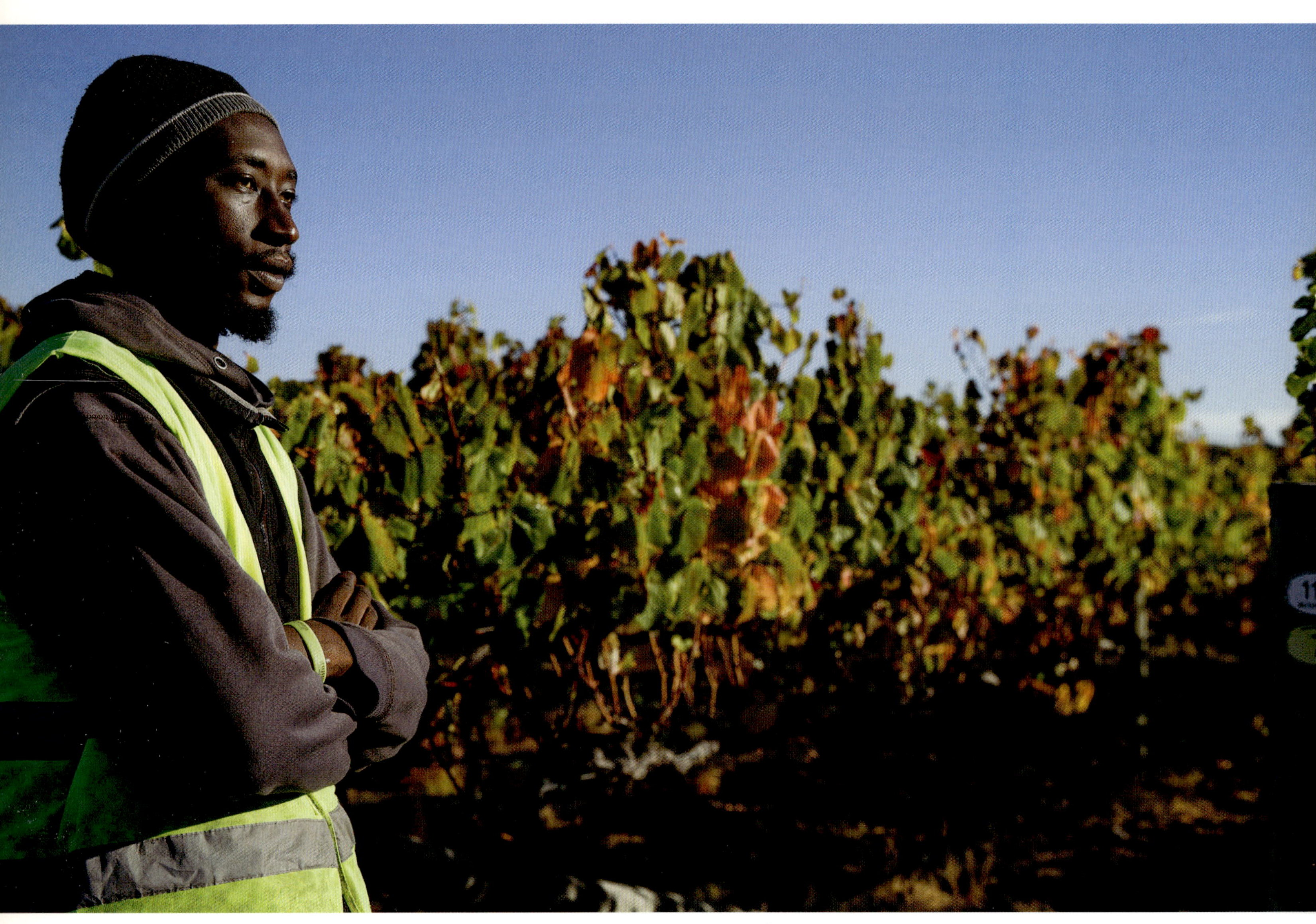

 Coffee break, vineyard worker, Sacred Hill Winery, Hastings

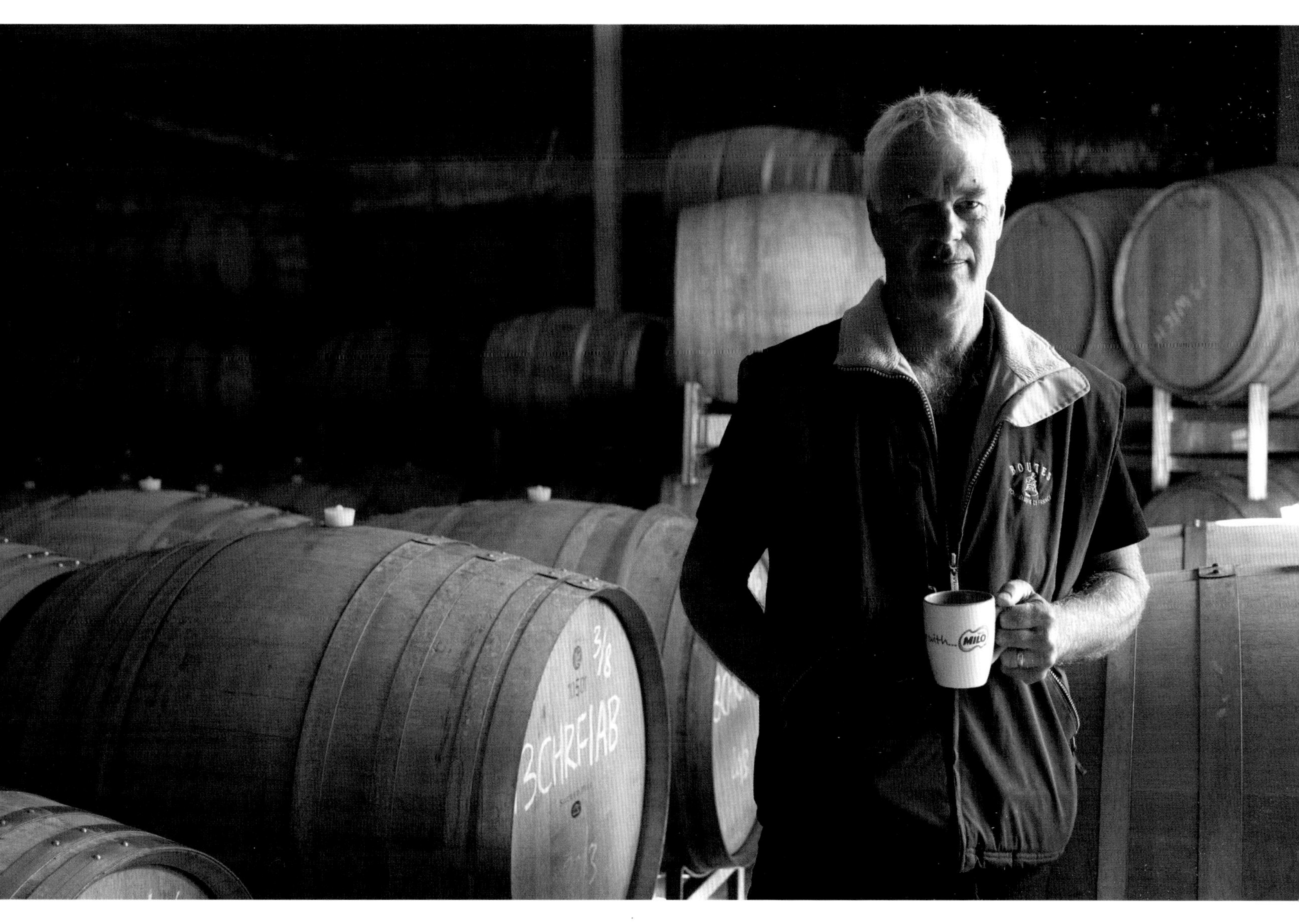

Coffee break, Tony Bish, Chief Winemaker, Sacred Hill Winery, Hastings

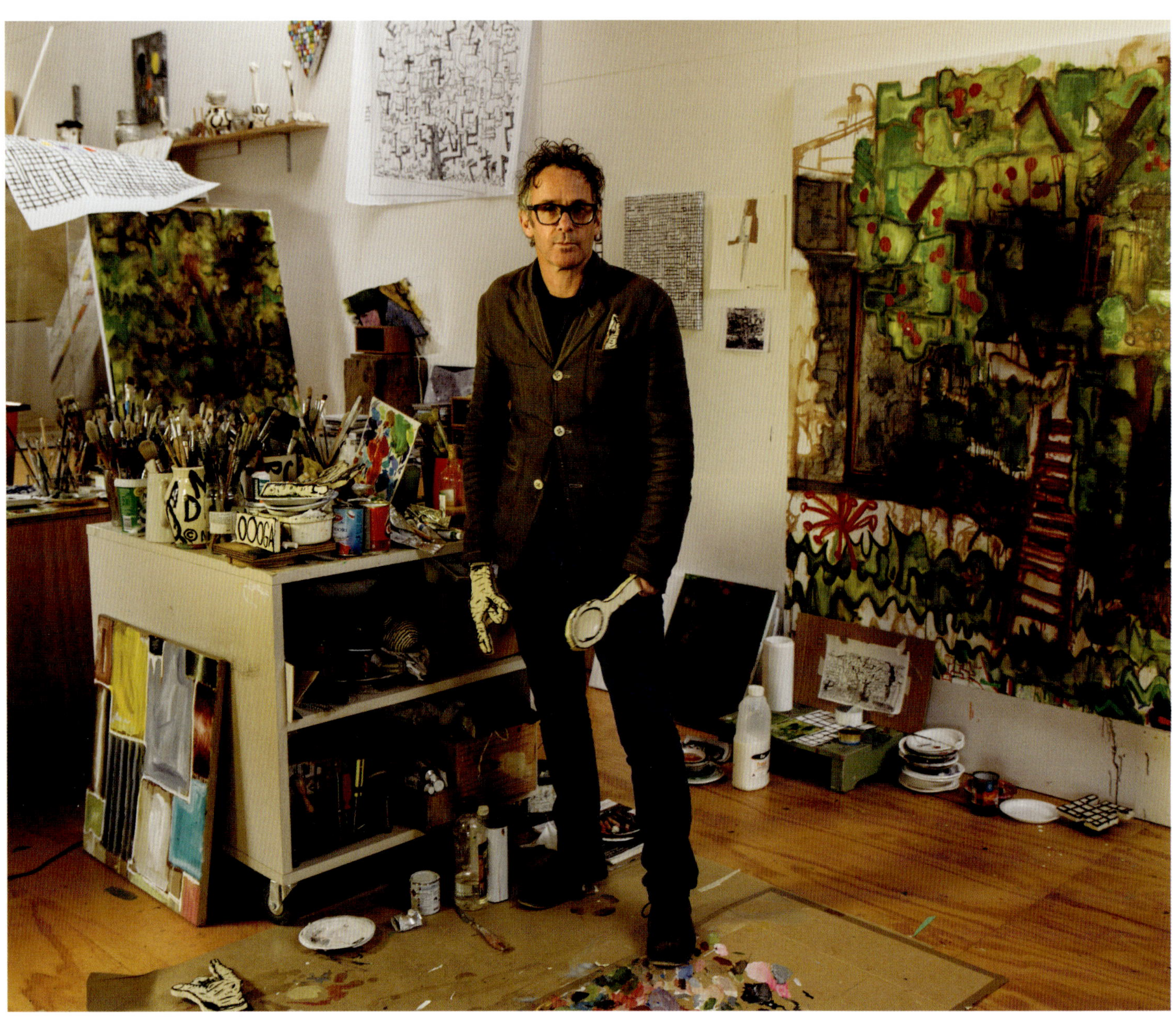

 Artist Martin Poppelwell at his studio on Napier Hill

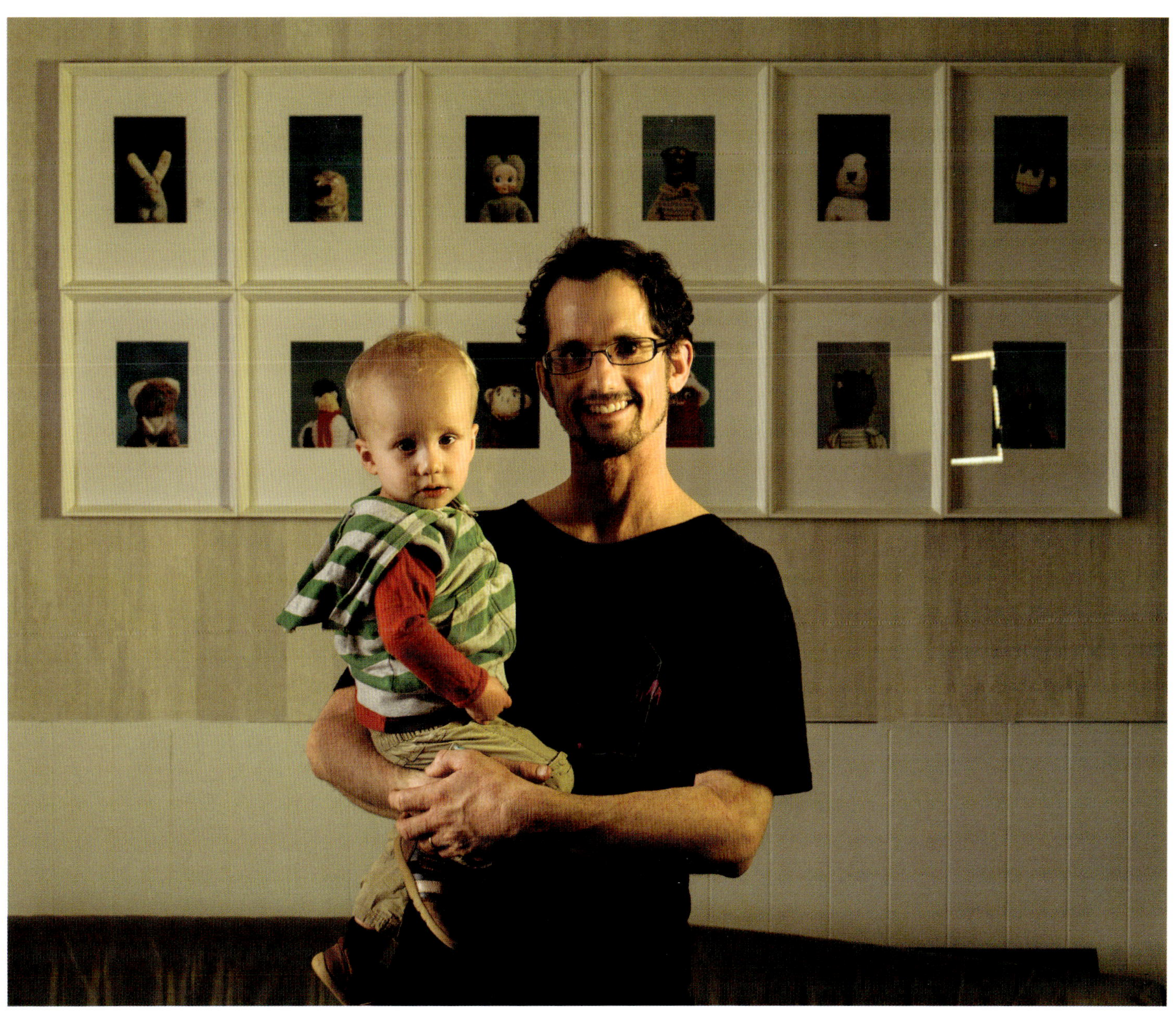

Artist Ben Pearce with son Oscar, Ahuriri, Napier

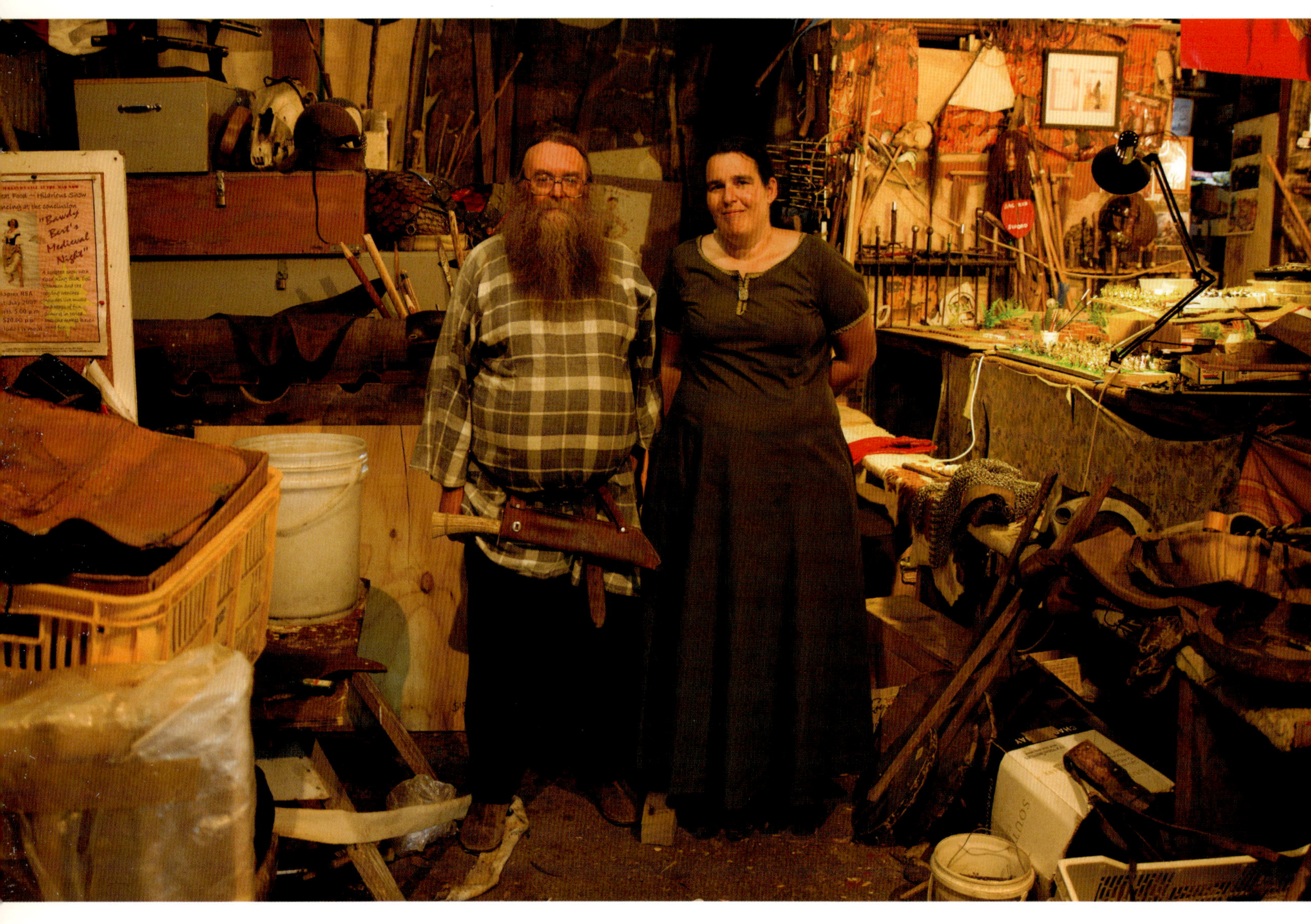

 Michael Webb and Mary Stephenson, Company of the Sacred Sword, Napier Medieval Club

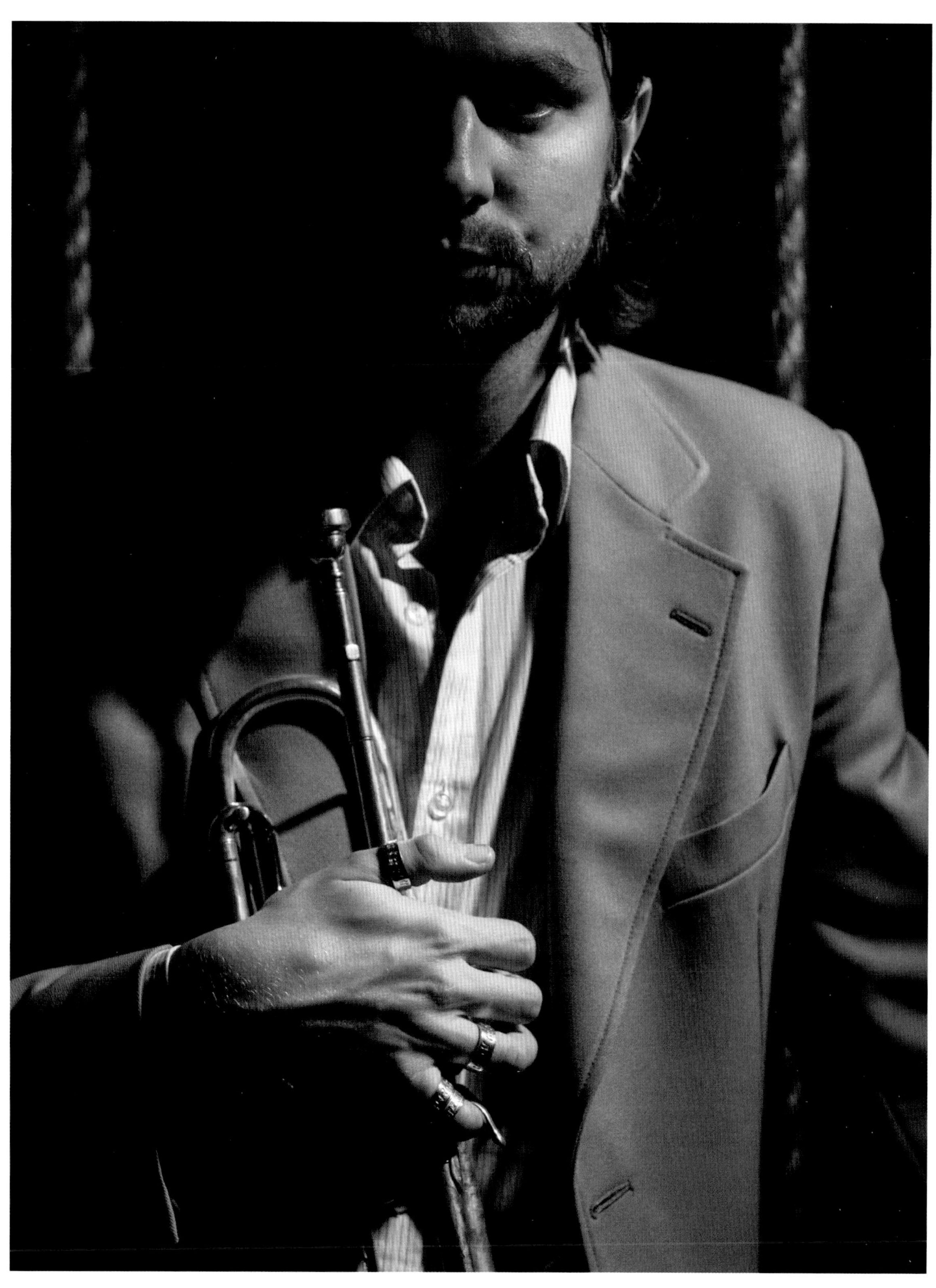

Musician Matt Mear, Hawkes Bay Opera House

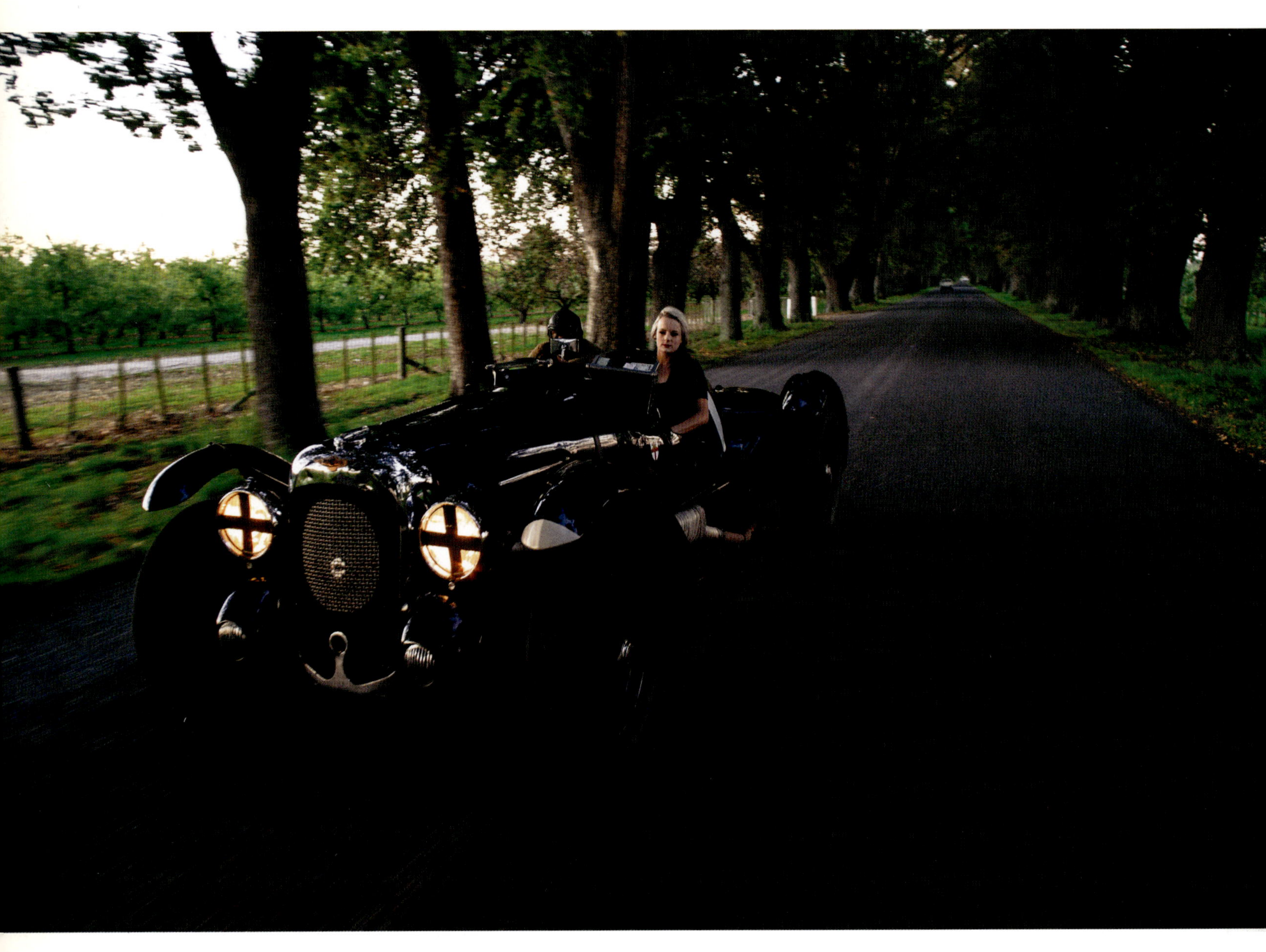

 Olive Holland in a 1938 Lagonda V12 Le Mans, Oak Avenue, Hastings

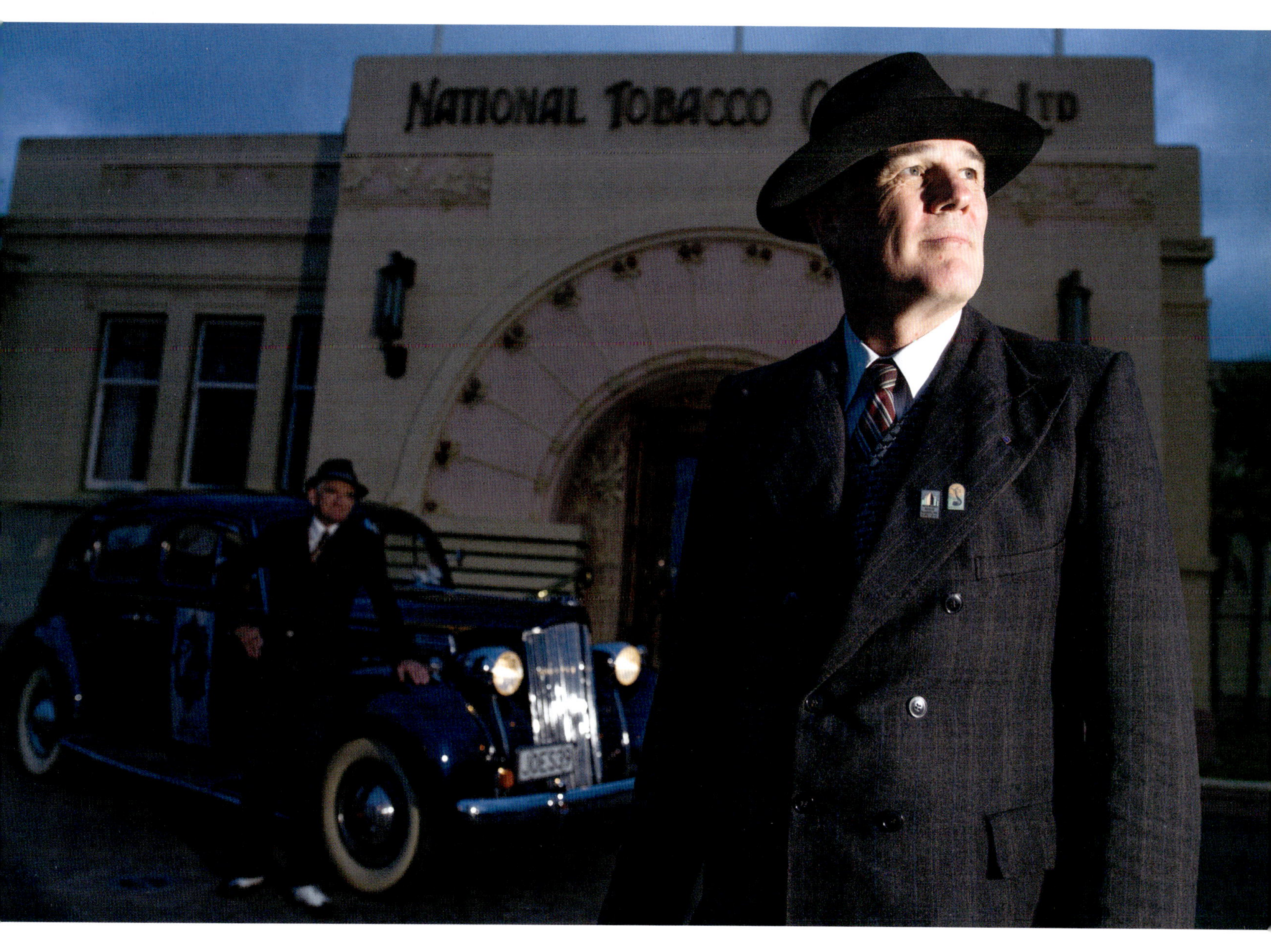

Graham Holley and Tony Mairs (background), with a 1939 Packard Six, Napier

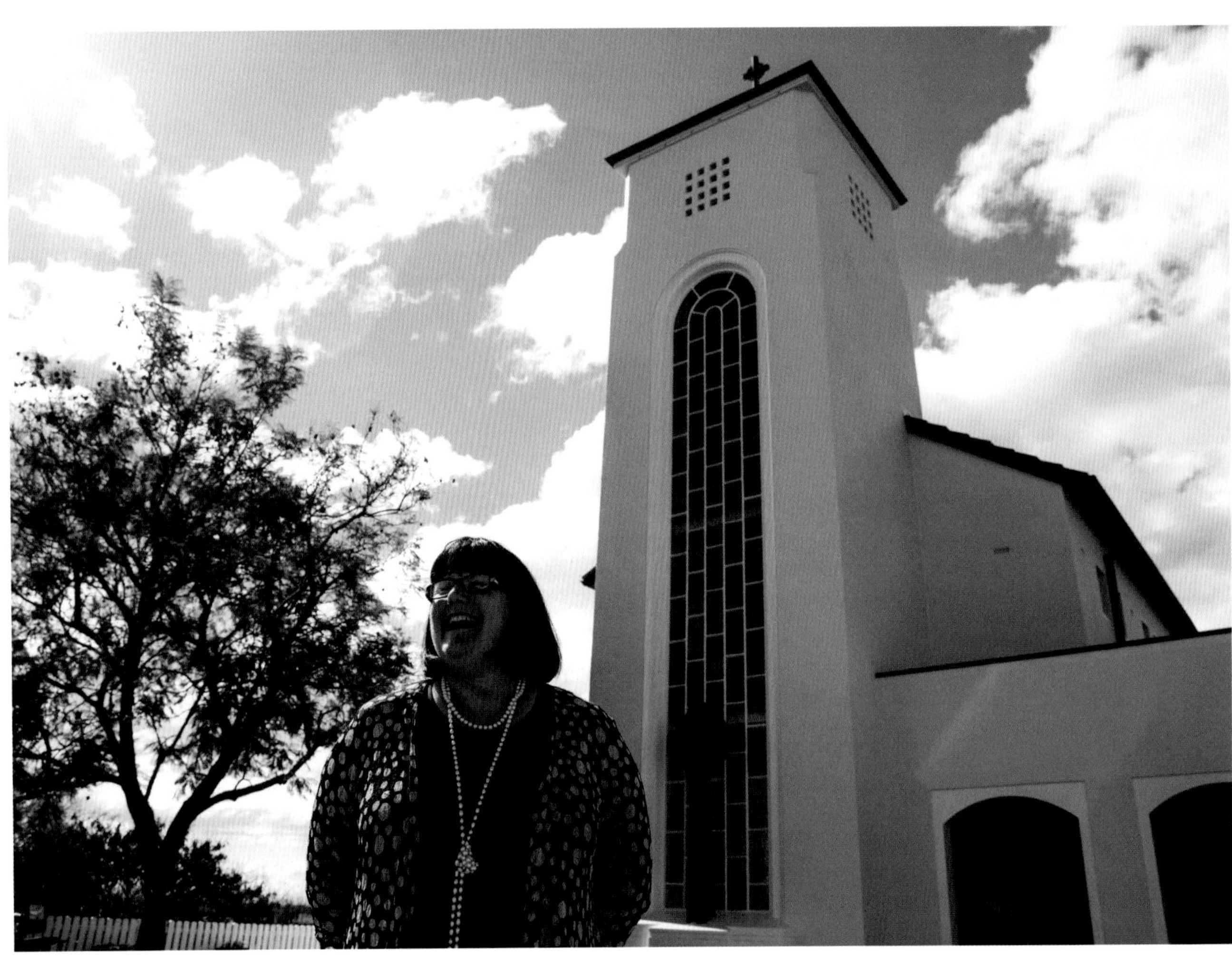

34 Pauline Duthie, Principal, Iona College, Havelock North

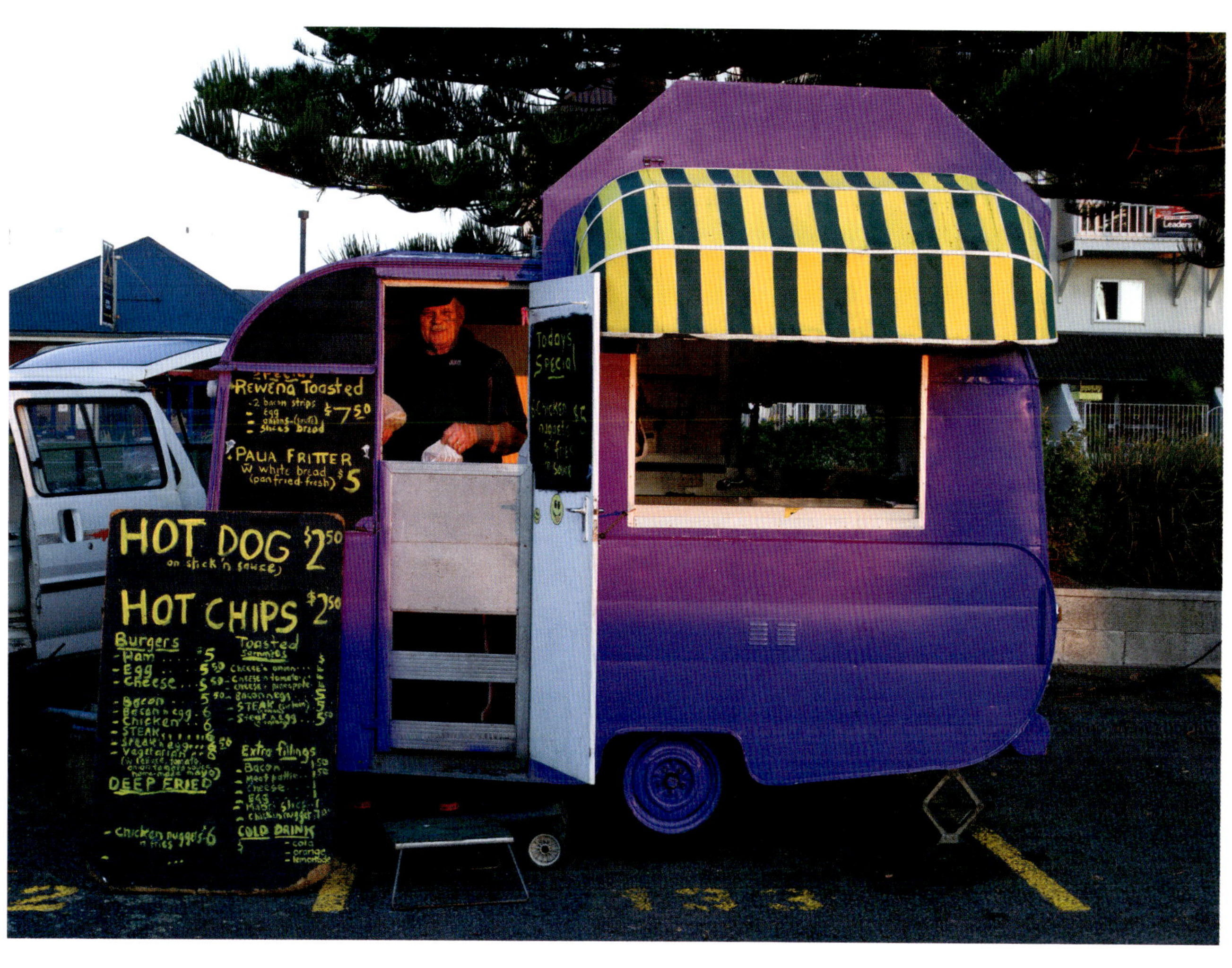
Rewena Toasted
2 bacon strips
$7.50
Paua Fritter
w white bread
(pan fried fresh) $5
Todays Special
HOT DOG $2.50
on stick 'n sauce)
HOT CHIPS $2.50
Burgers
Ham $5
Egg $5.50
Cheese $5.50
Bacon $5.50
Chicken $6
Steak
Toasted Sammies
Extra fillings
Bacon
Cheese
DEEP FRIED
COLD DRINK
cola
orange

WHATUNGARONGARO TE TANGATA TOI TU WHENUA.

AS MAN DISAPPEARS FROM SIGHT, THE LAND REMAINS.

 Driveway at first light, Haumoana, Hawke's Bay

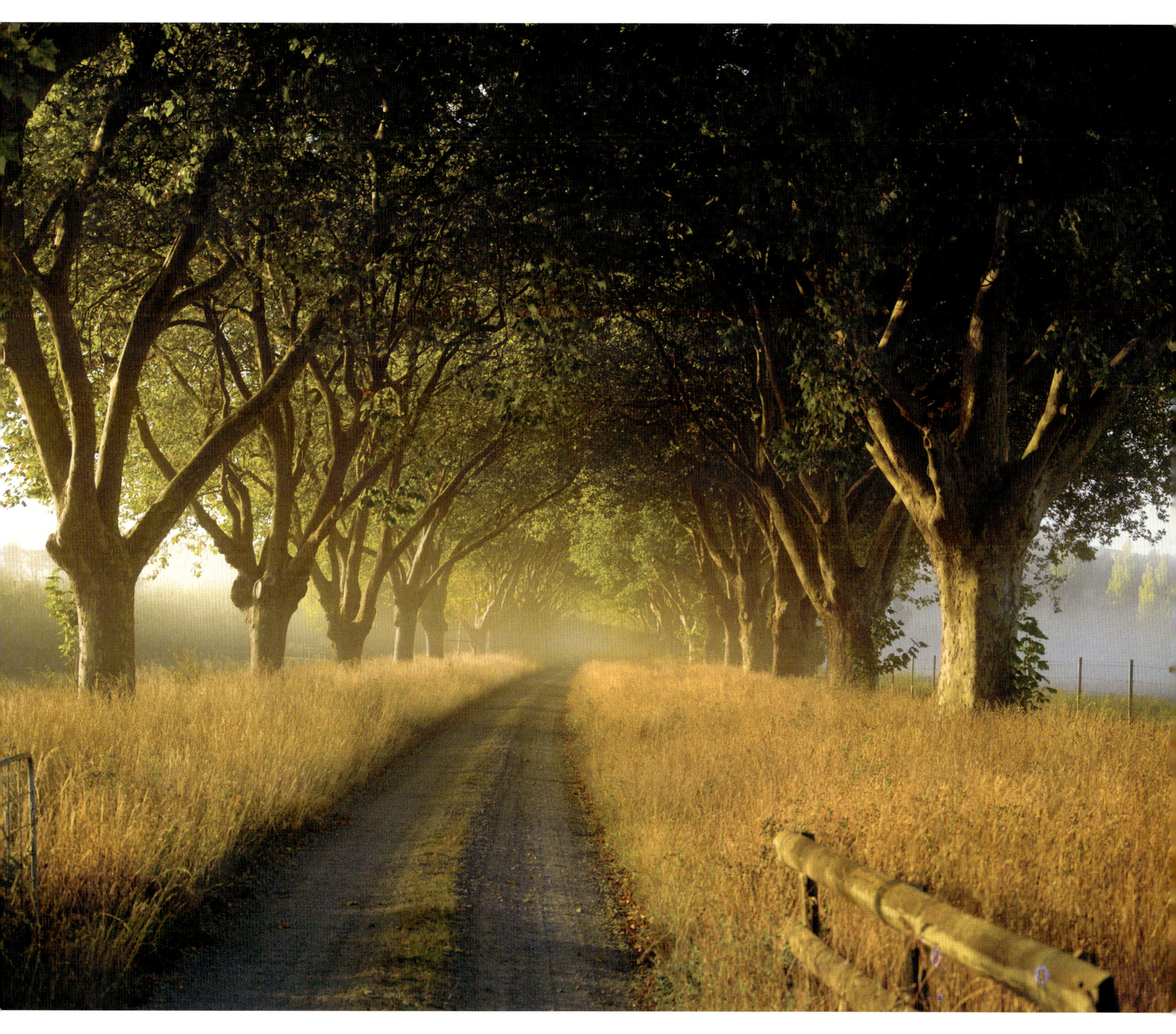

PORTRAIT OF OUR LAND

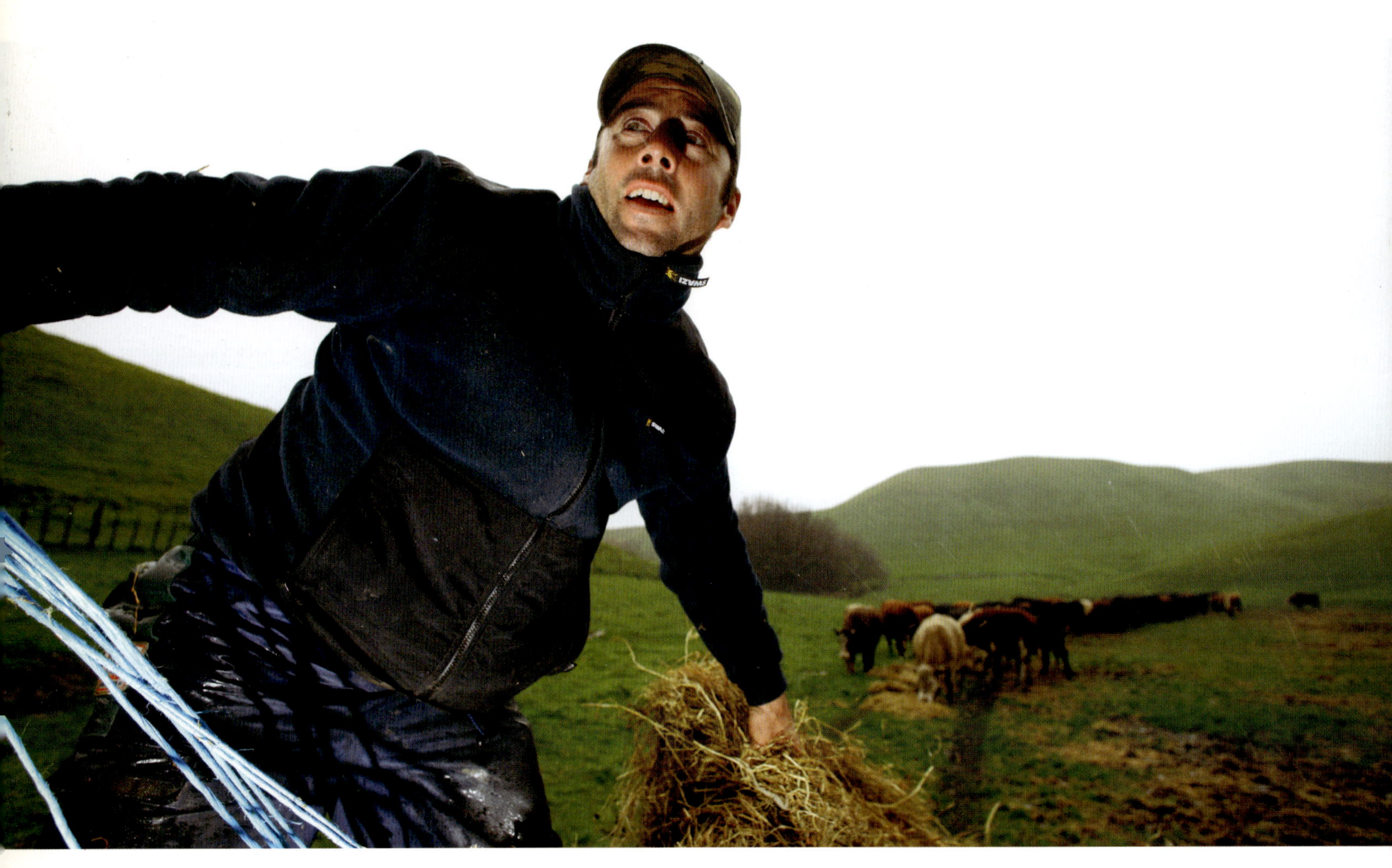

 Matt Nilsson feeding stock at Cape Estate, Te Awanga

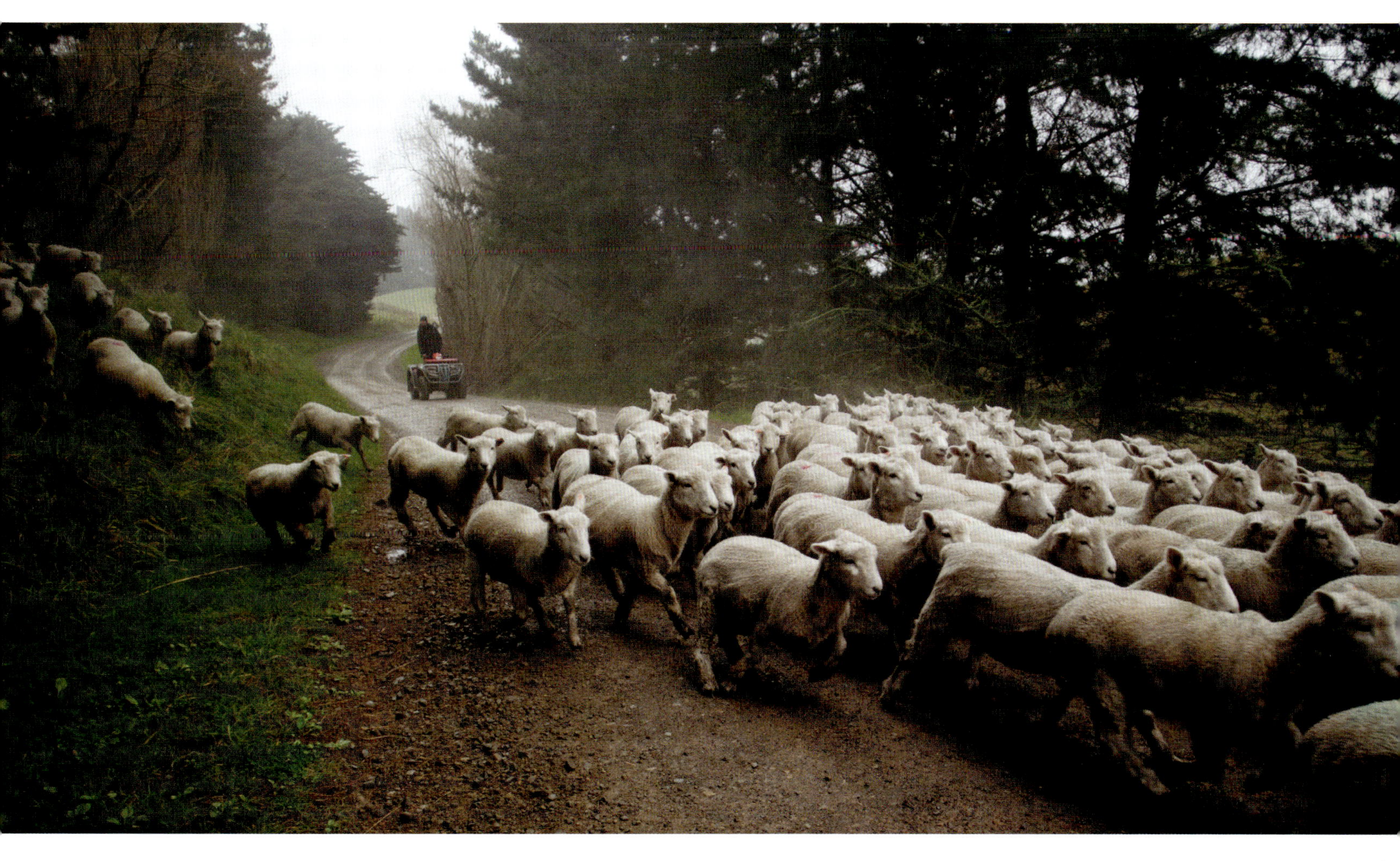

Droving sheep, Central Hawke's Bay

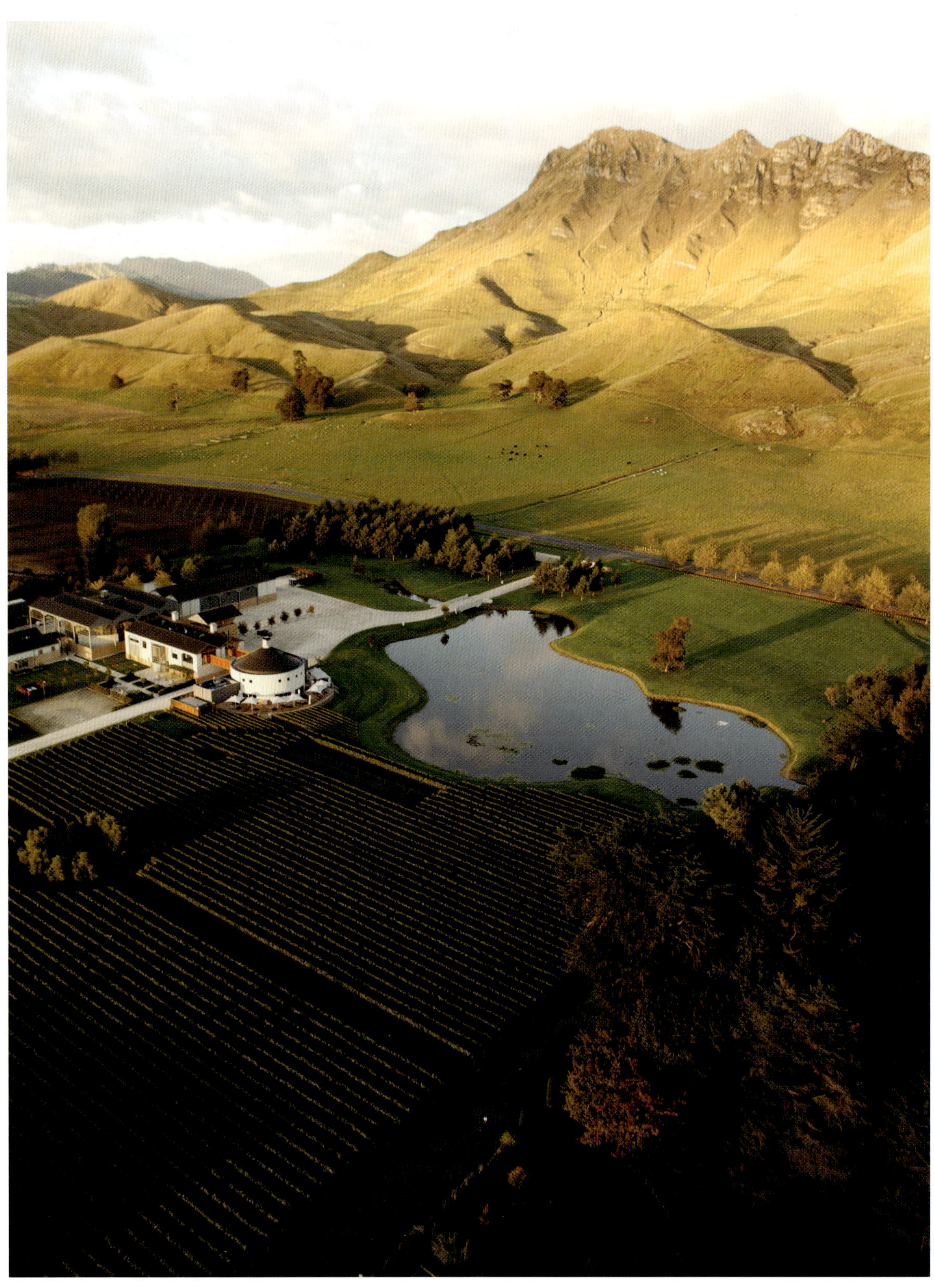

 Craggy Range Winery, Tukituki Valley, Havelock North

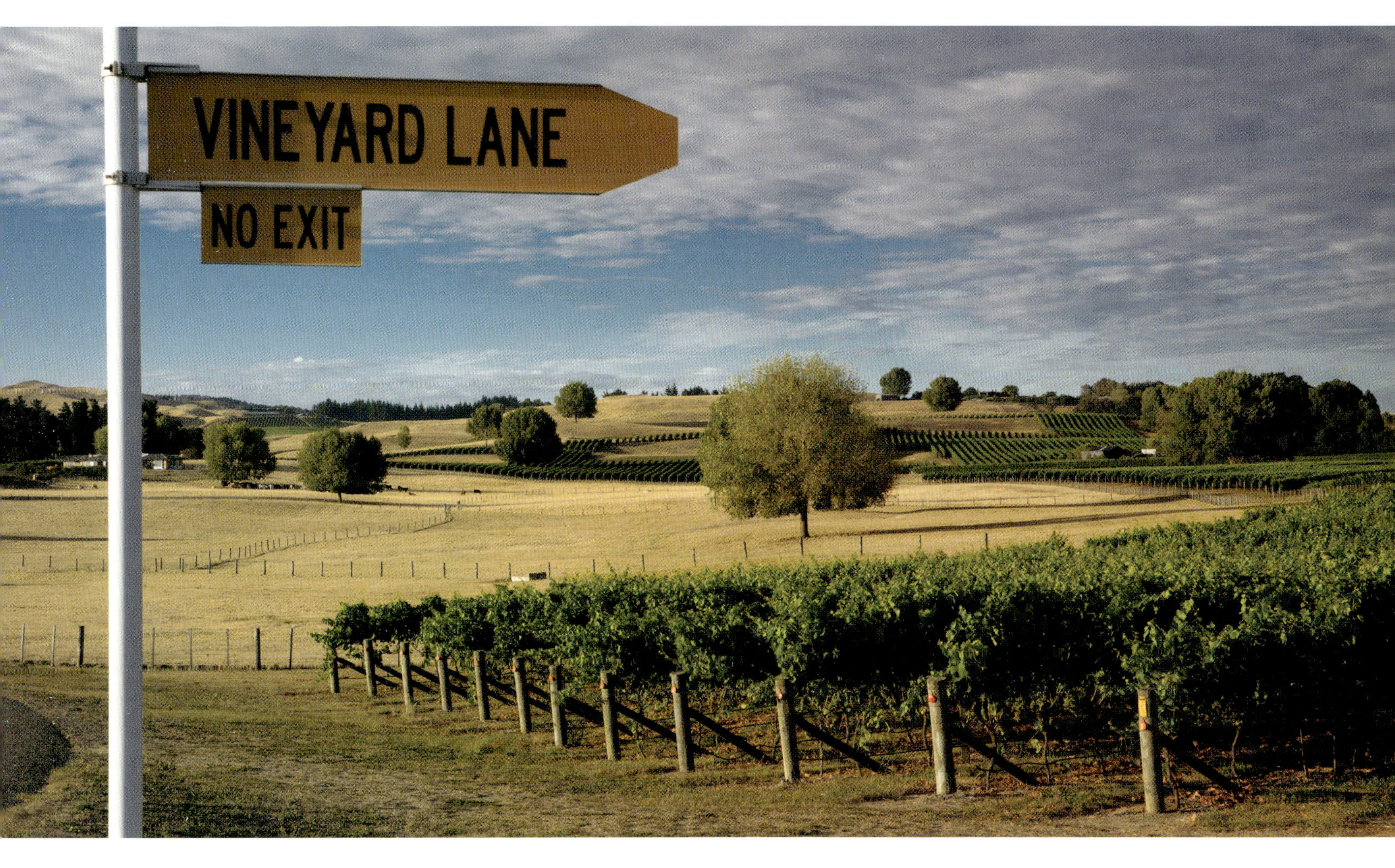

Vineyard Lane, Parkhill Estate, Haumoana

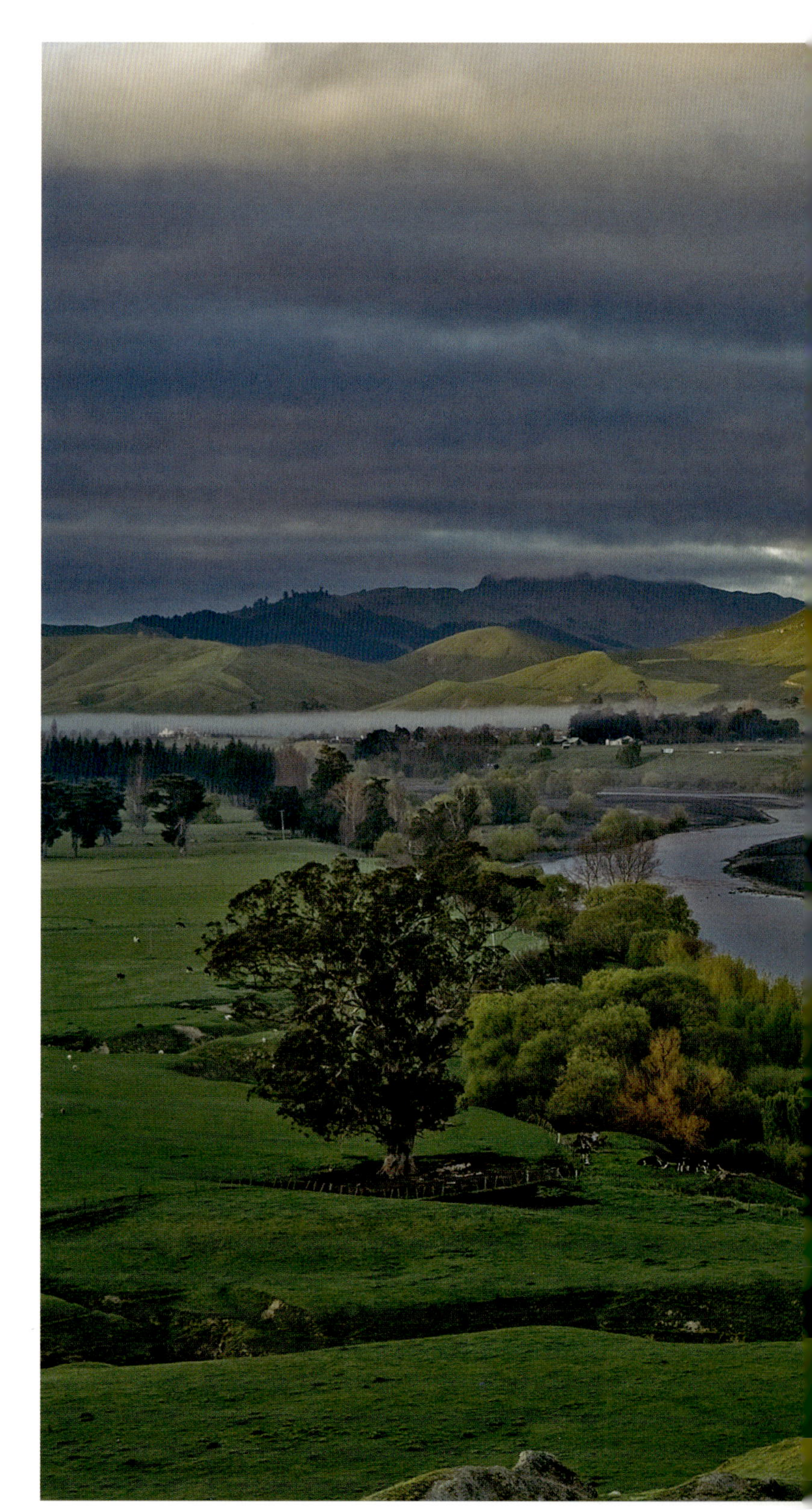

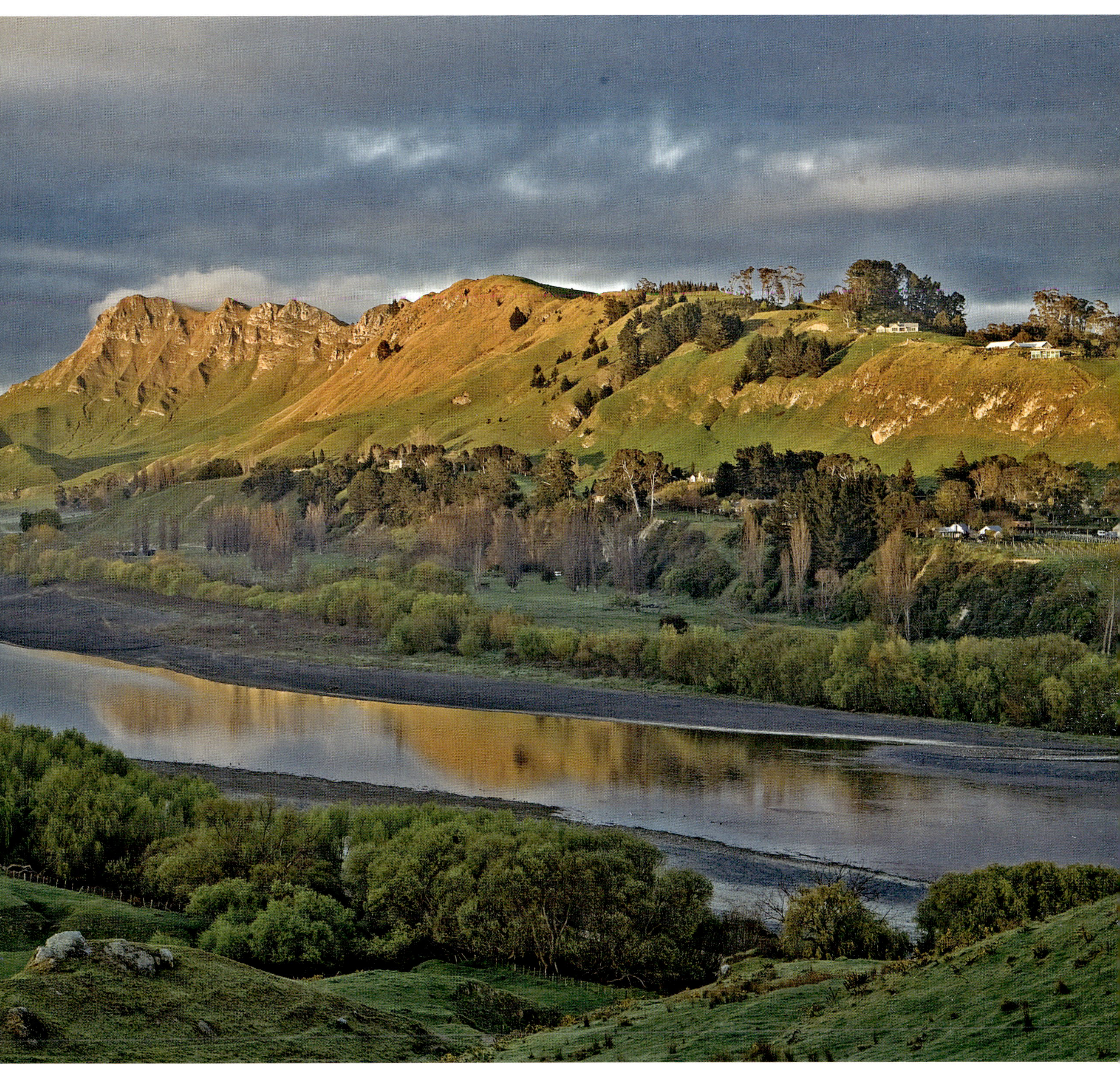

Early morning, Te Mata Peak and the Tukituki River

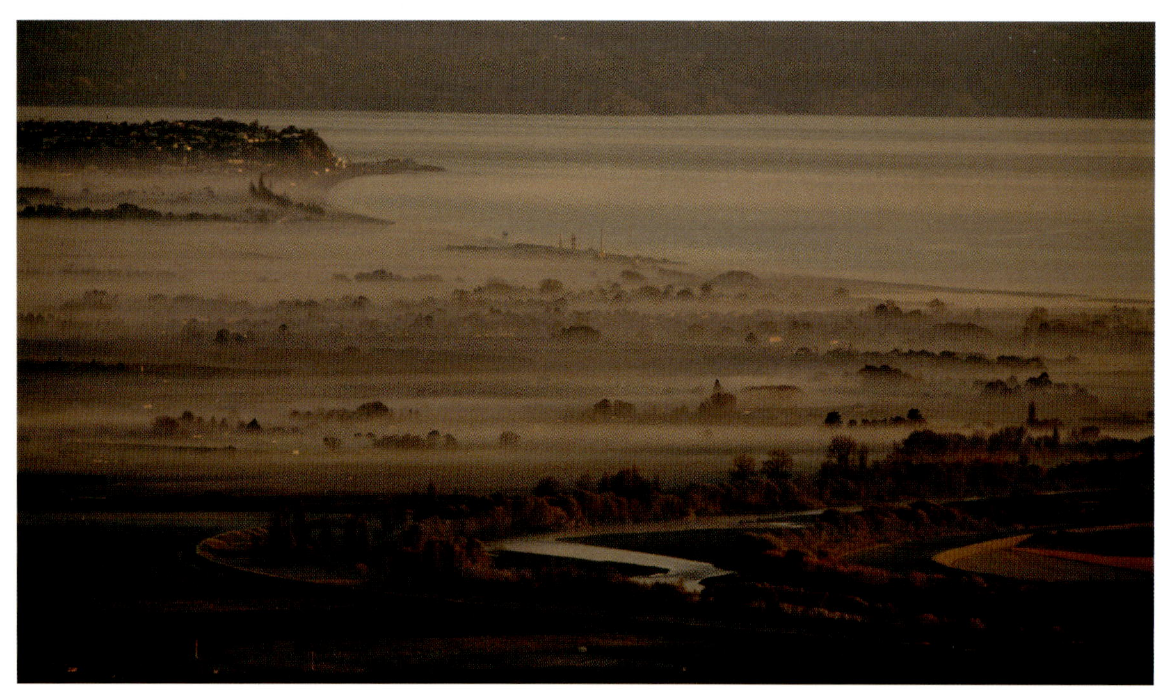

 Misty morning looking towards Bluff Hill, Napier

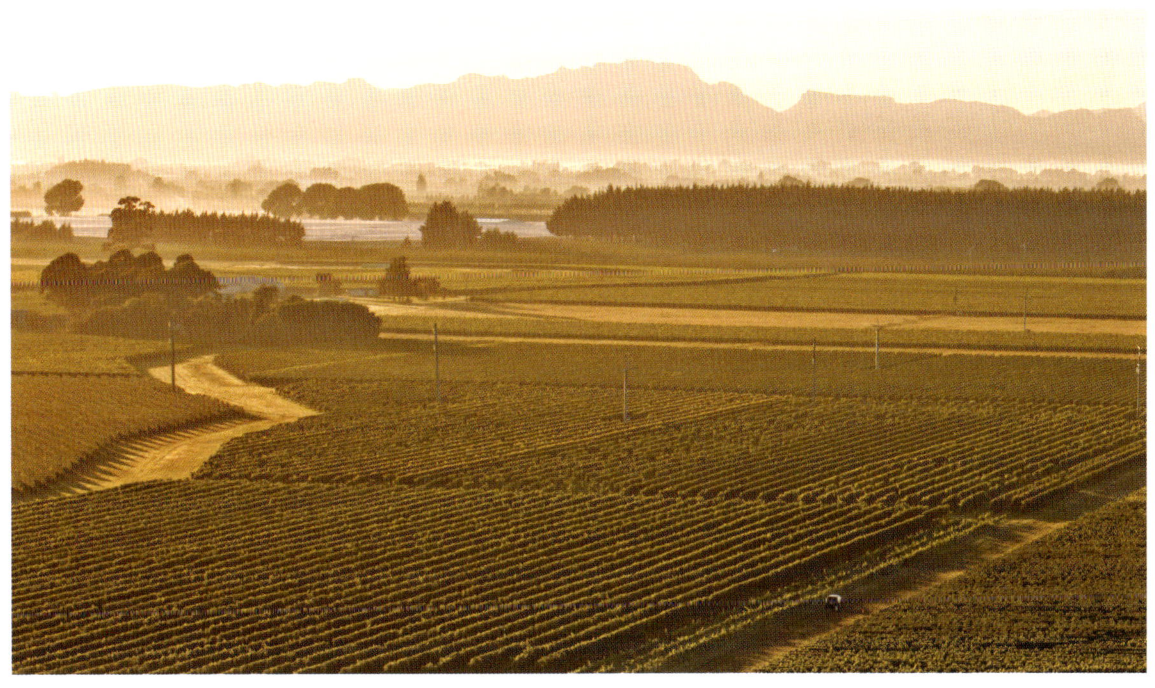

Gimblett Gravels wine growing district with 'The Sleeping Giant' (Te Mata Peak) in the background

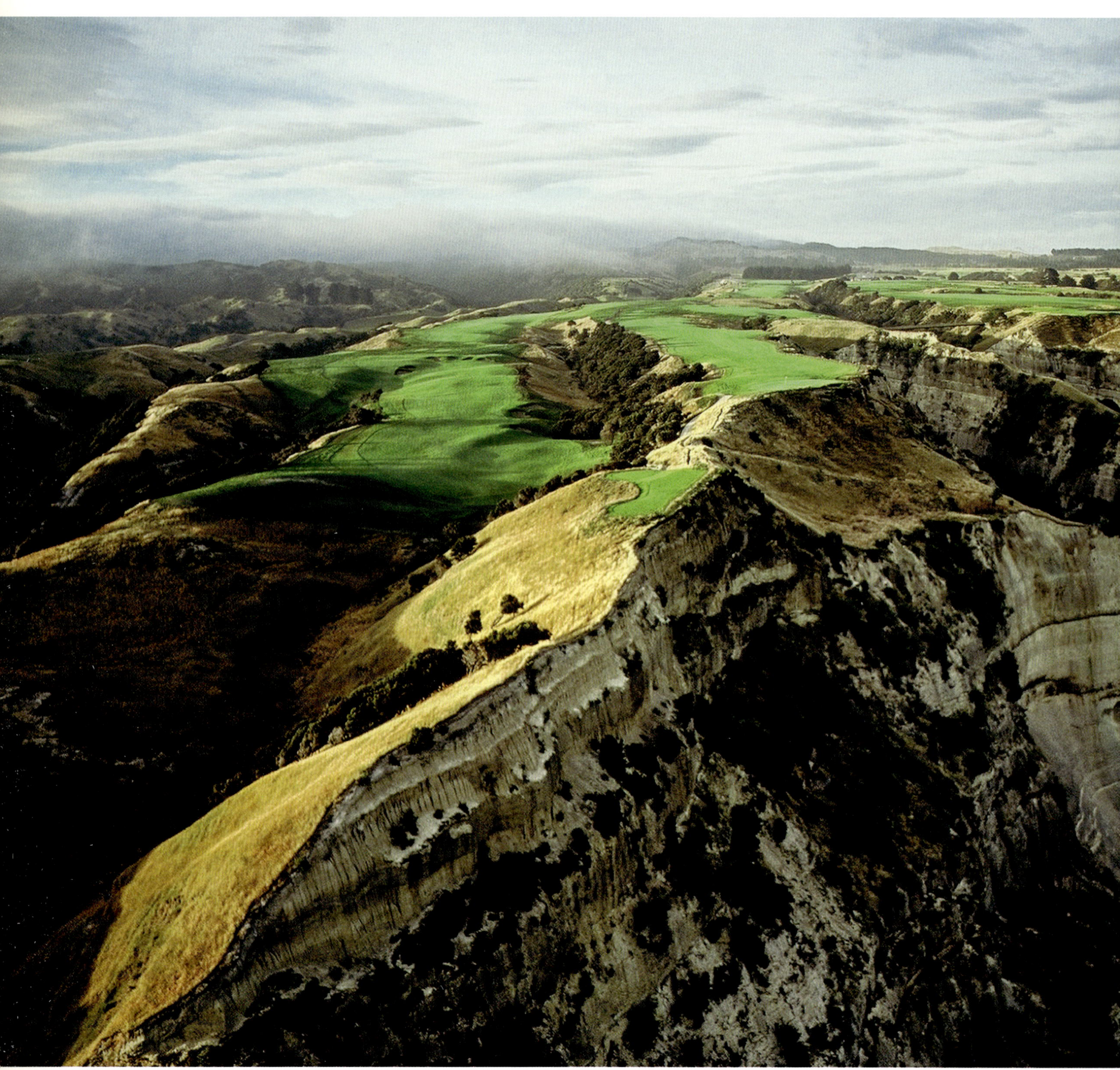

46 View of Cape Kidnappers Golf Course

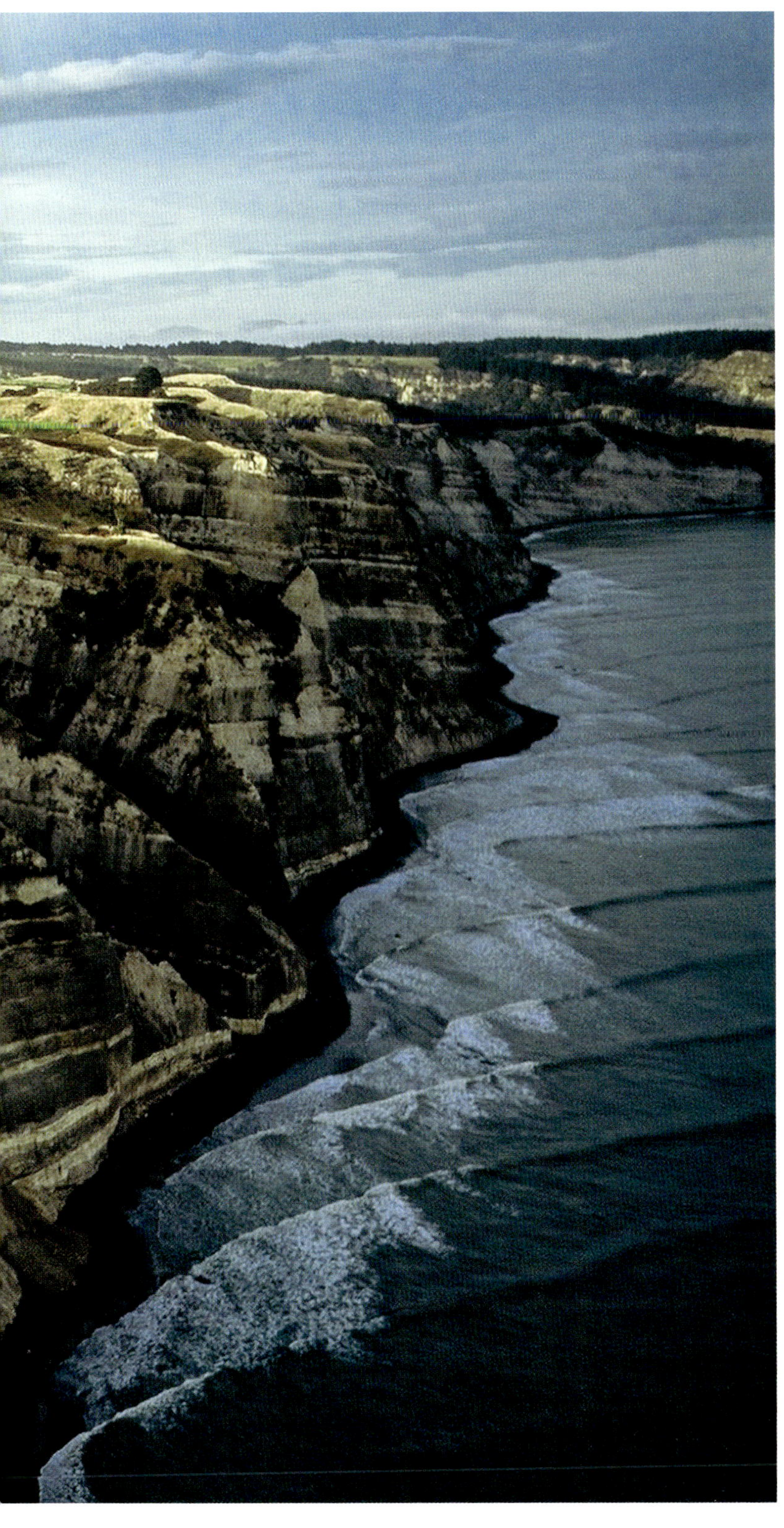

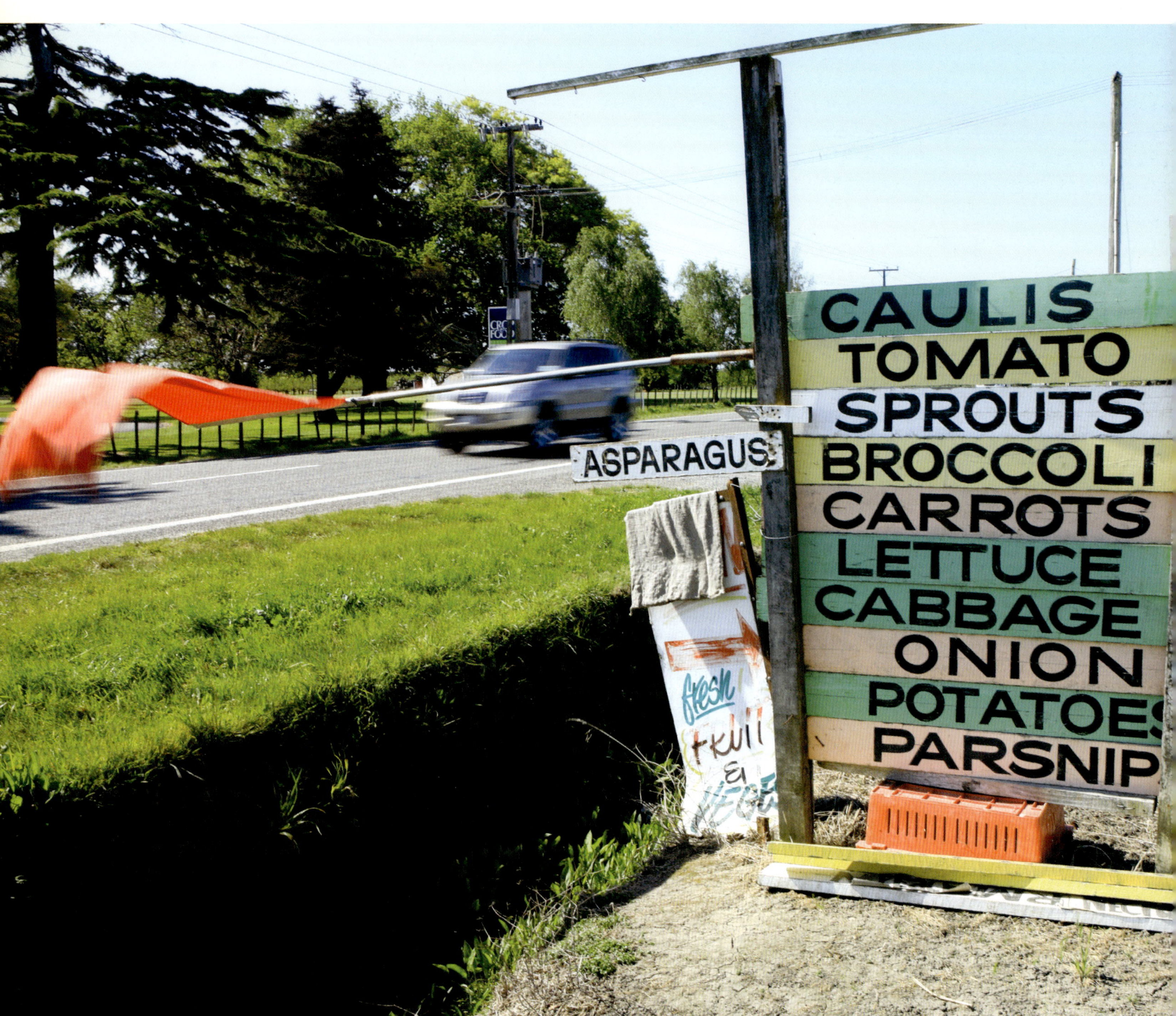

 Joe's Market Garden, Lawn Road, Hastings District

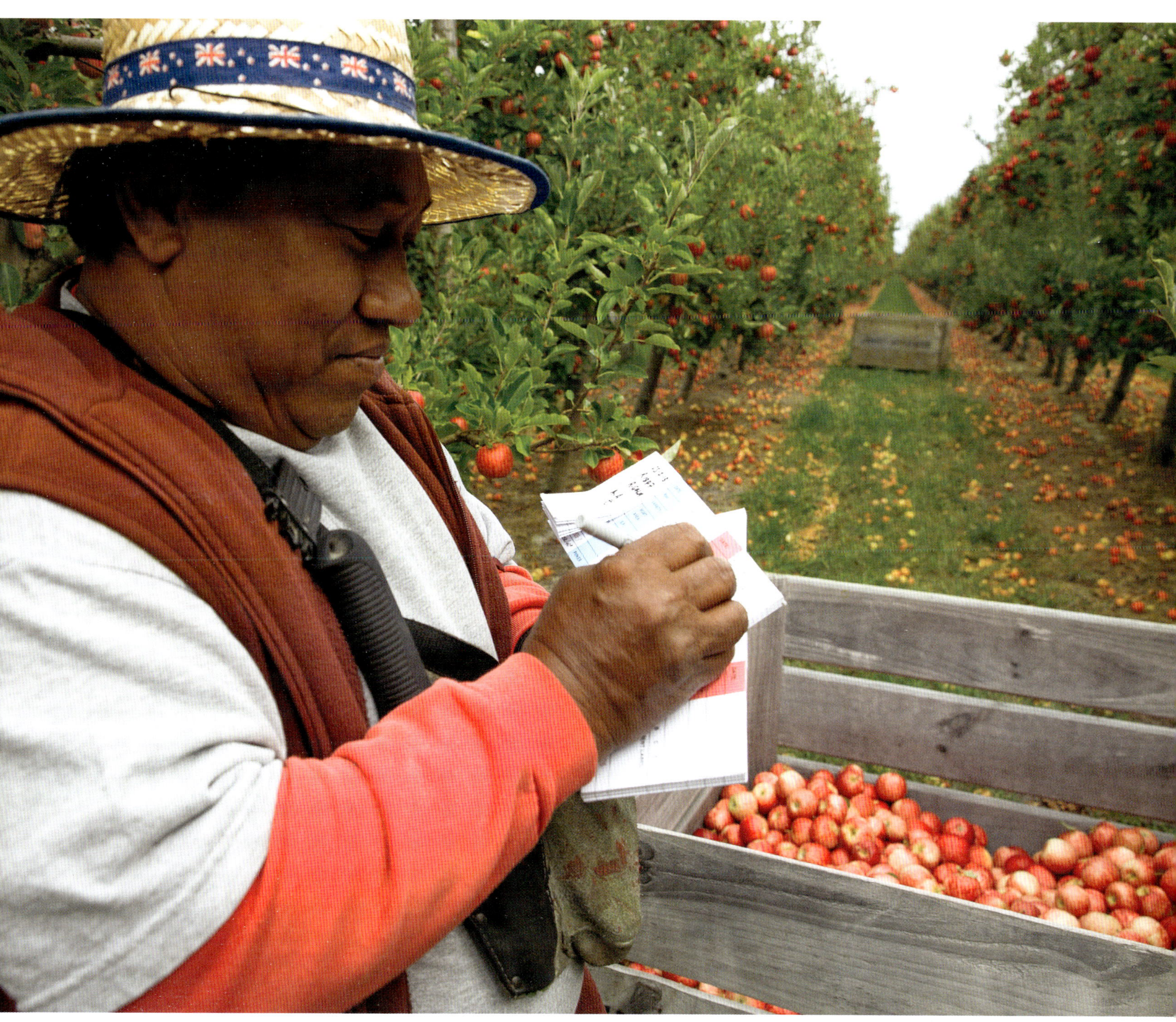

Fruit picker keeping bin tally, Hastings

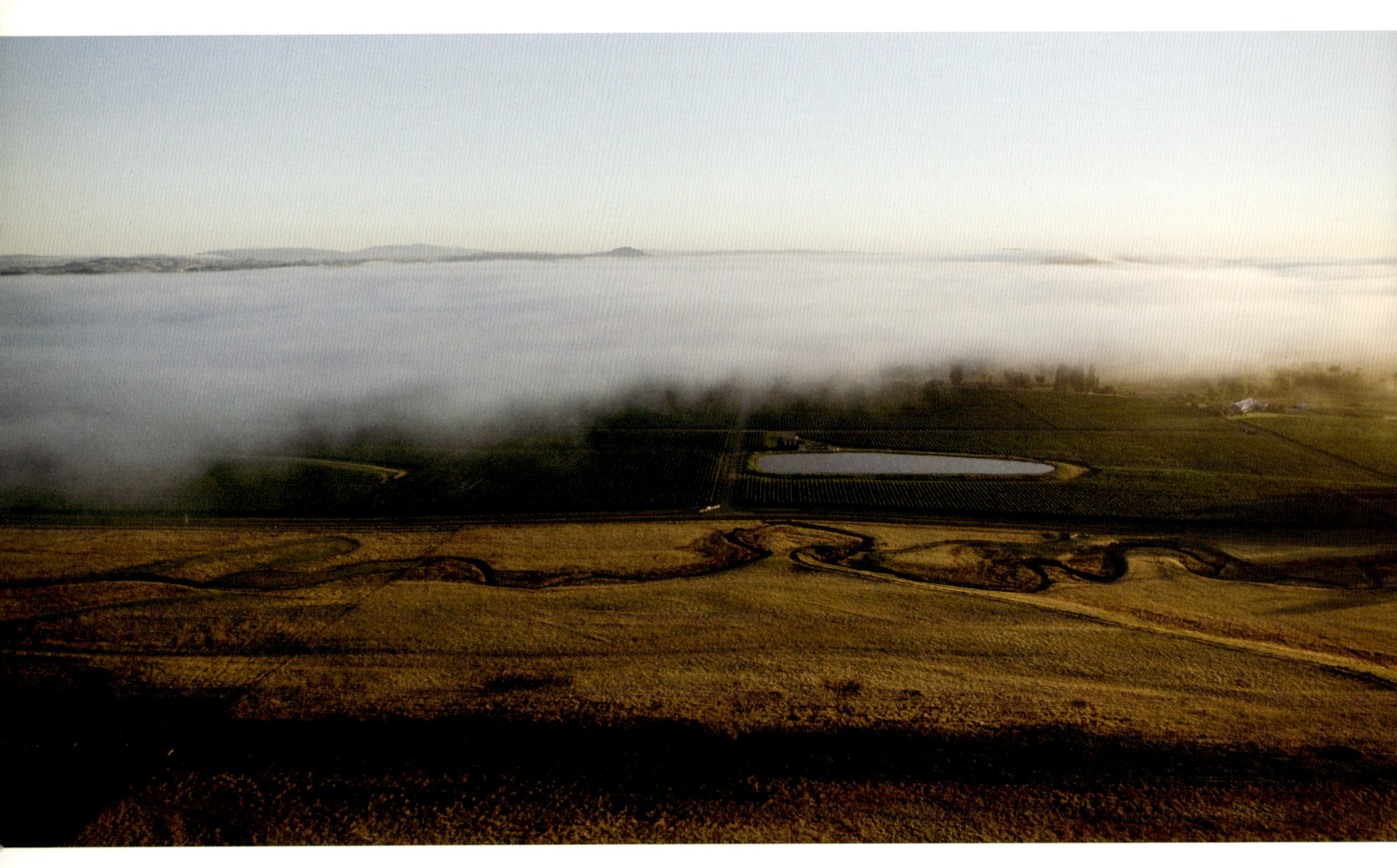

 View of Maraekakaho, Hastings District

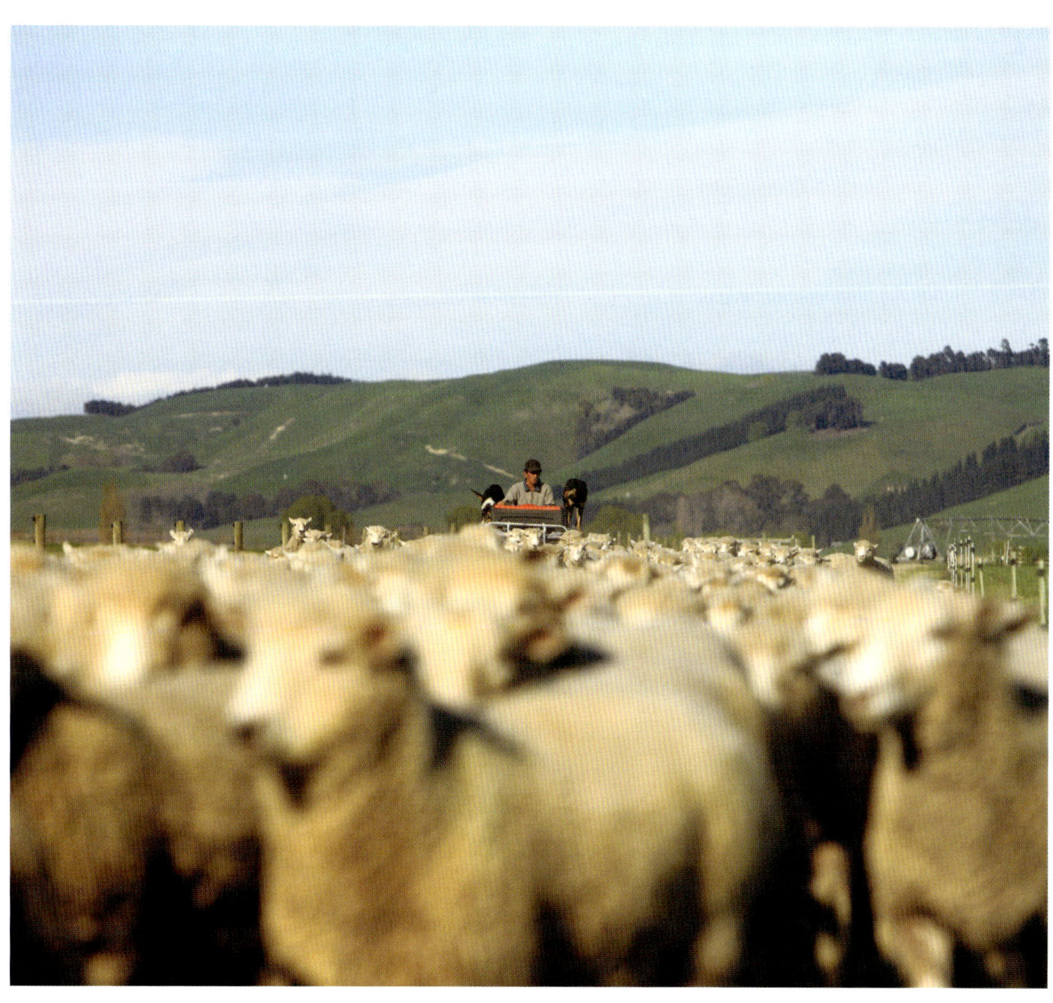

Mustering sheep, Te Hauke, south of Hastings

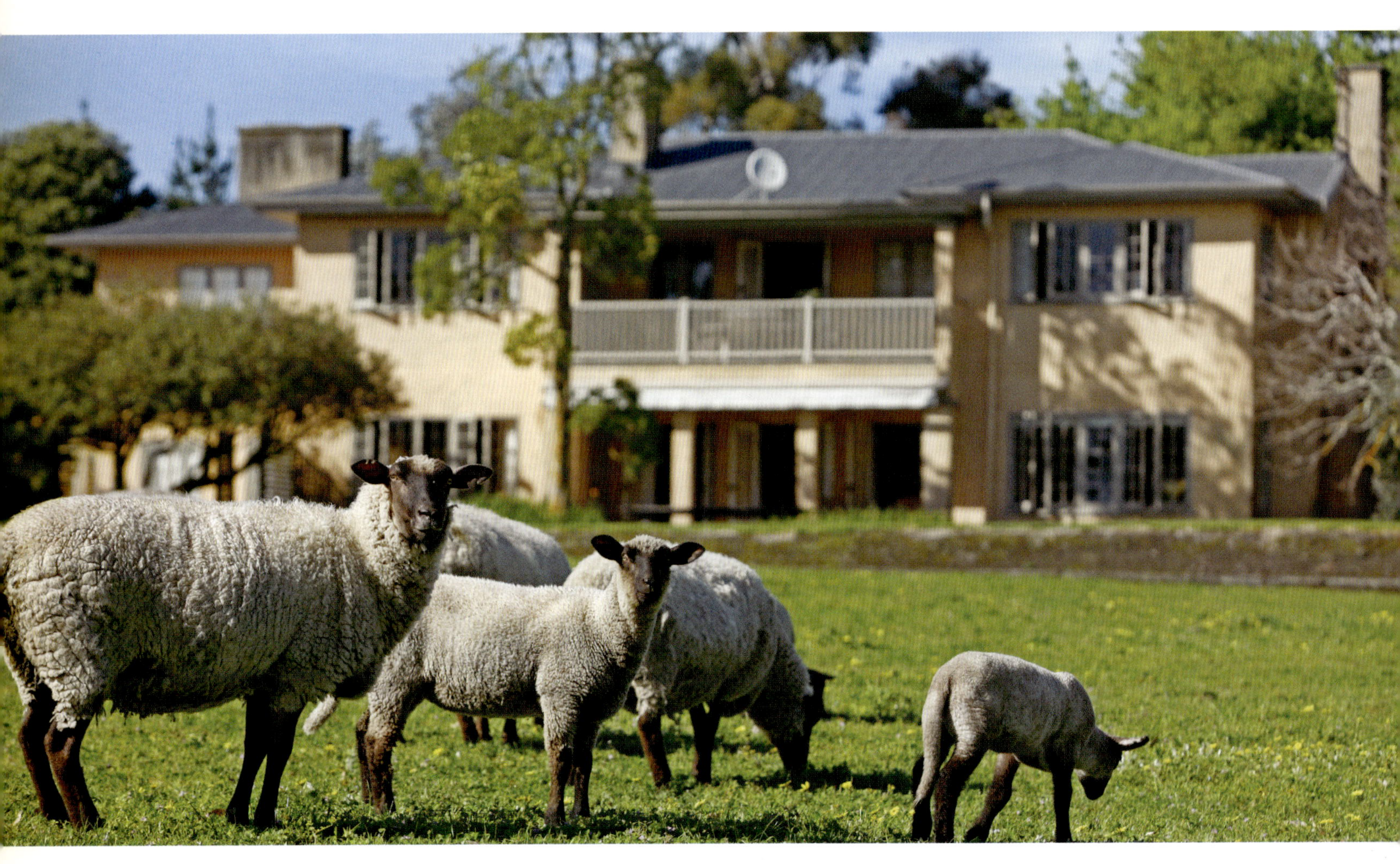

 Summerlee luxury retreat, Te Awanga

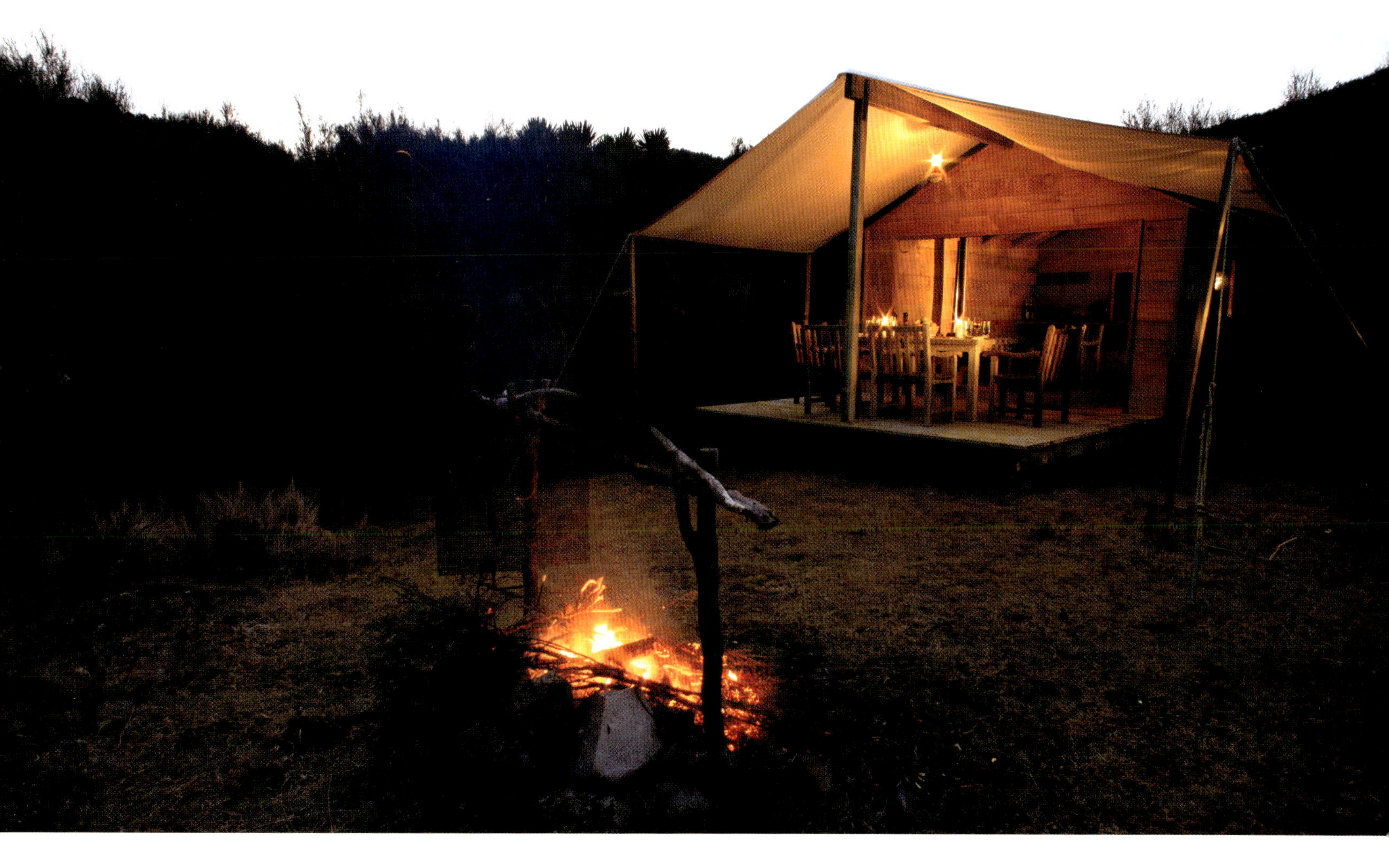

Upmarket safari camp at Poronui Ranch on the Mohaka River

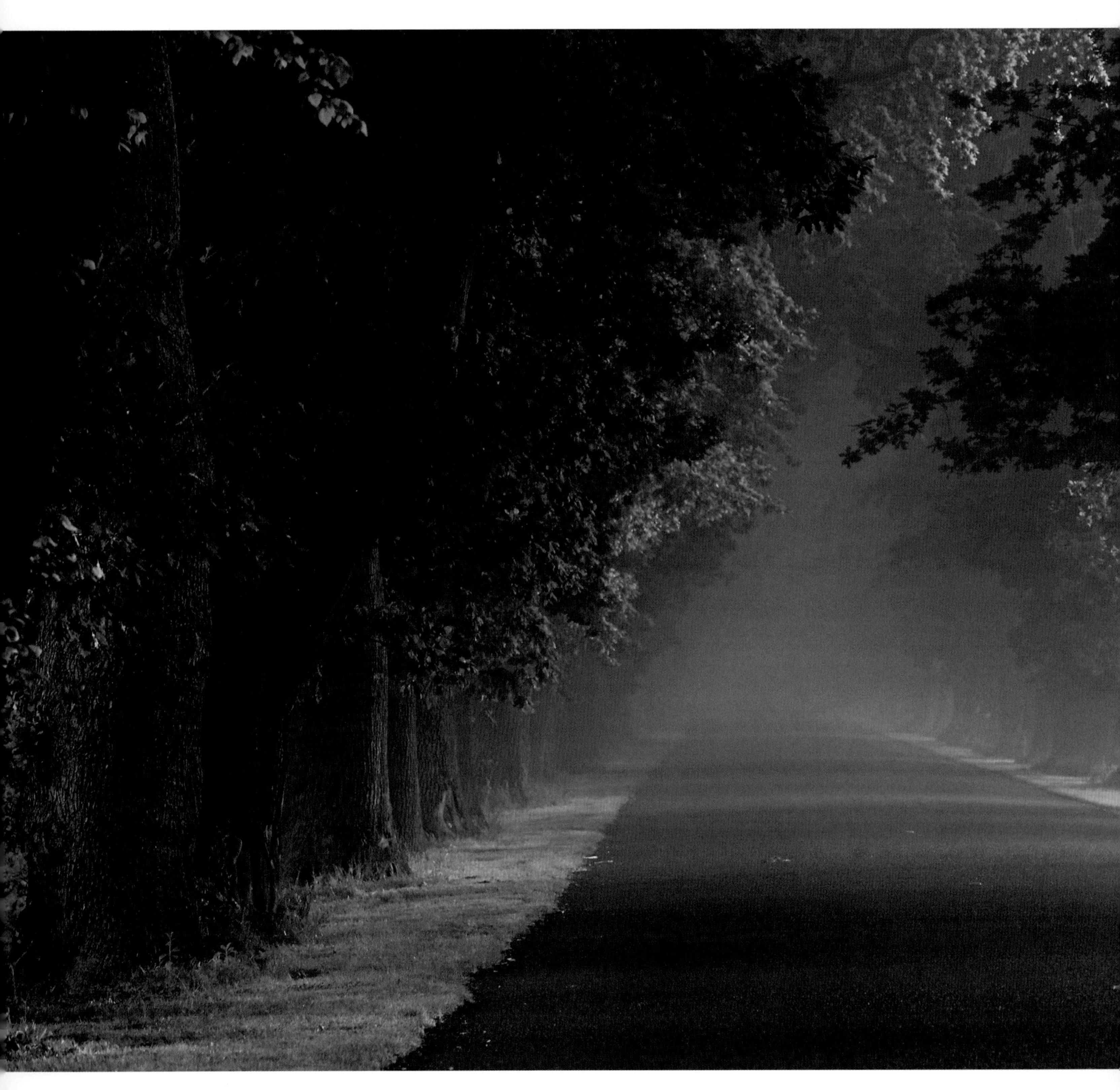

54 'Oak Avenue' (Ormond Road), planted in the 1860s, Hastings

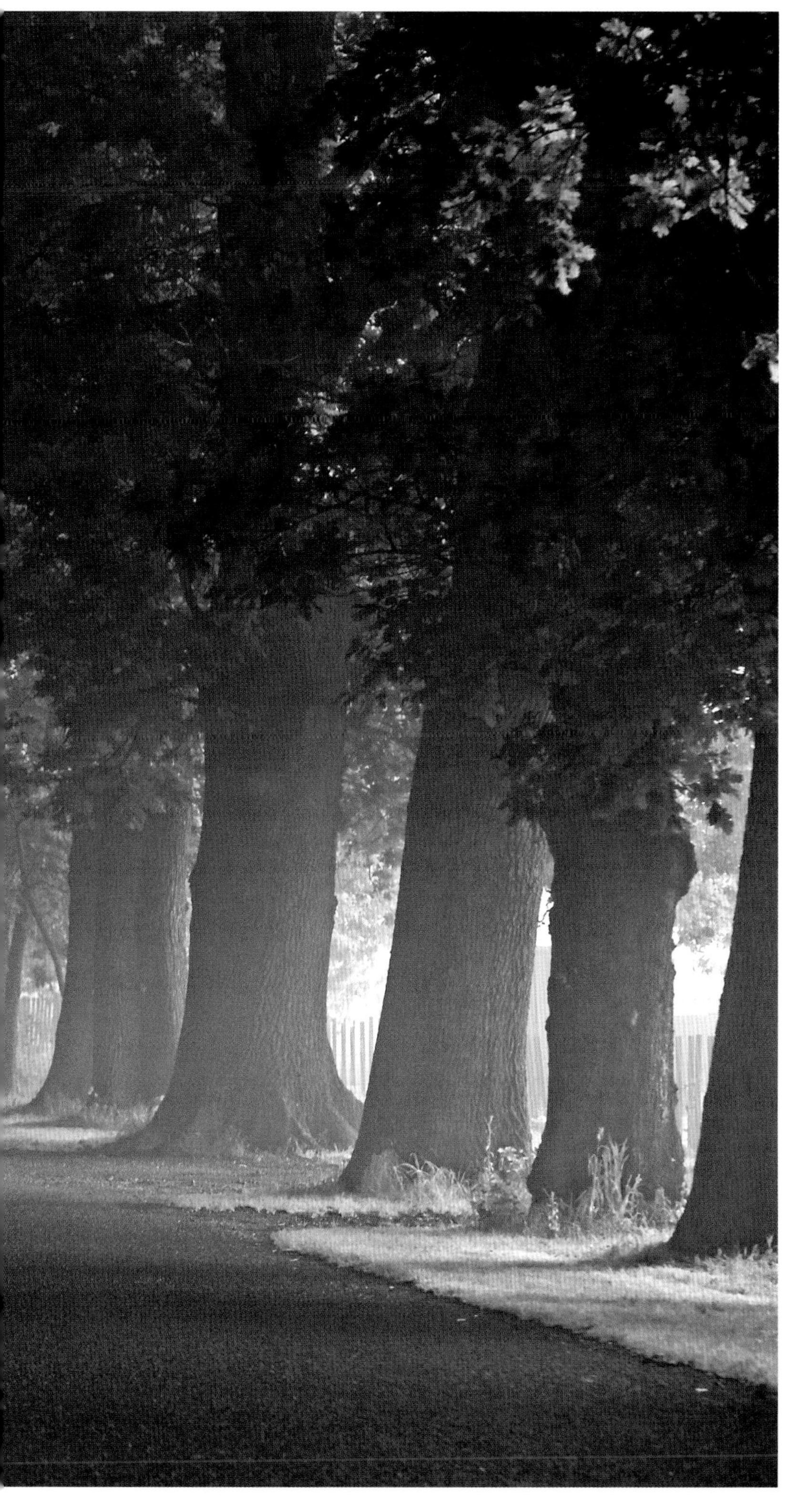

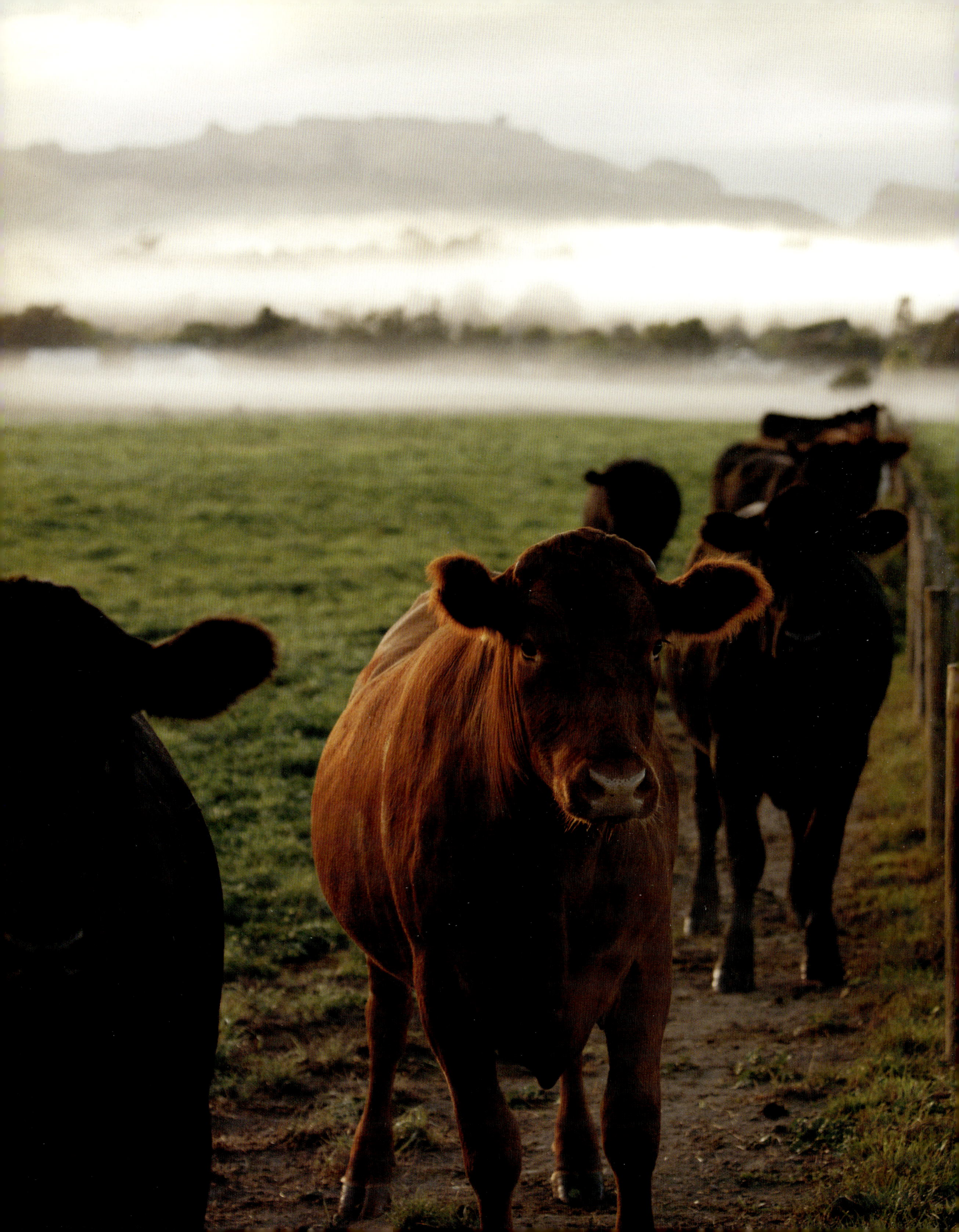

Grazing cattle, rural Havelock North

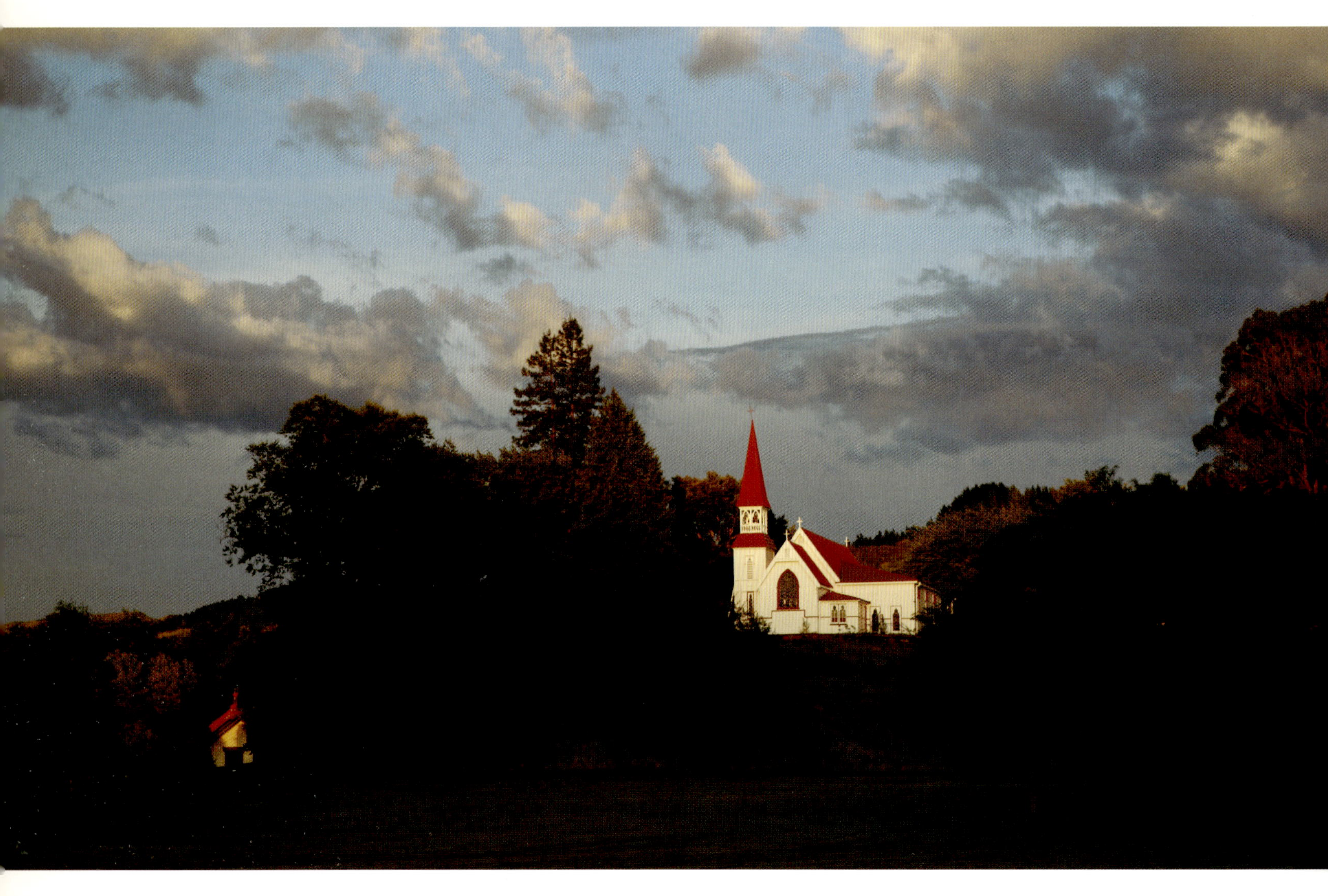

 Te Aute College Chapel built in 1900, Te Aute, south of Hastings

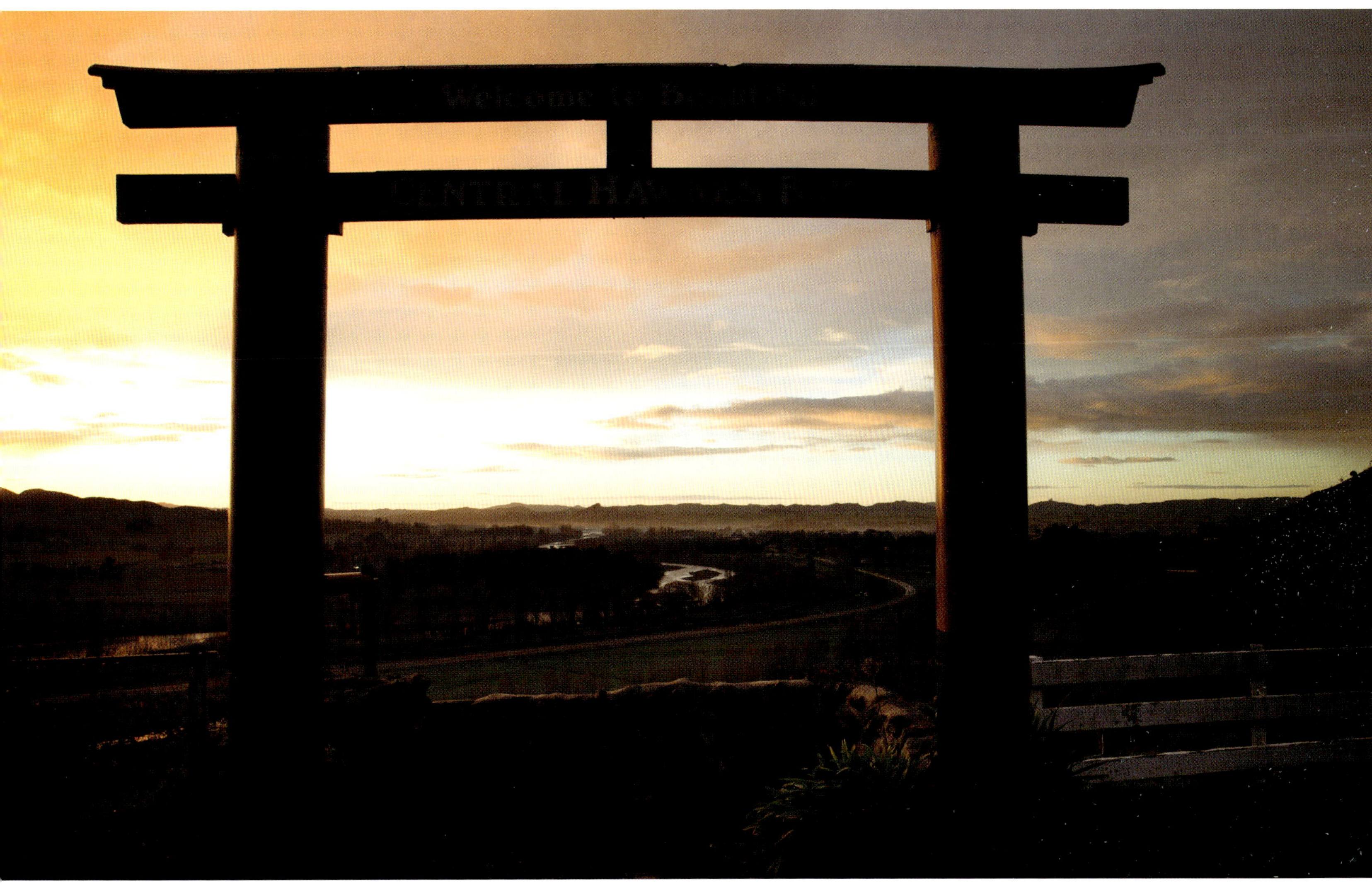

Lookout on Pukeora Hill, overlooking Waipukurau, Central Hawke's Bay

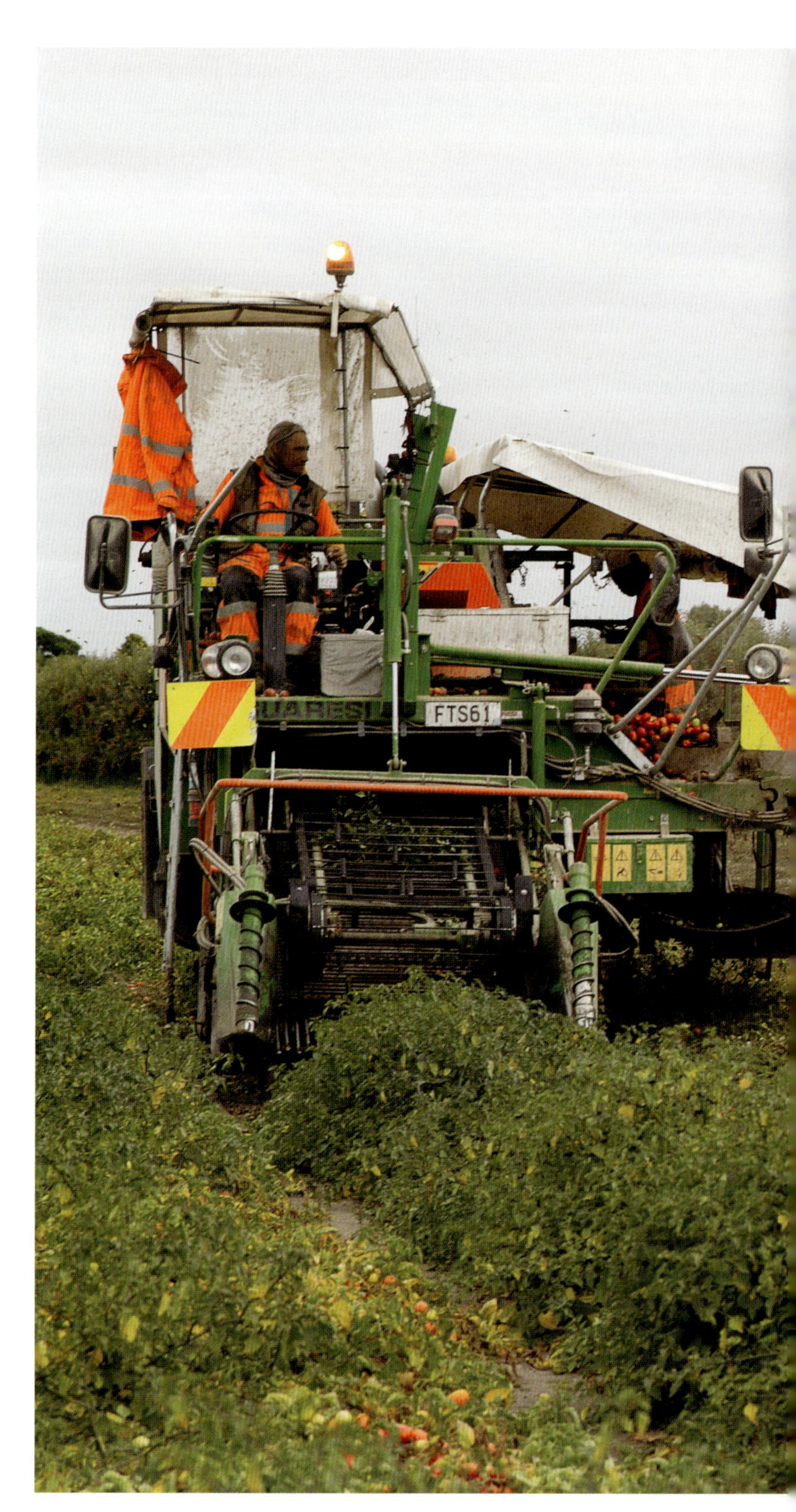
FTS61

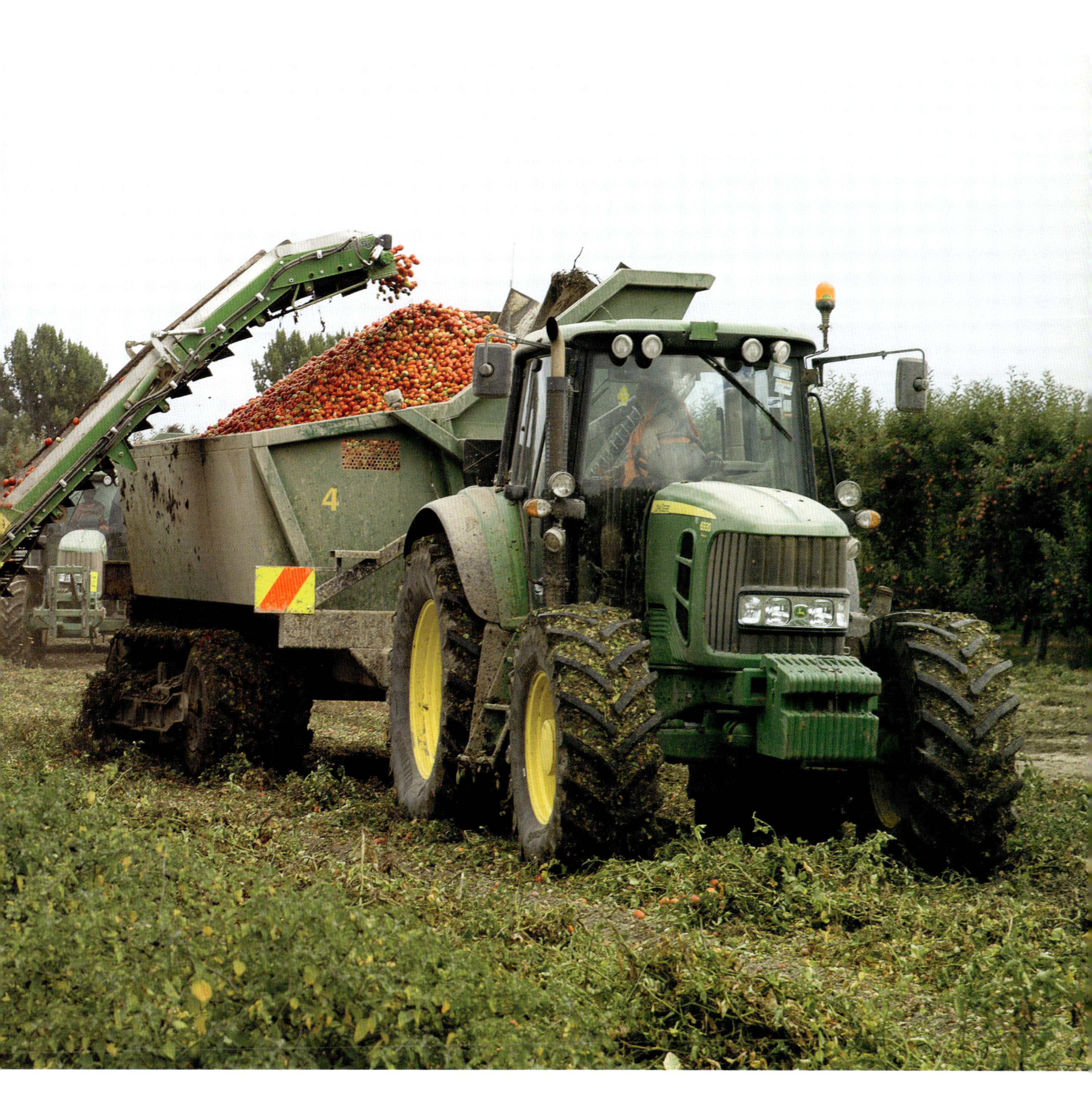

Tomato harvesting, Hastings District

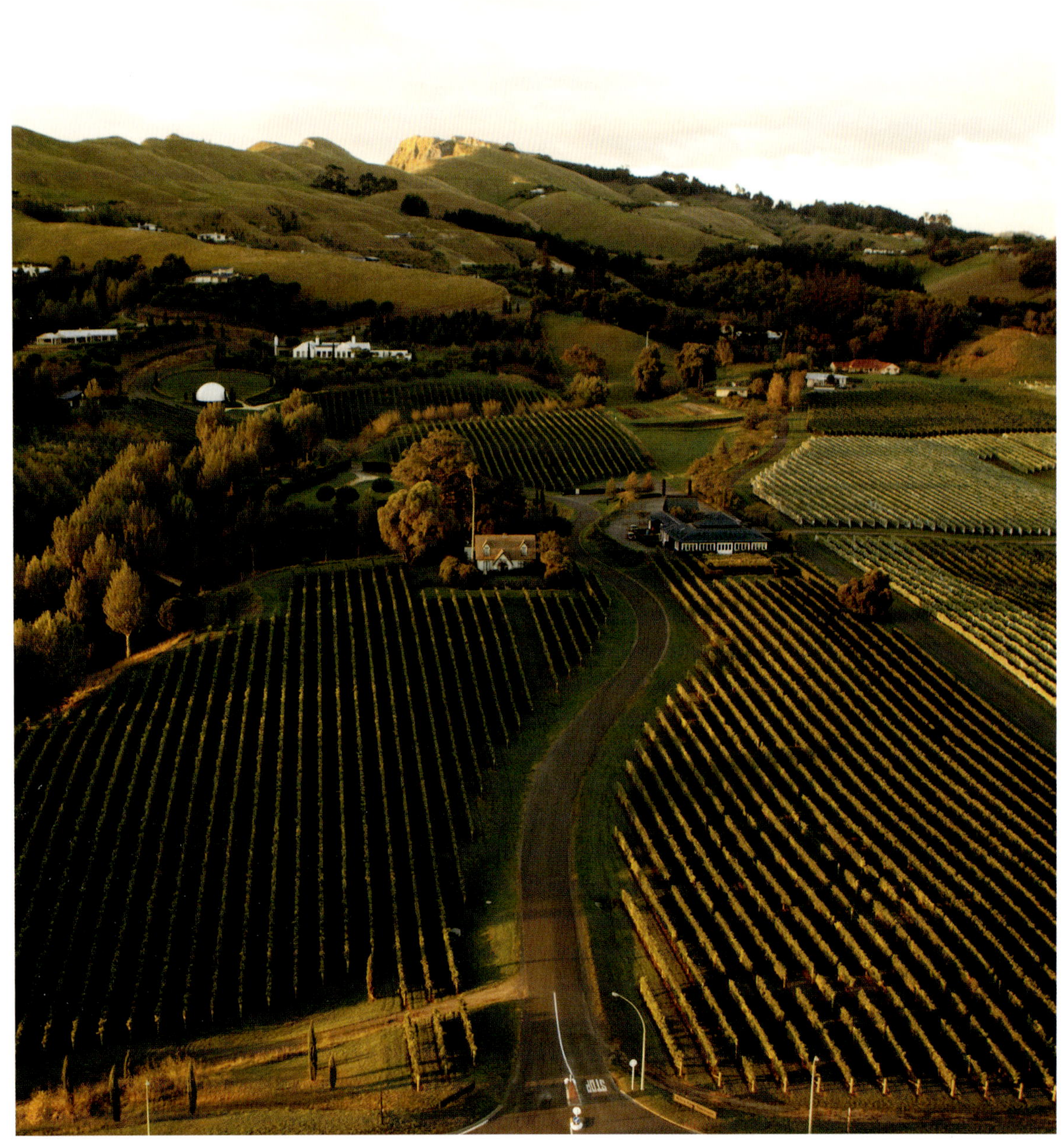

 Aerial view of vineyard at Black Barn Winery, Havelock North

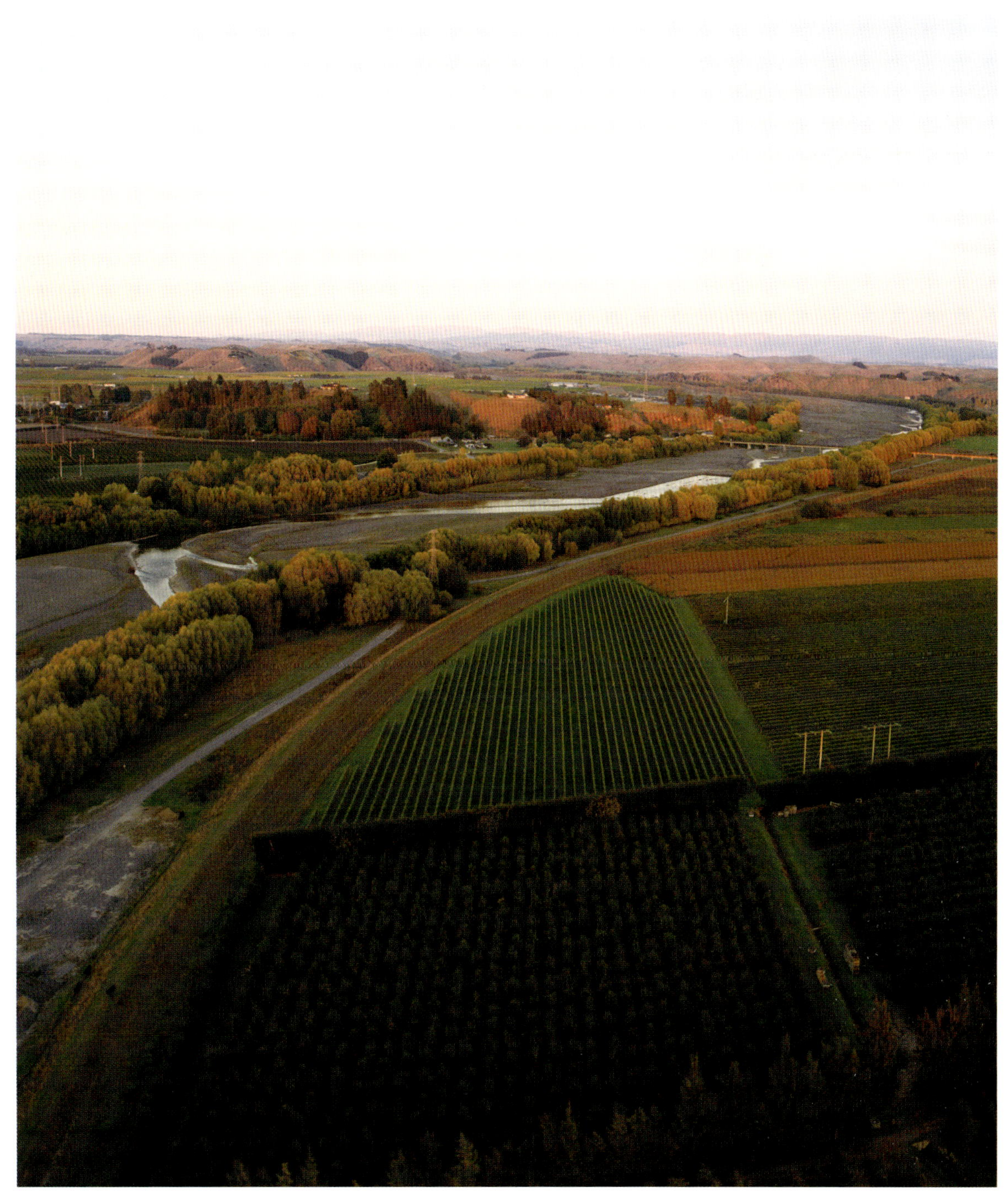

Aerial view of Ngaruroro River, Fernhill, Hastings

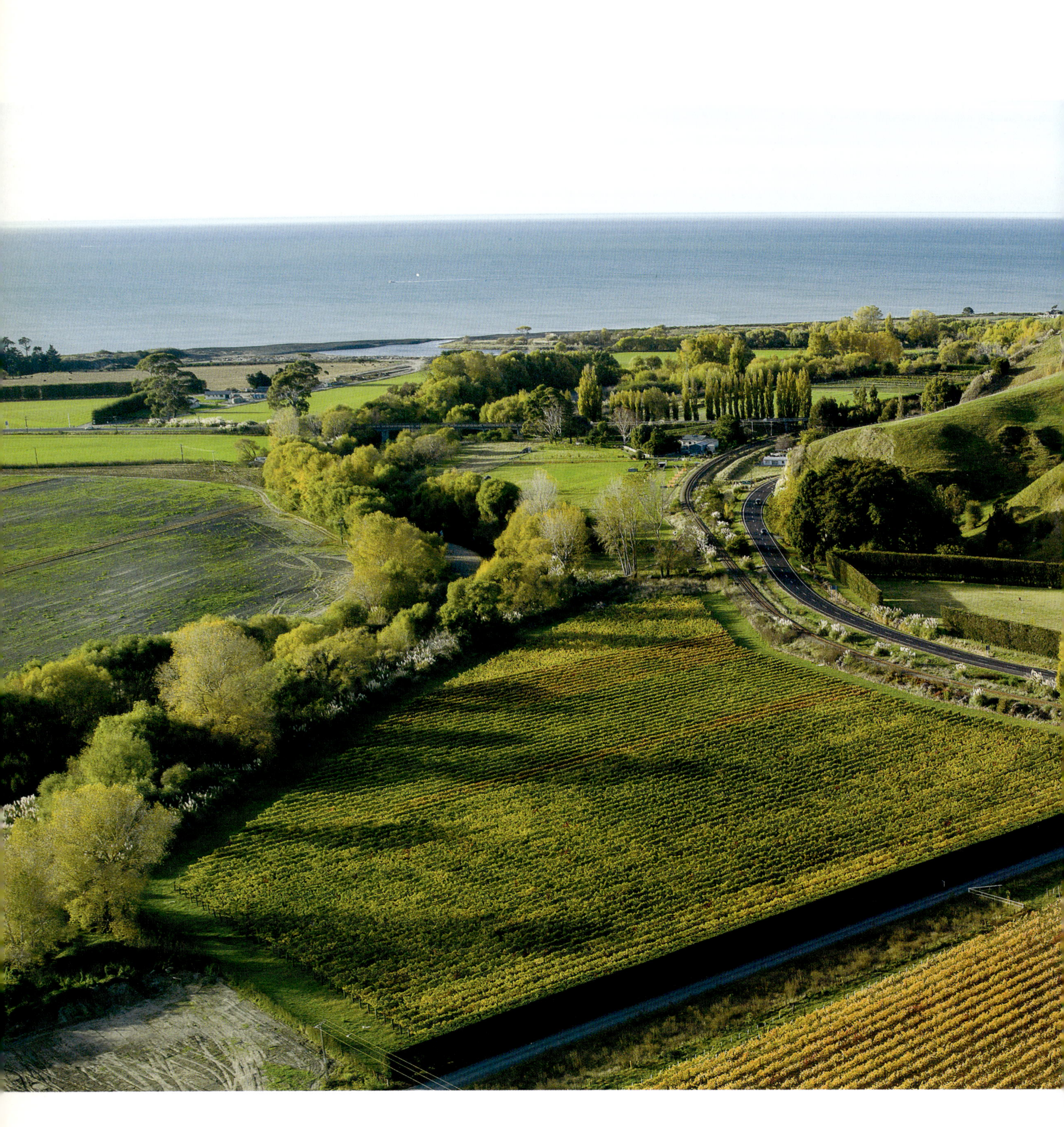

 Aerial view over Esk Valley looking towards Bluff Hill, Napier and Cape Kidnappers

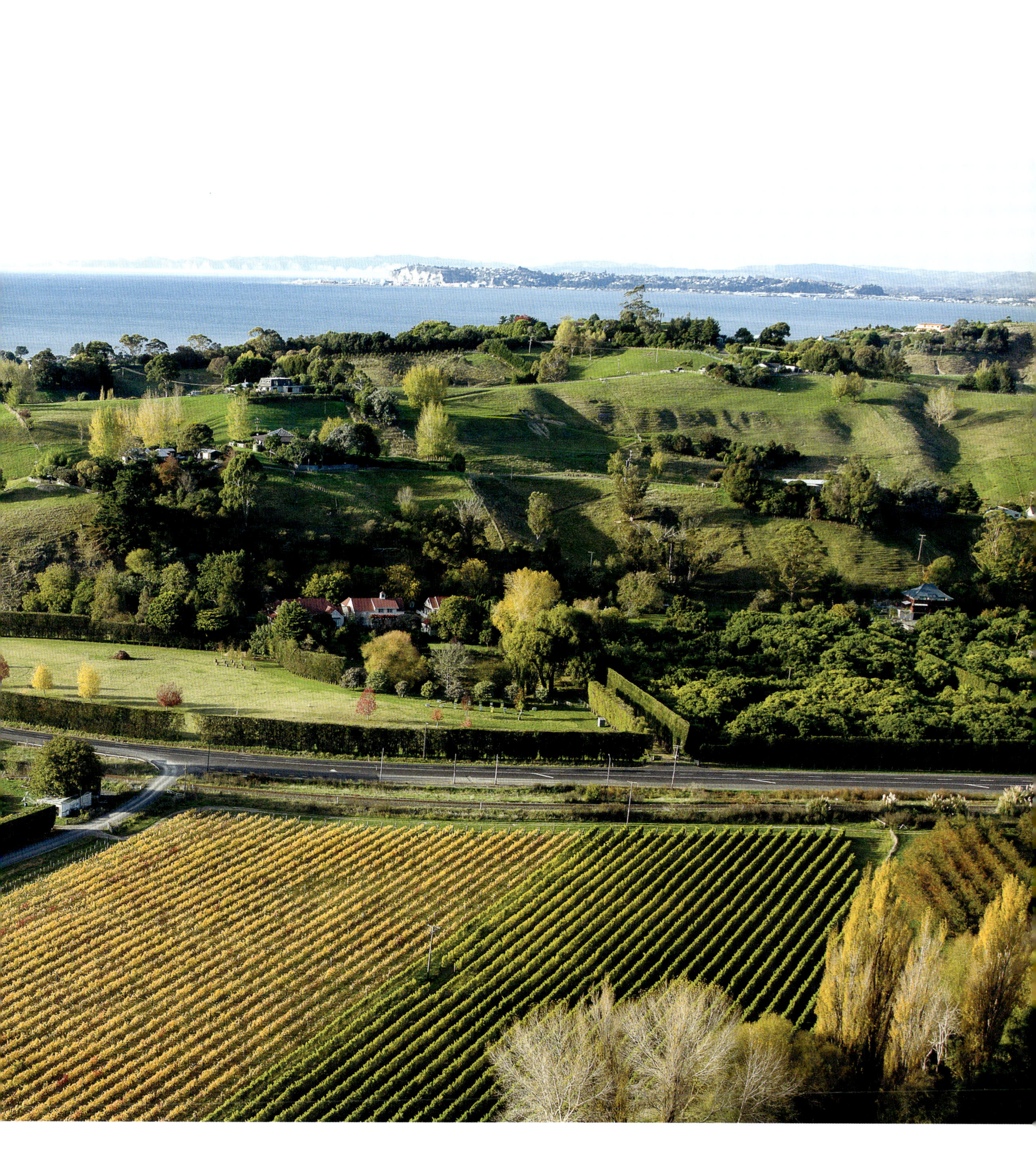

NĀKU I HANGA TŌKU WHARE HEI HAUMARU WHAKARURUHAU.

I HAVE BUILT MY HOUSE AS A SHELTER TO WITHSTAND THE ELEMENTS OF NATURE.

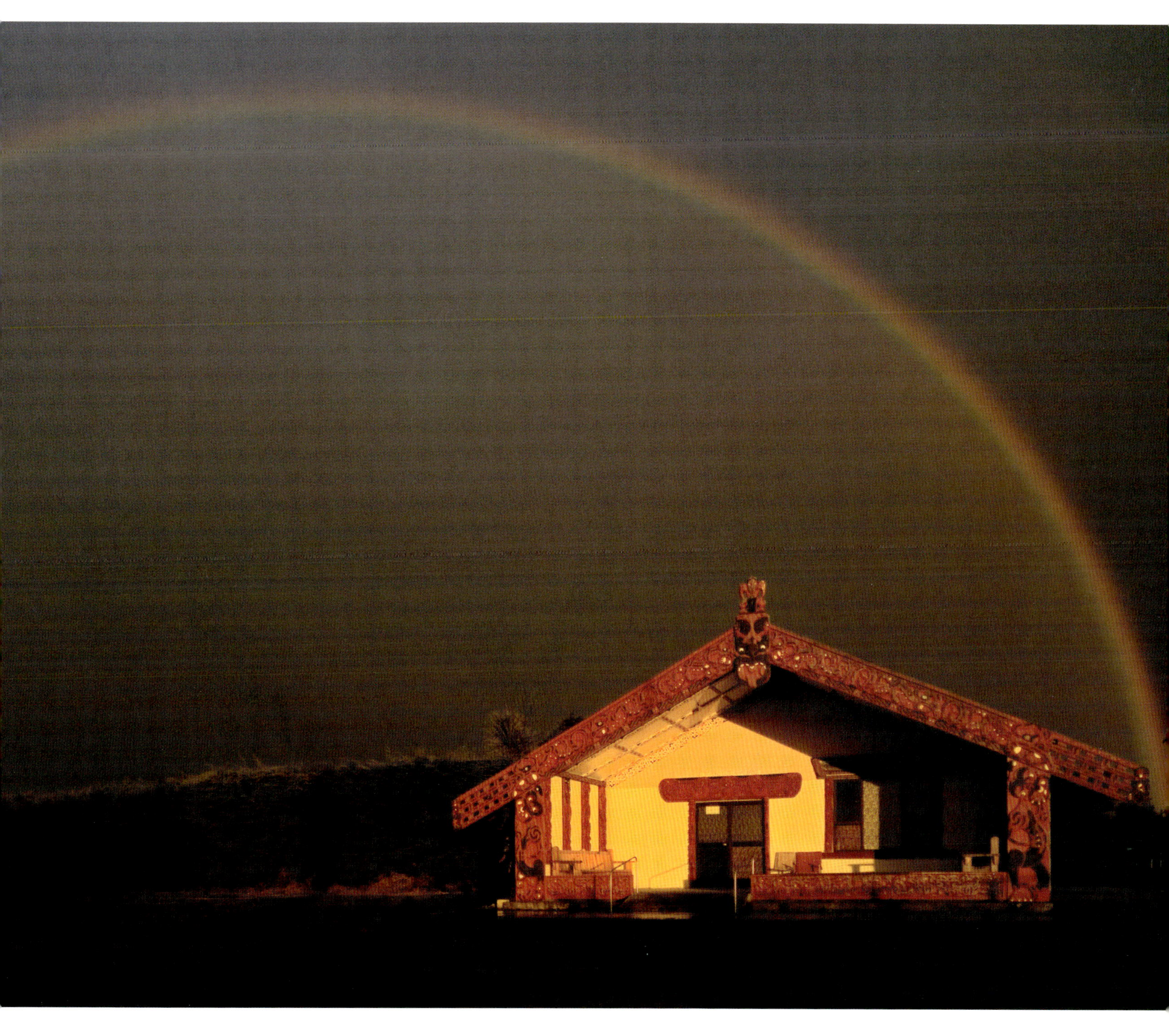

PORTRAIT OF OUR PLACES

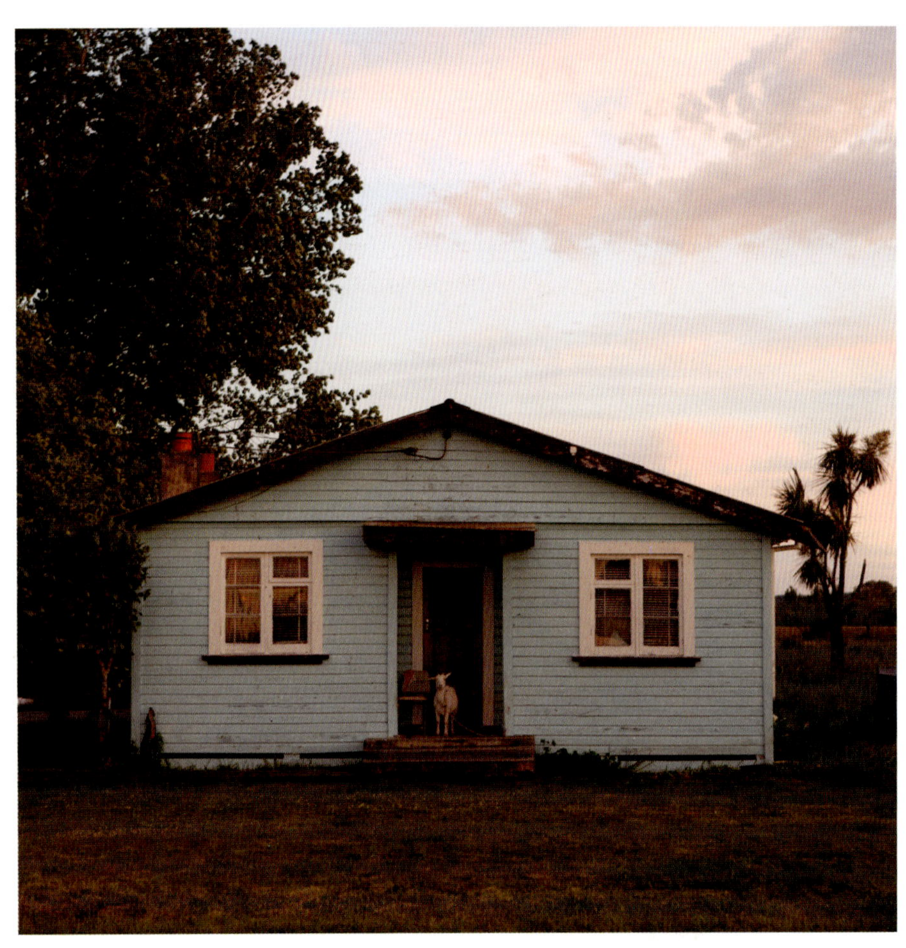

 House and goat, Lawn Road, Hastings District

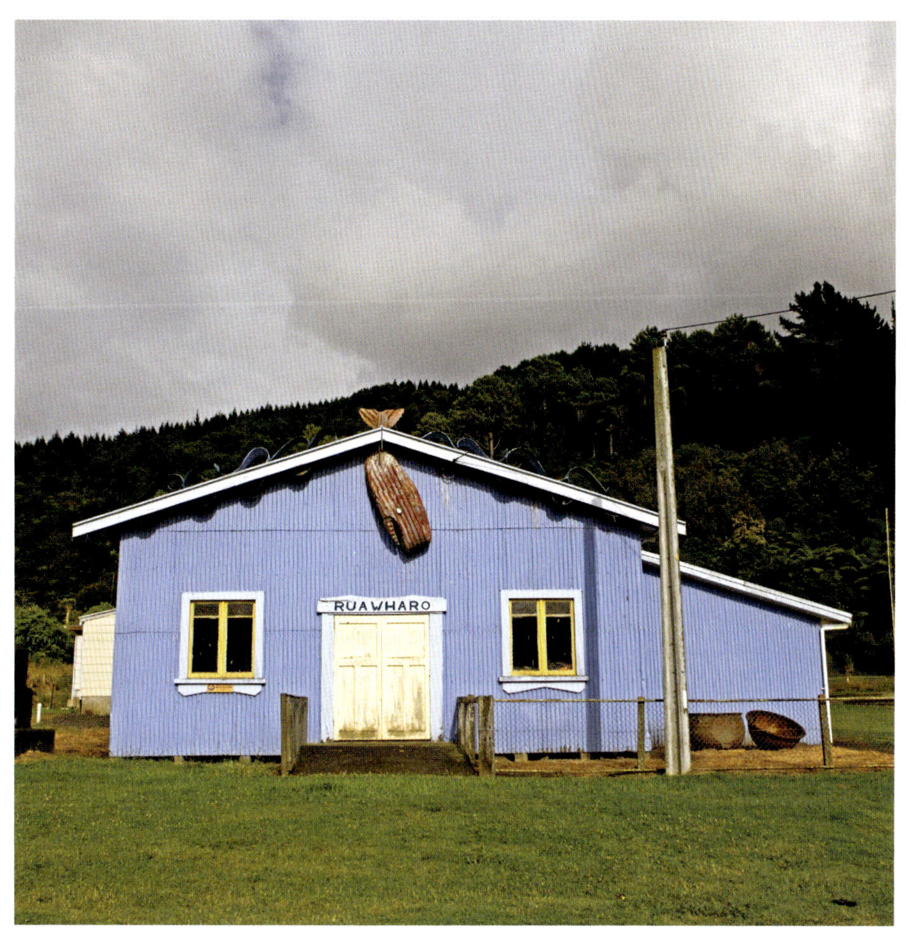

Ruawharo Marae, Opoutama, Mahia Peninsula

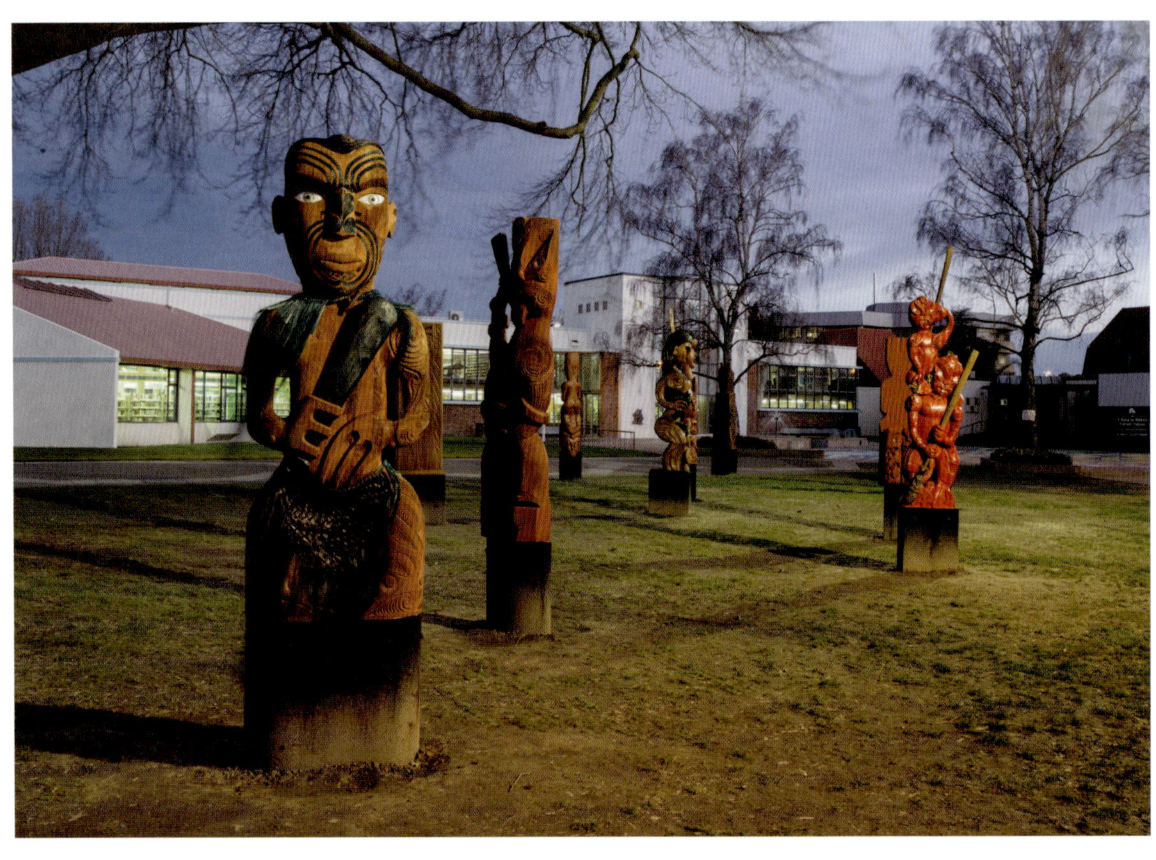

70 Carved pou, each depicting an ancestor as part of the Nga Marae o Heretaunga project, Civic Centre, Hastings

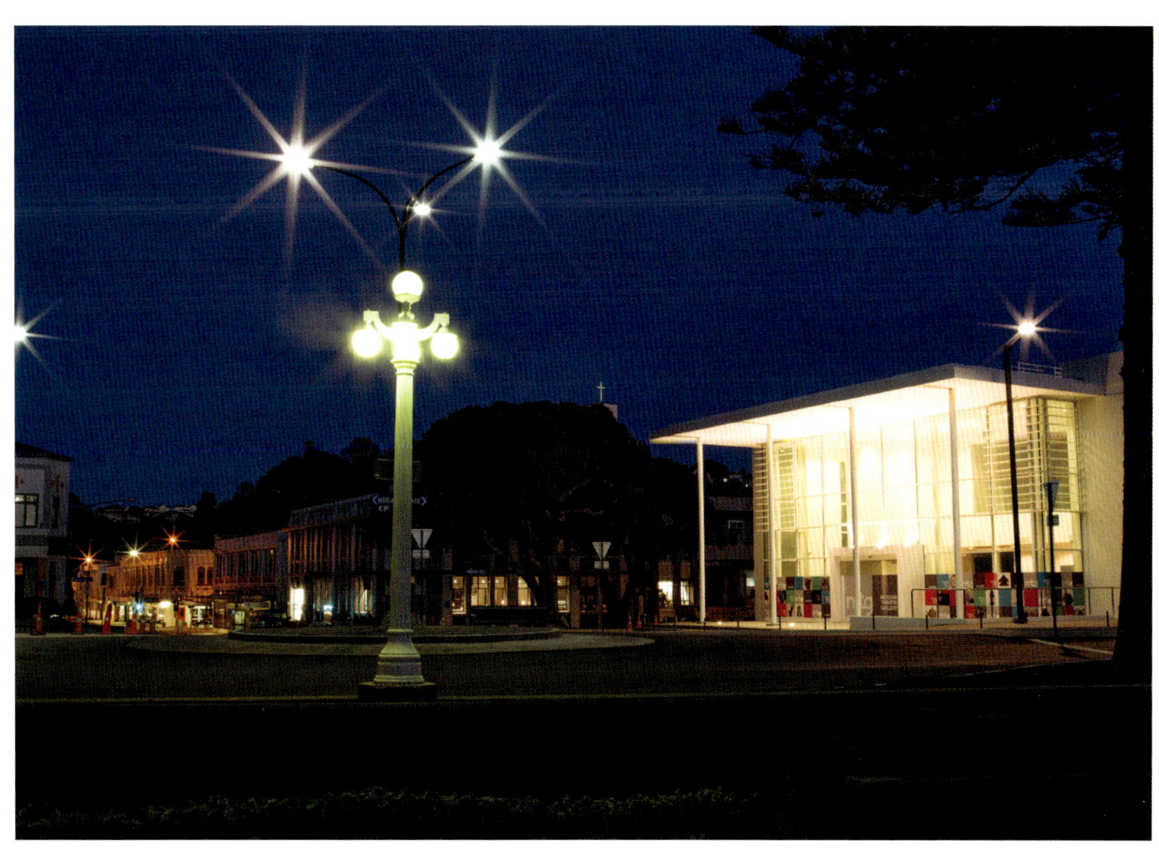

Museum, Theatre, Gallery (MTG), Napier, officially opened September 2013

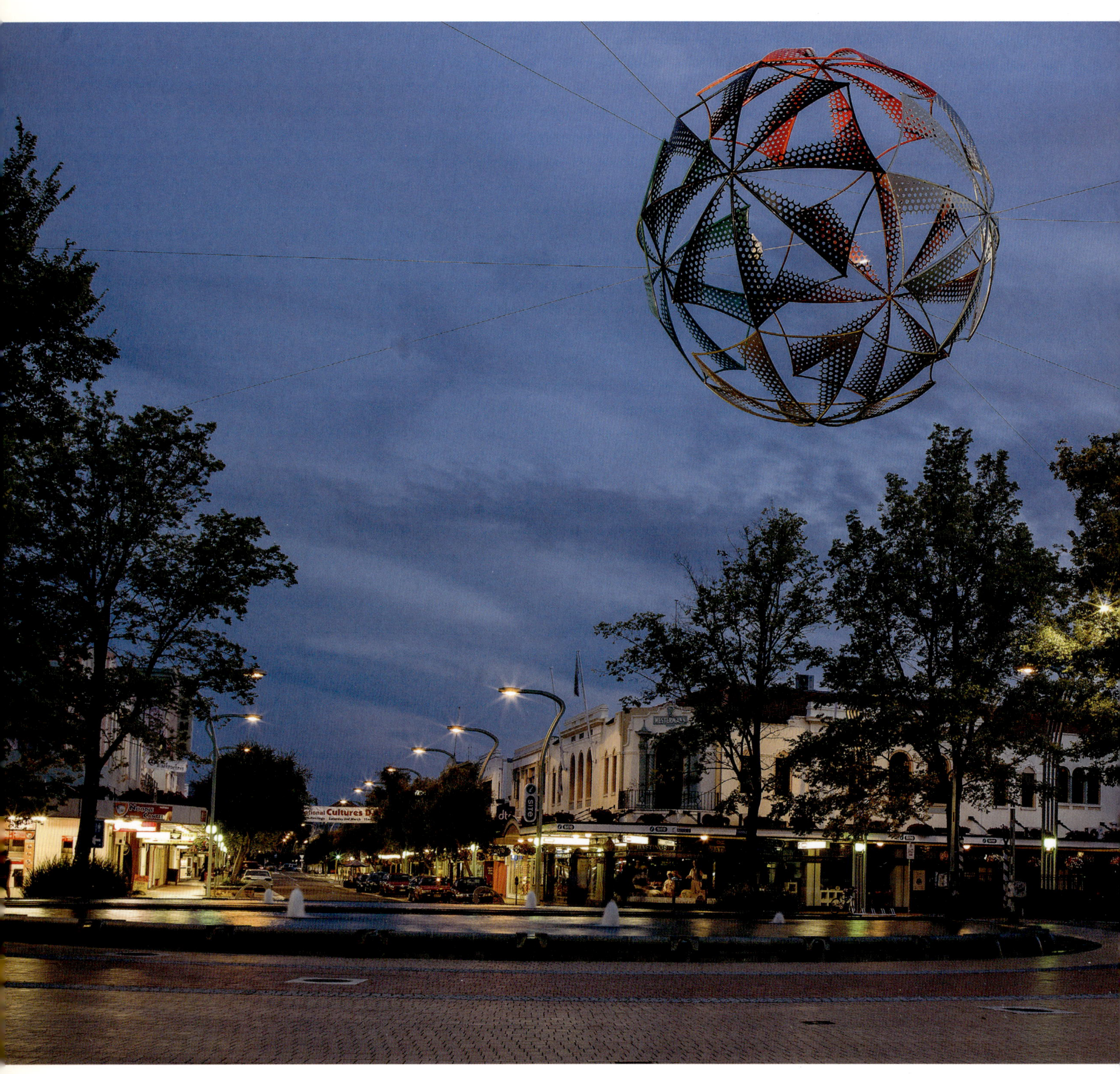

 ‘Suntrap’ sculpture by Neil Dawson, central Hastings

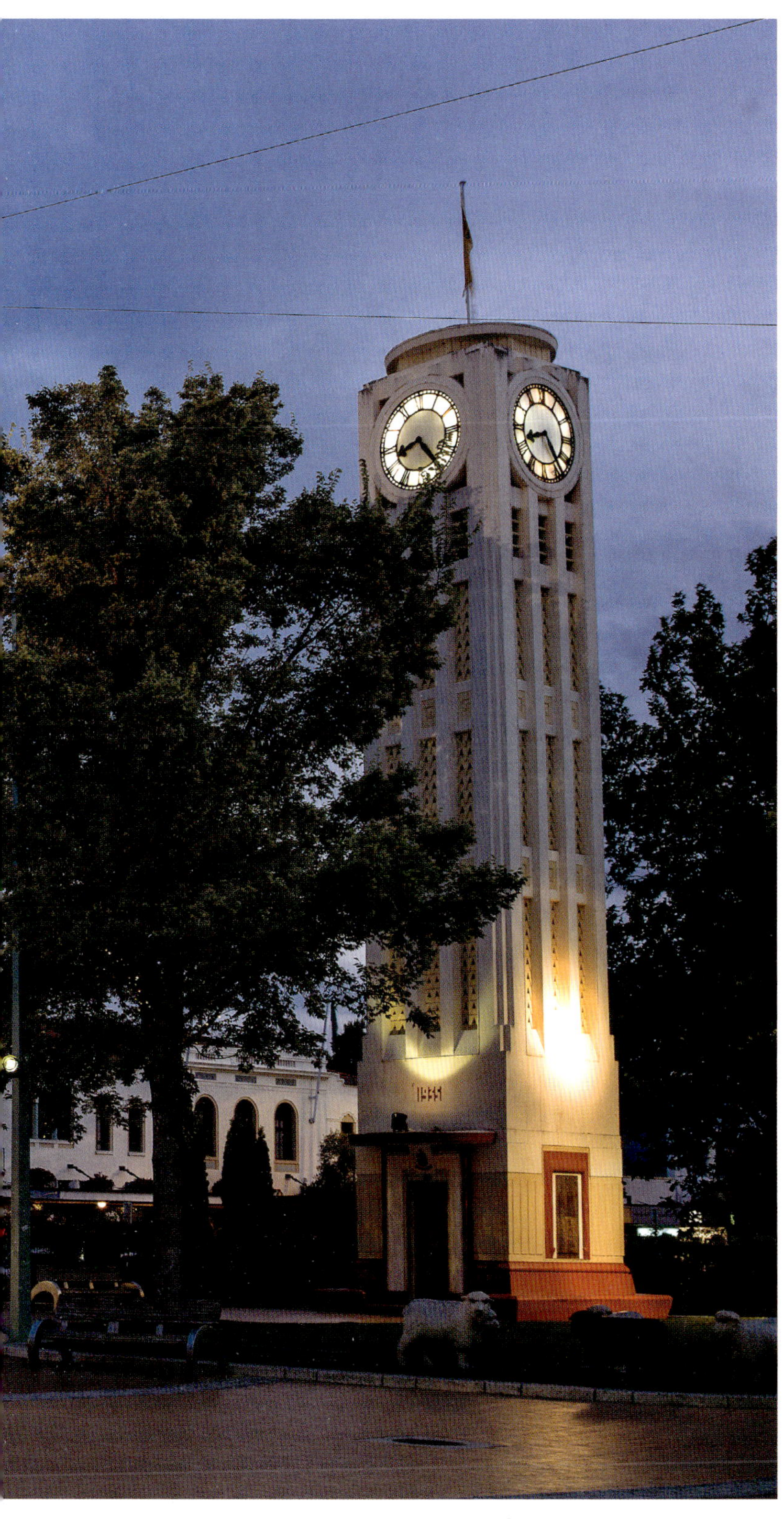

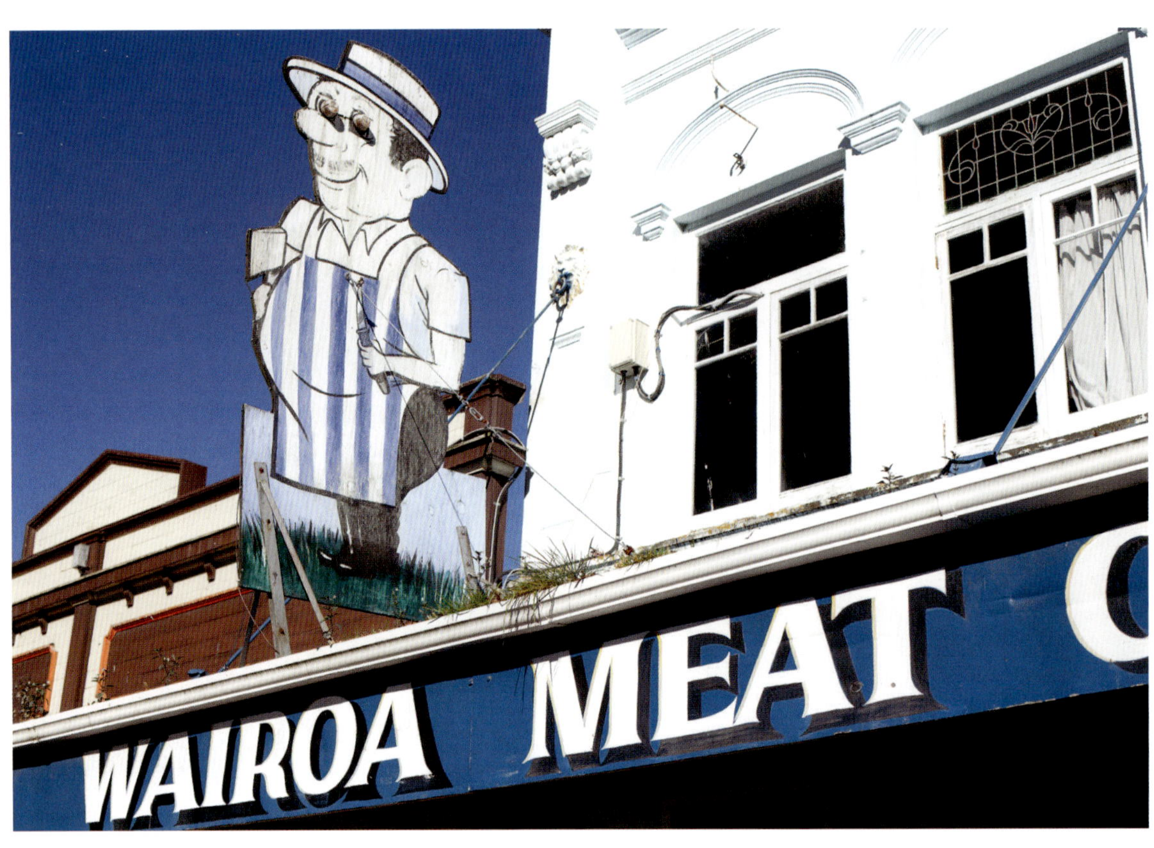

 Wairoa Meat Company, Wairoa, Northern Hawke's Bay

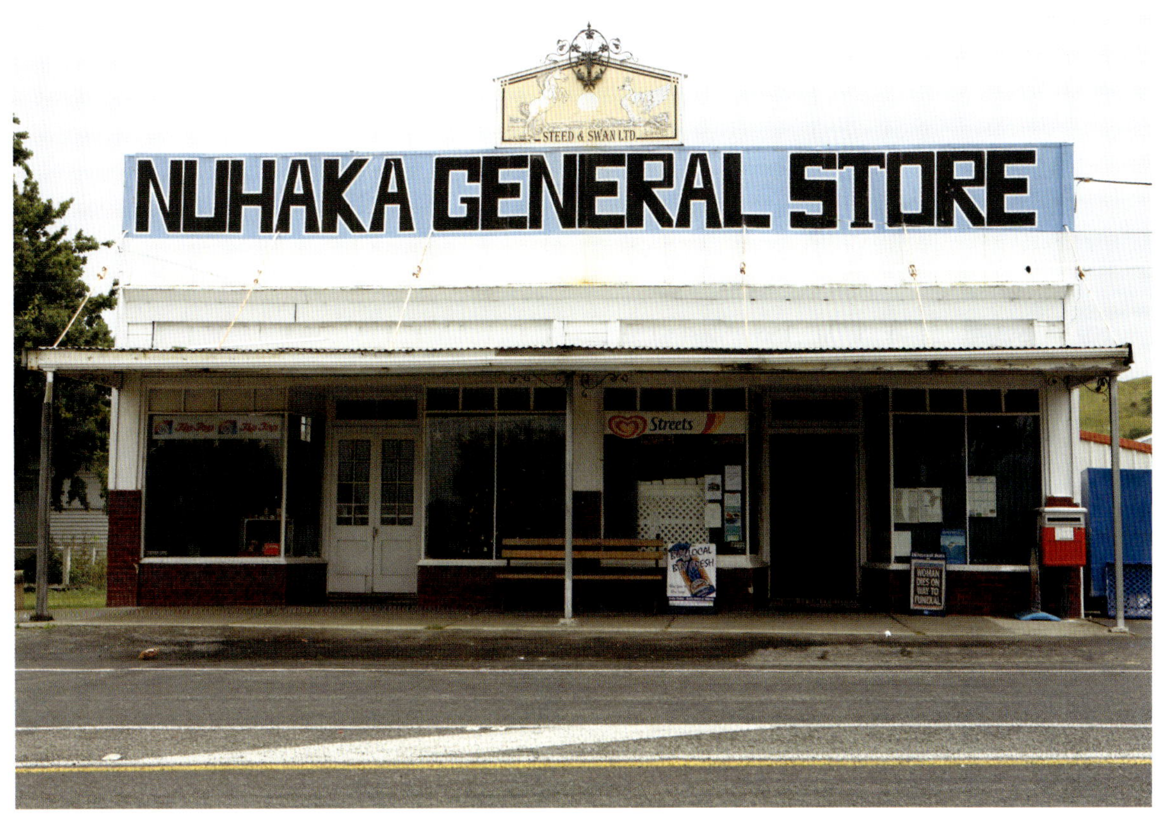
STEED & SWAN LTD
NUHAKA GENERAL STORE
Streets
WOMAN DIES ON WAY TO FUNERAL

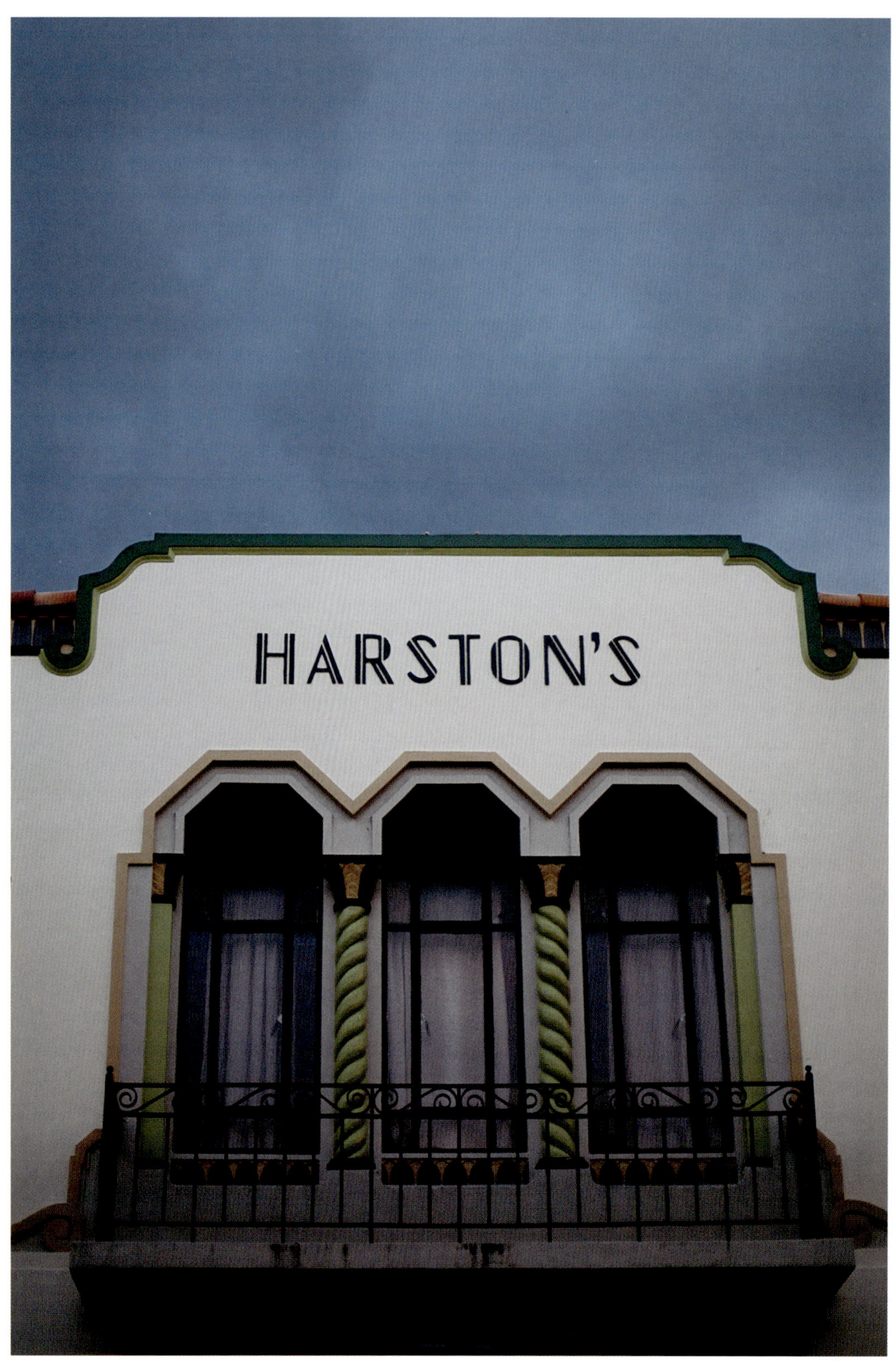

 The historic Harston's building, 1930, survivor of the 1931 Napier Earthquake

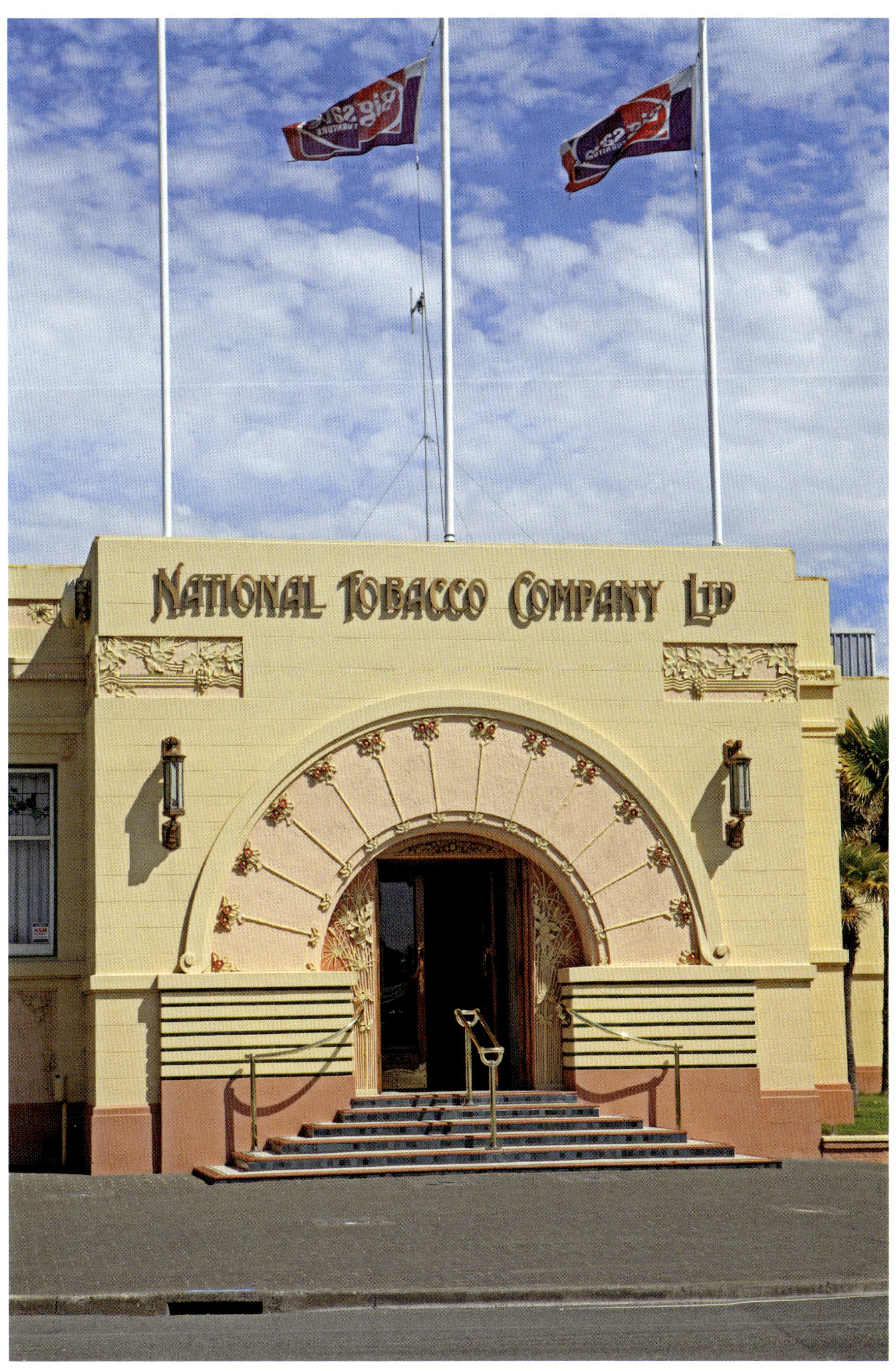

The National Tobacco Company Building (Rothman's Building), designed by architect Louis Hay in the Art Deco style

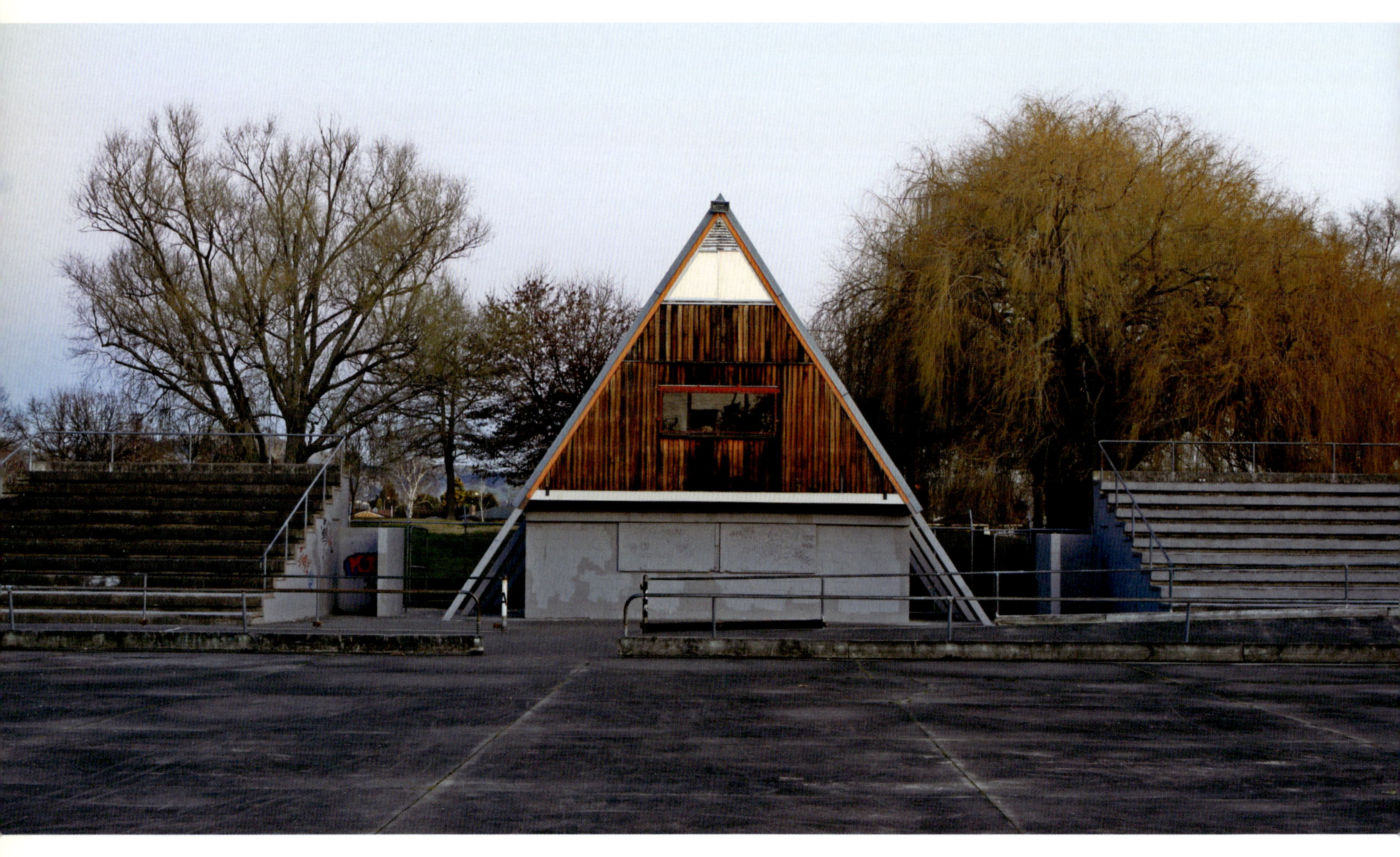

 Roller skating rink, Windsor Park, Hastings

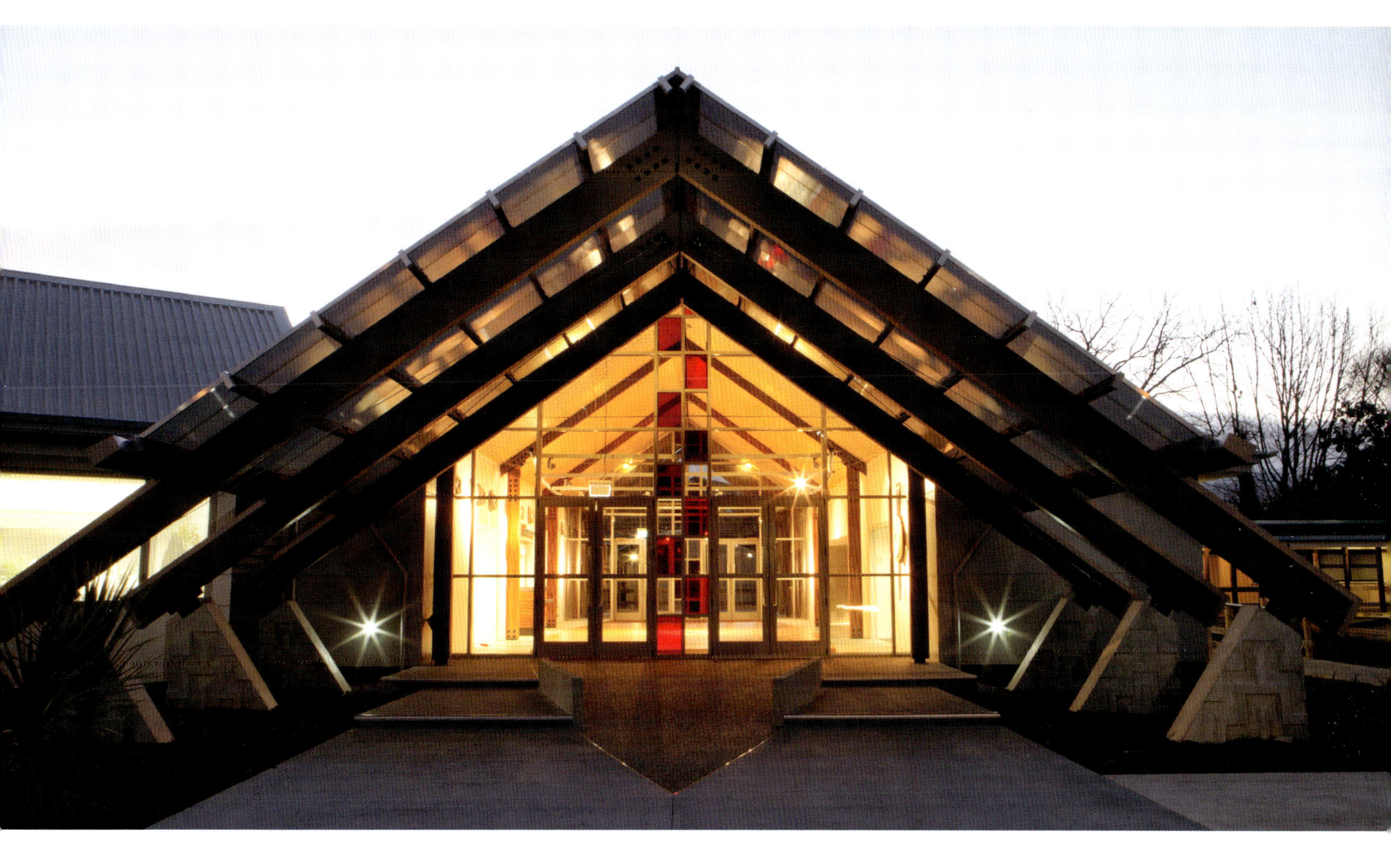

Te Ūranga Waka building, Faculty of Māori Studies, Eastern Institute of Technology (EIT)

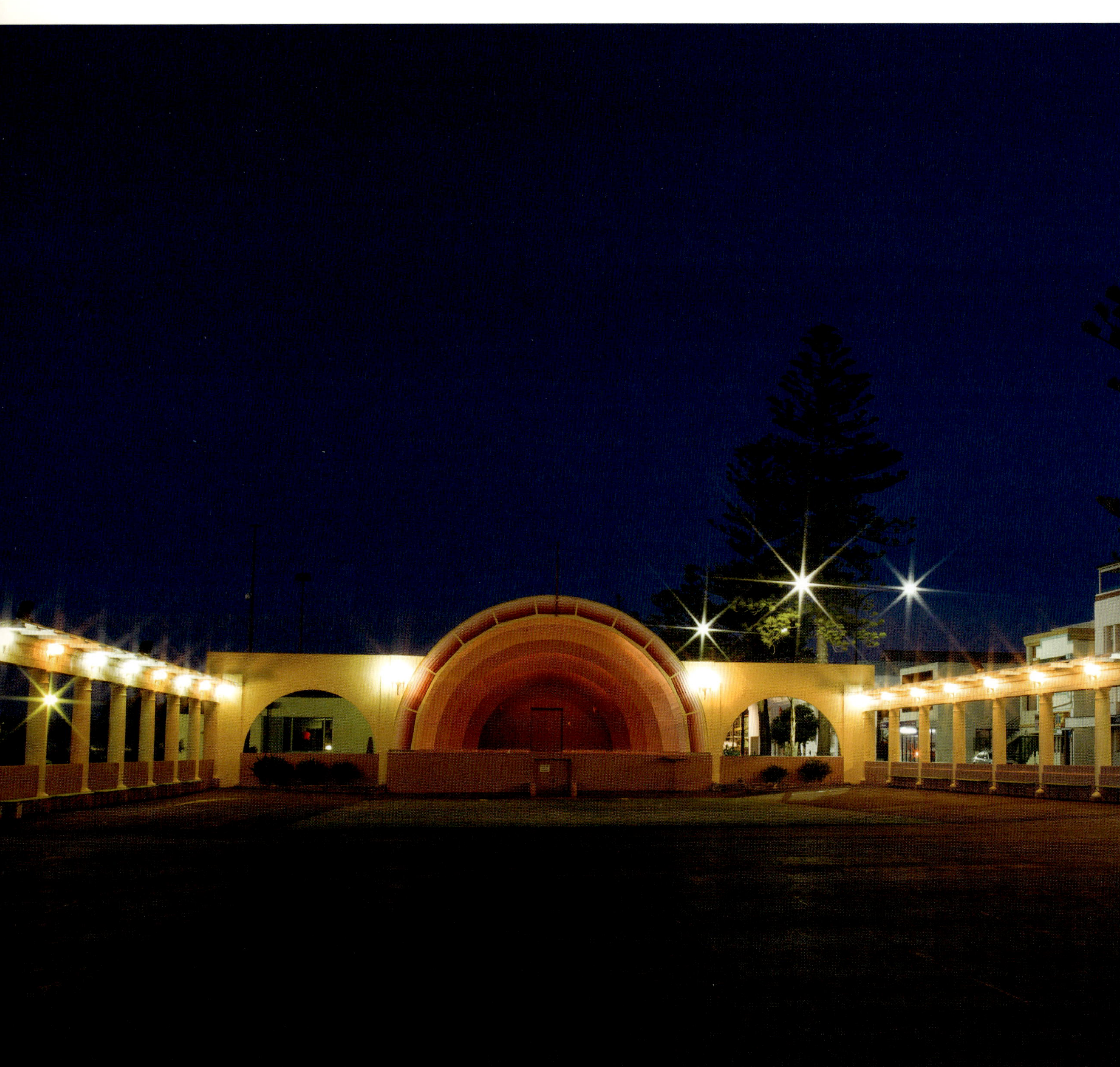

 The historic Soundshell and Dome, Marine Parade, Napier

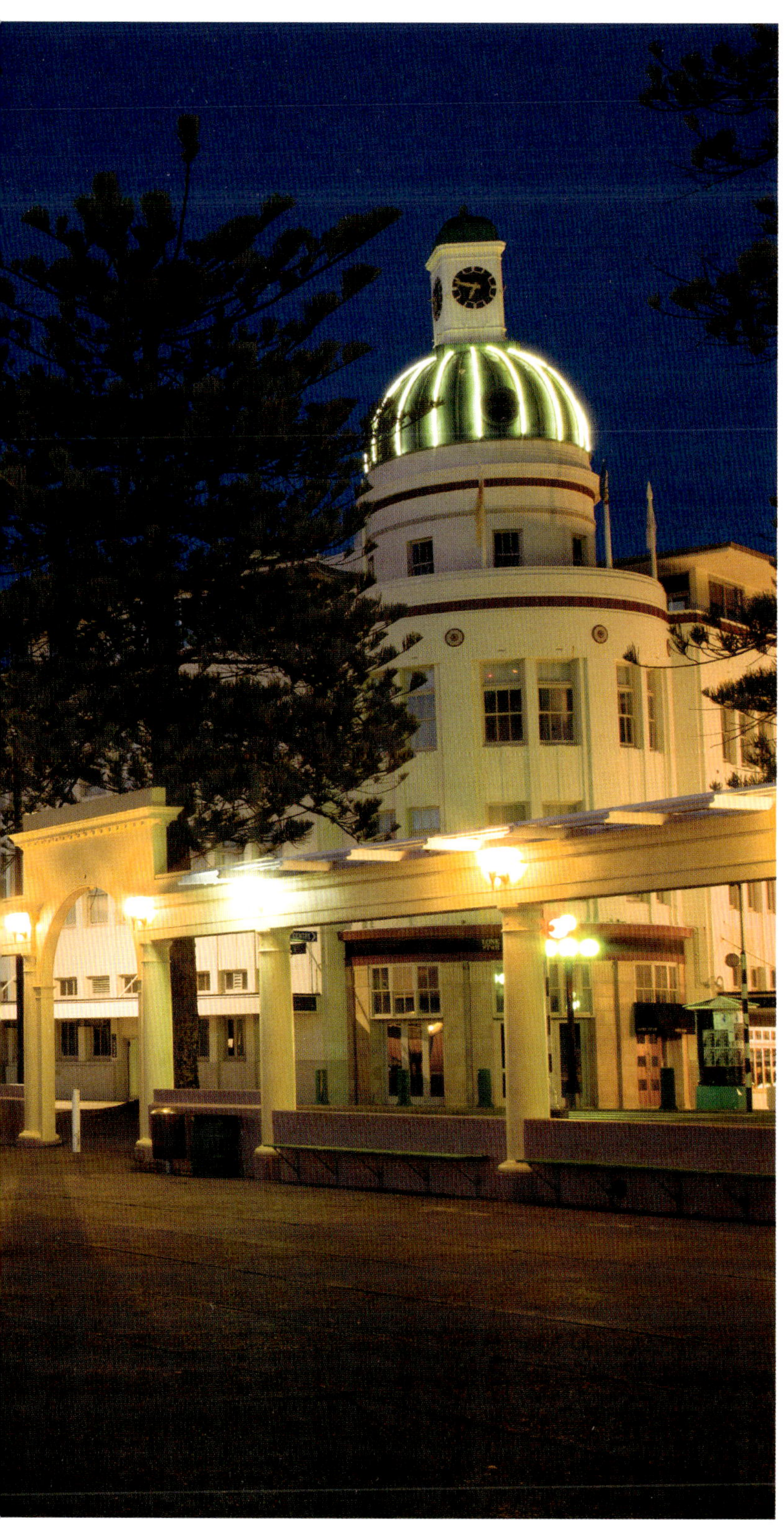

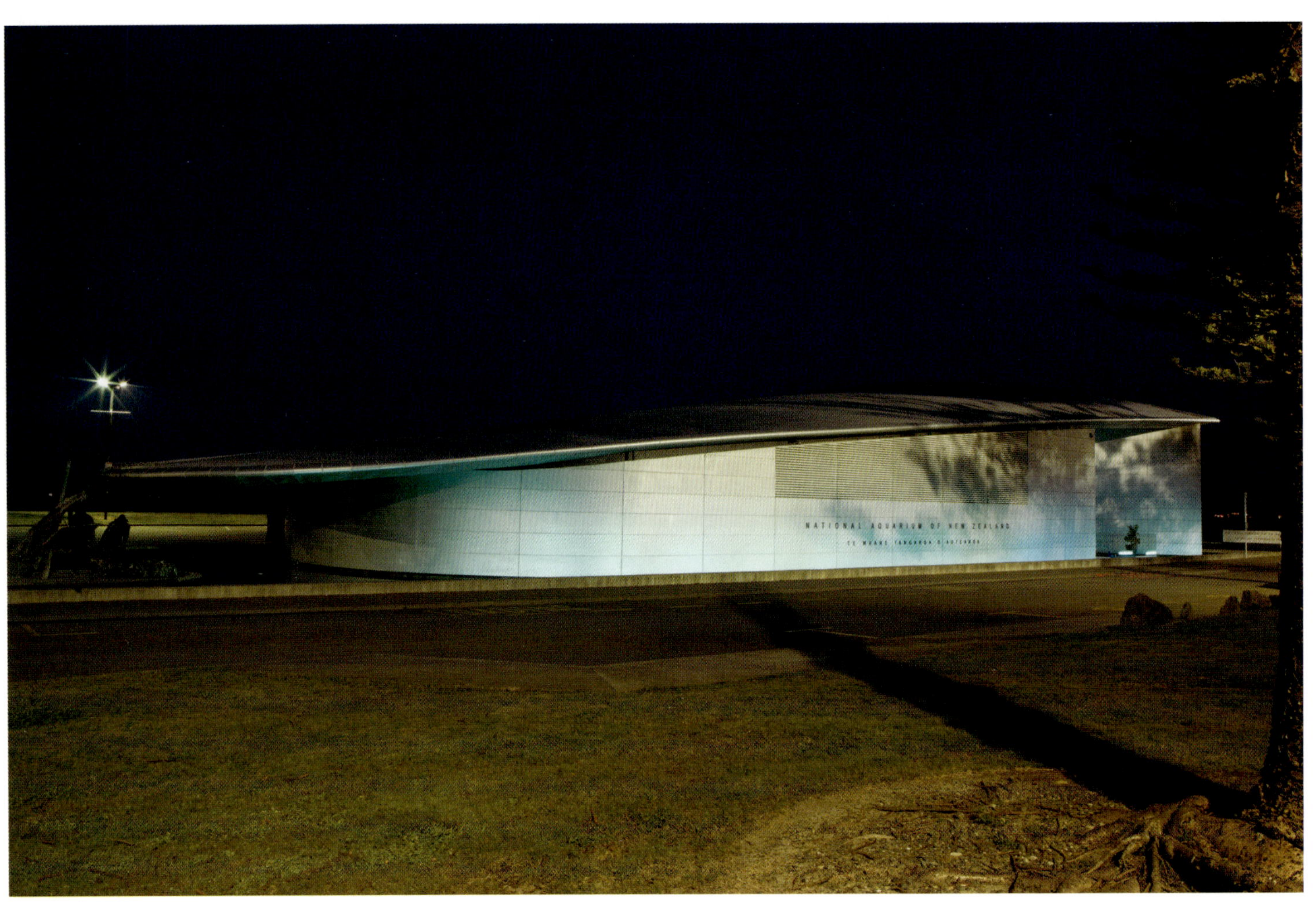

 National Aquarium of New Zealand, Marine Parade, Napier

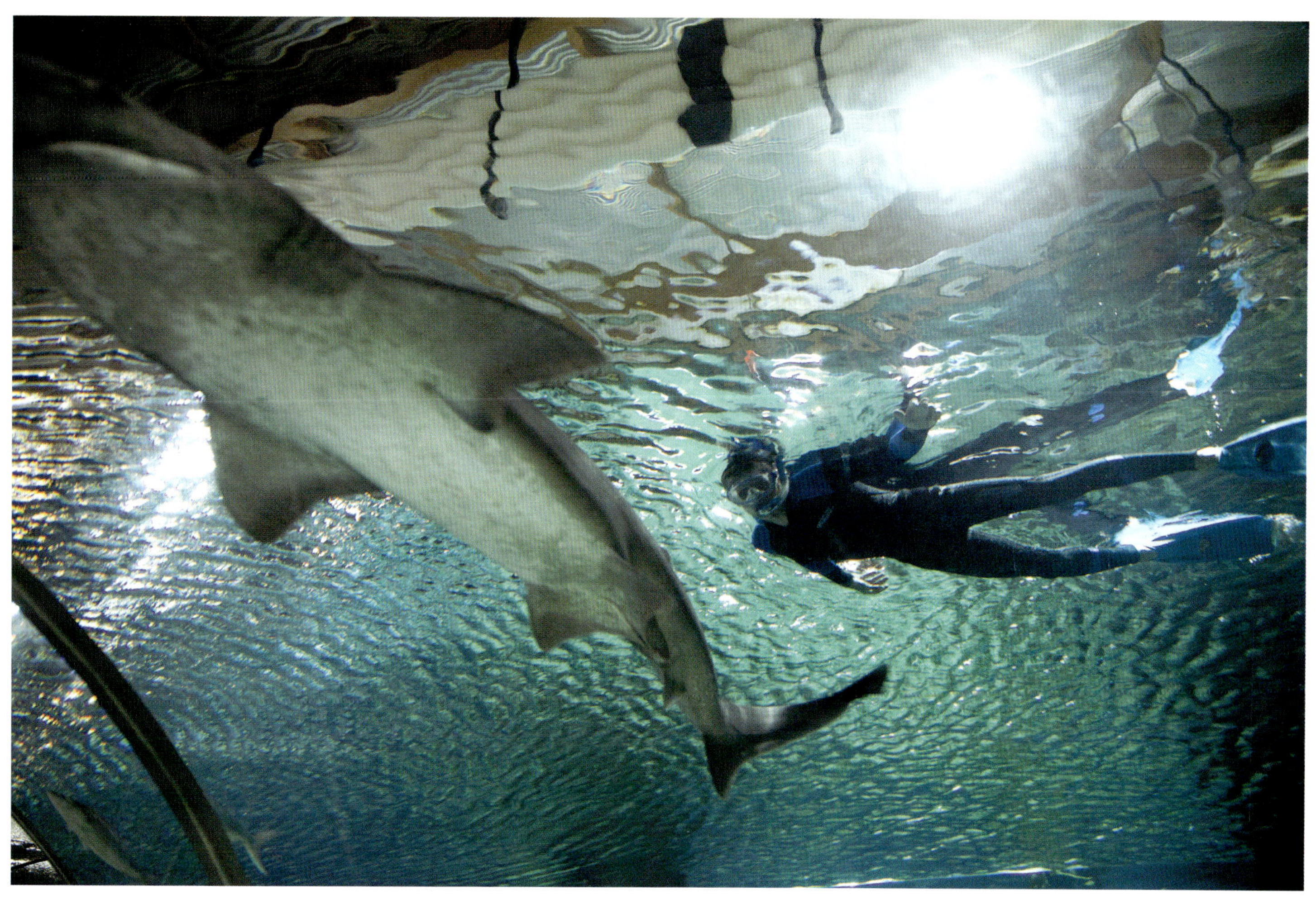

Swimming with sharks, National Aquarium of New Zealand, Napier

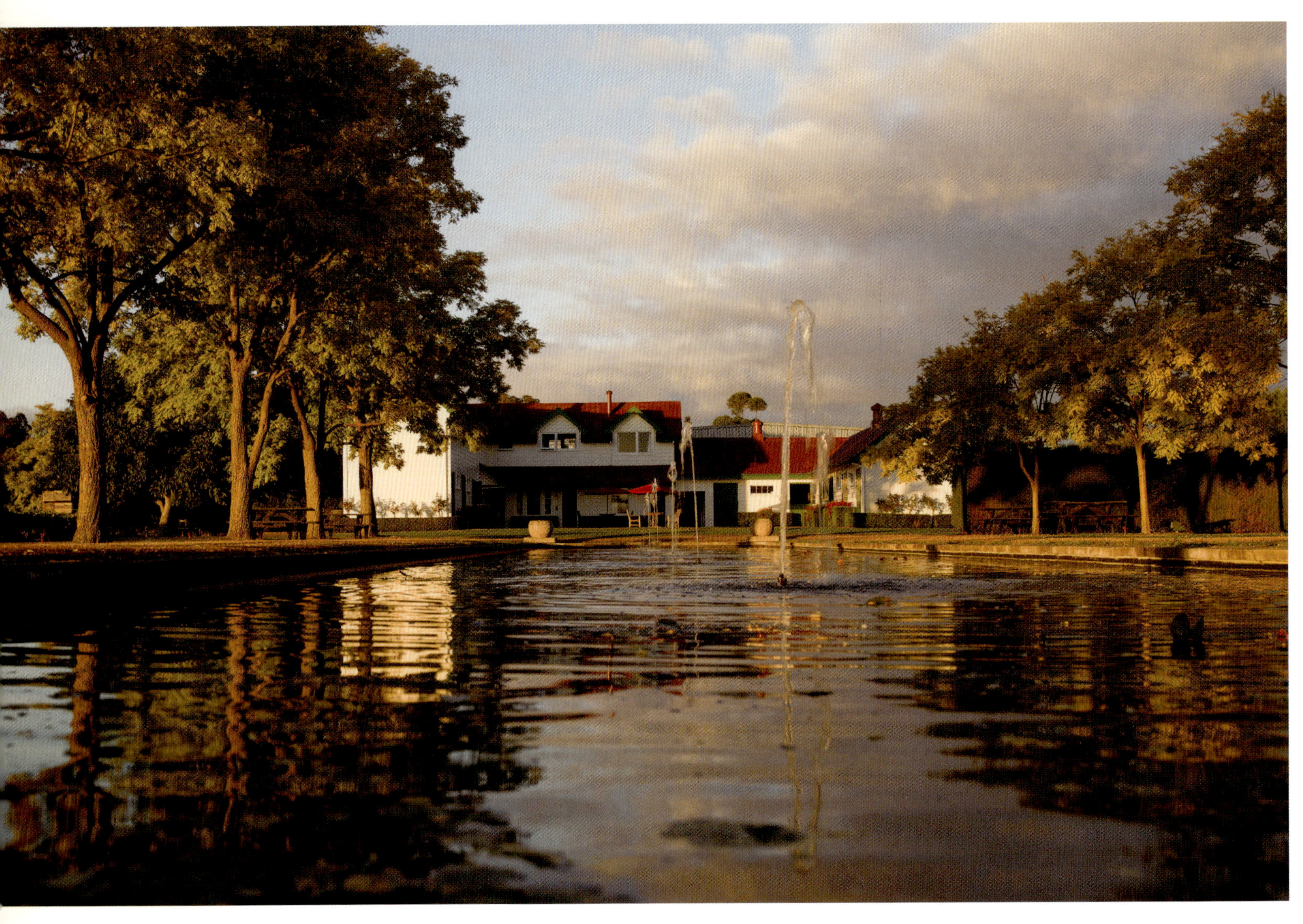

 Ngatarawa Winery, orignially built as stables in 1890, Bridge Pa, Hastings

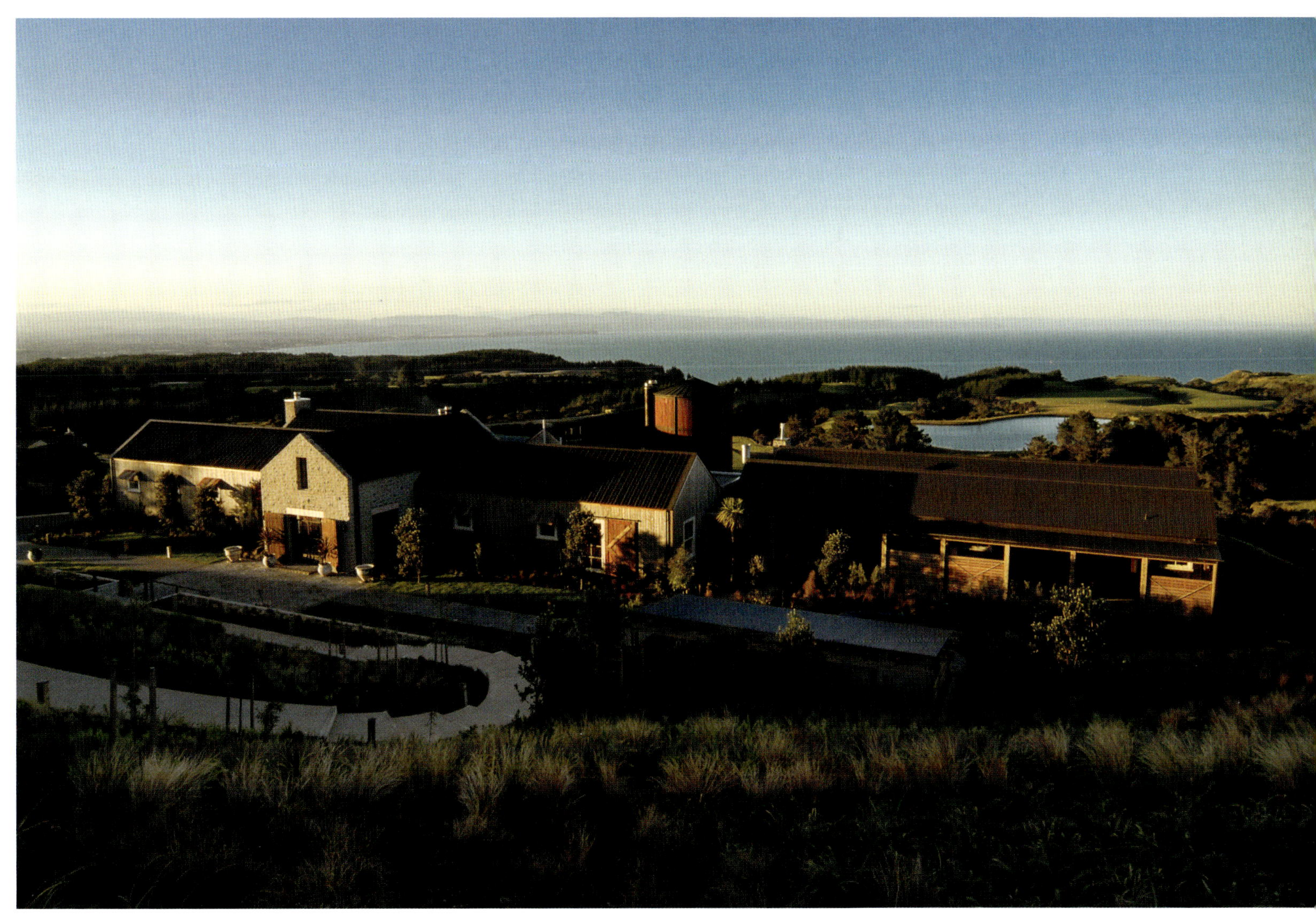

Luxury lodge, The Farm at Cape Kidnappers

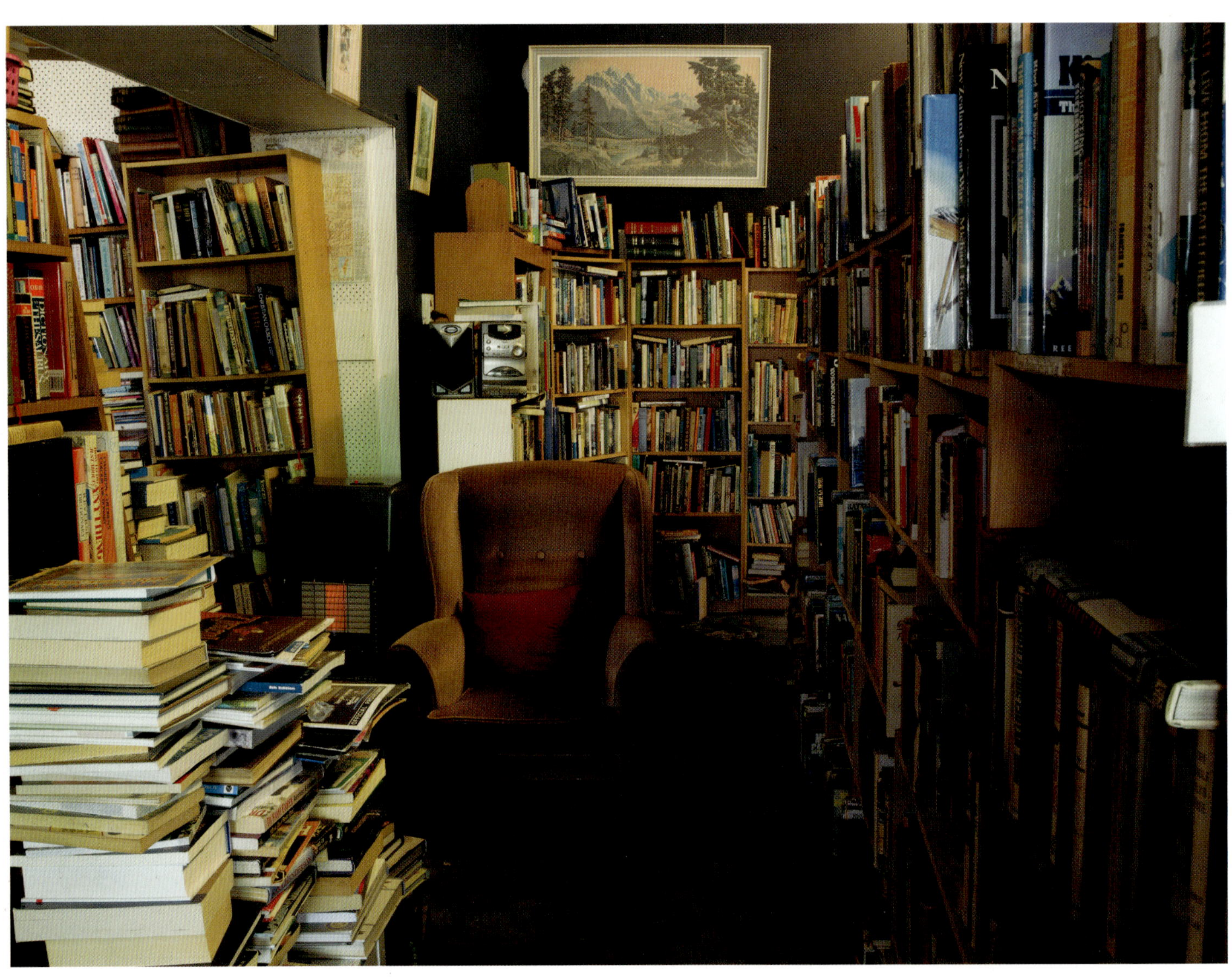

 'The Little Book Shop', Napier

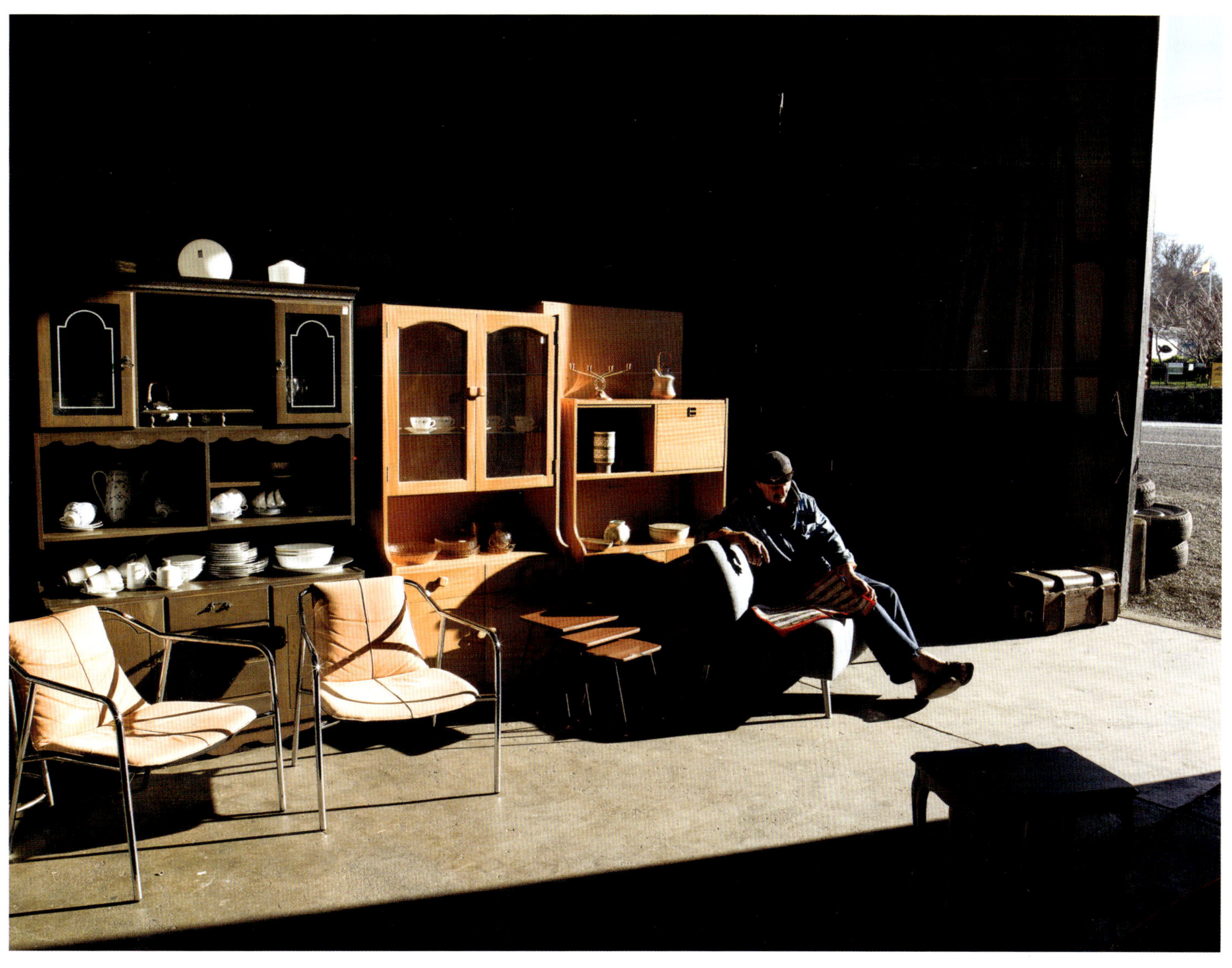

Mike Clough's second hand shop 'Shed 169', Pukehou, Central Hawke's Bay

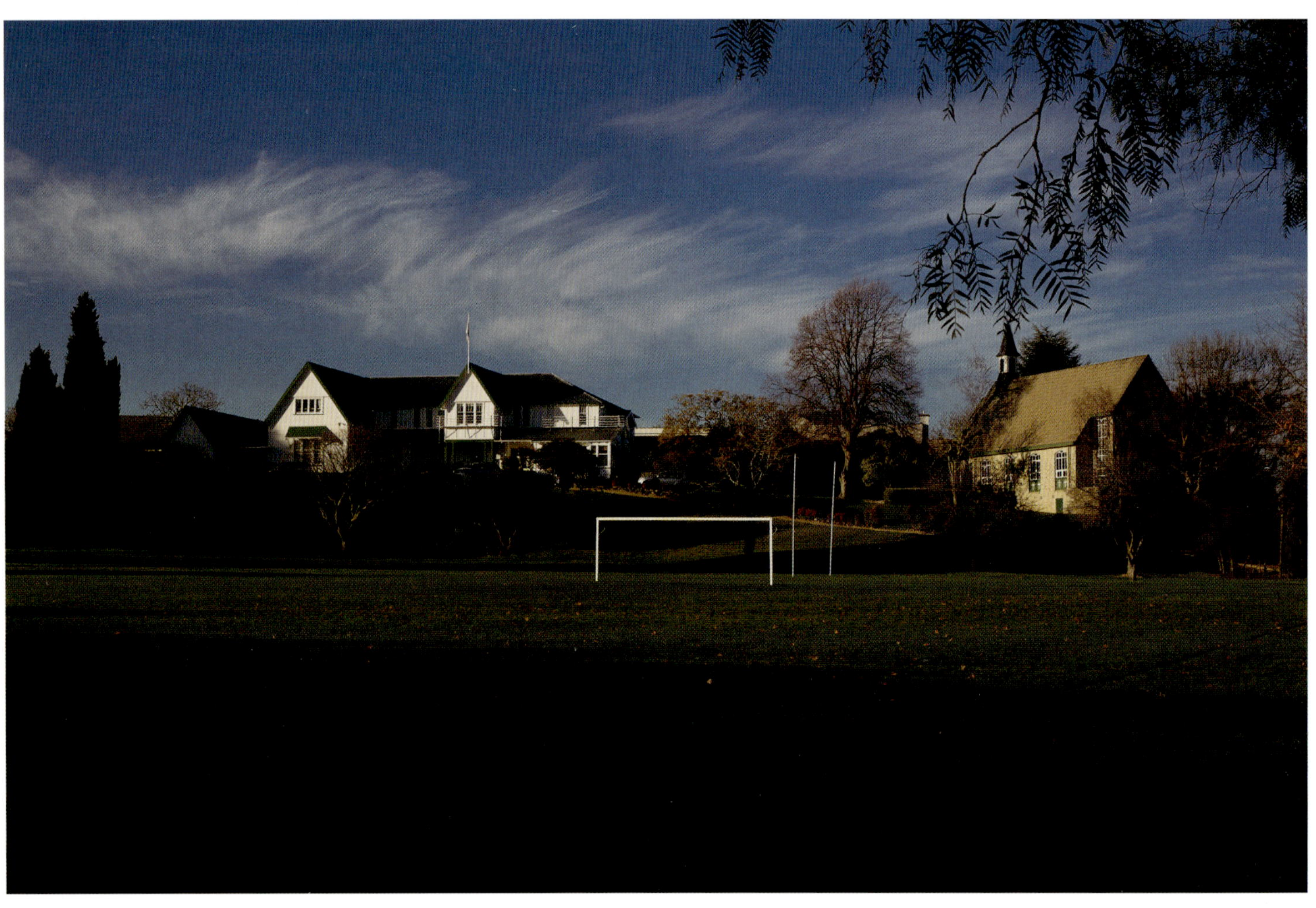

 Hereworth School, Havelock North

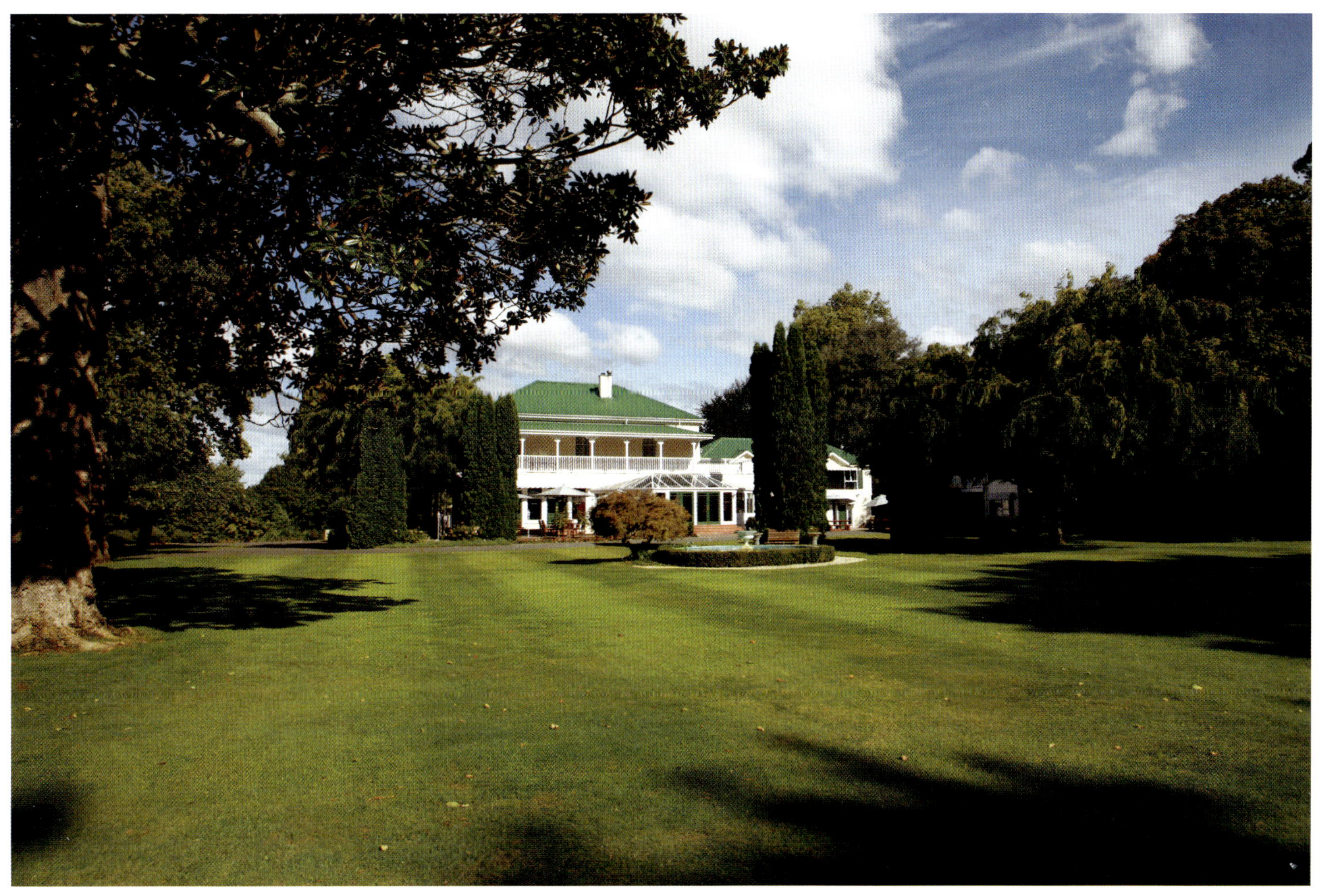

Mangapapa Lodge, Napier Road, Havelock North

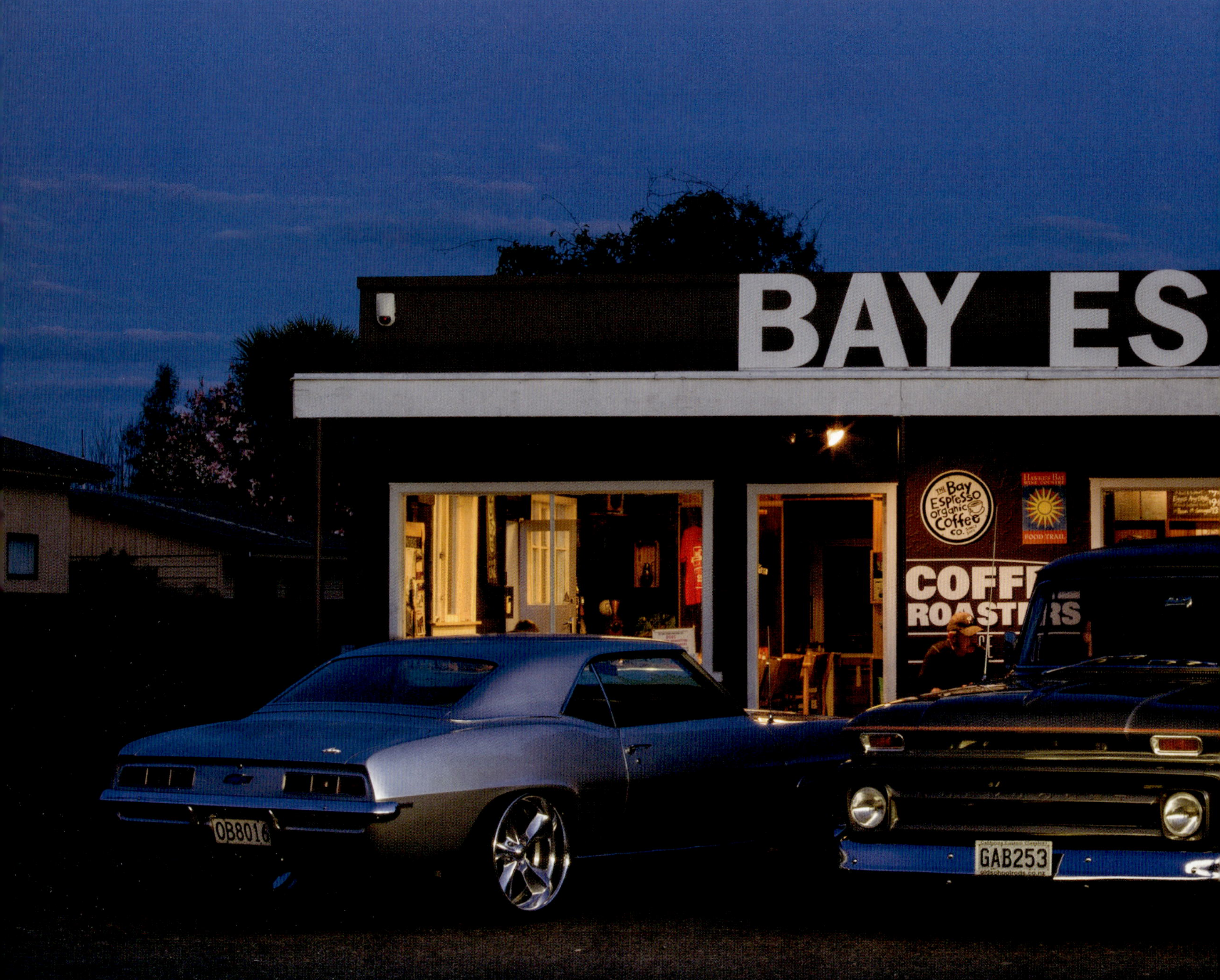
BAY ES
The Bay Espresso organic Coffee Co.
OB8016
GAB253

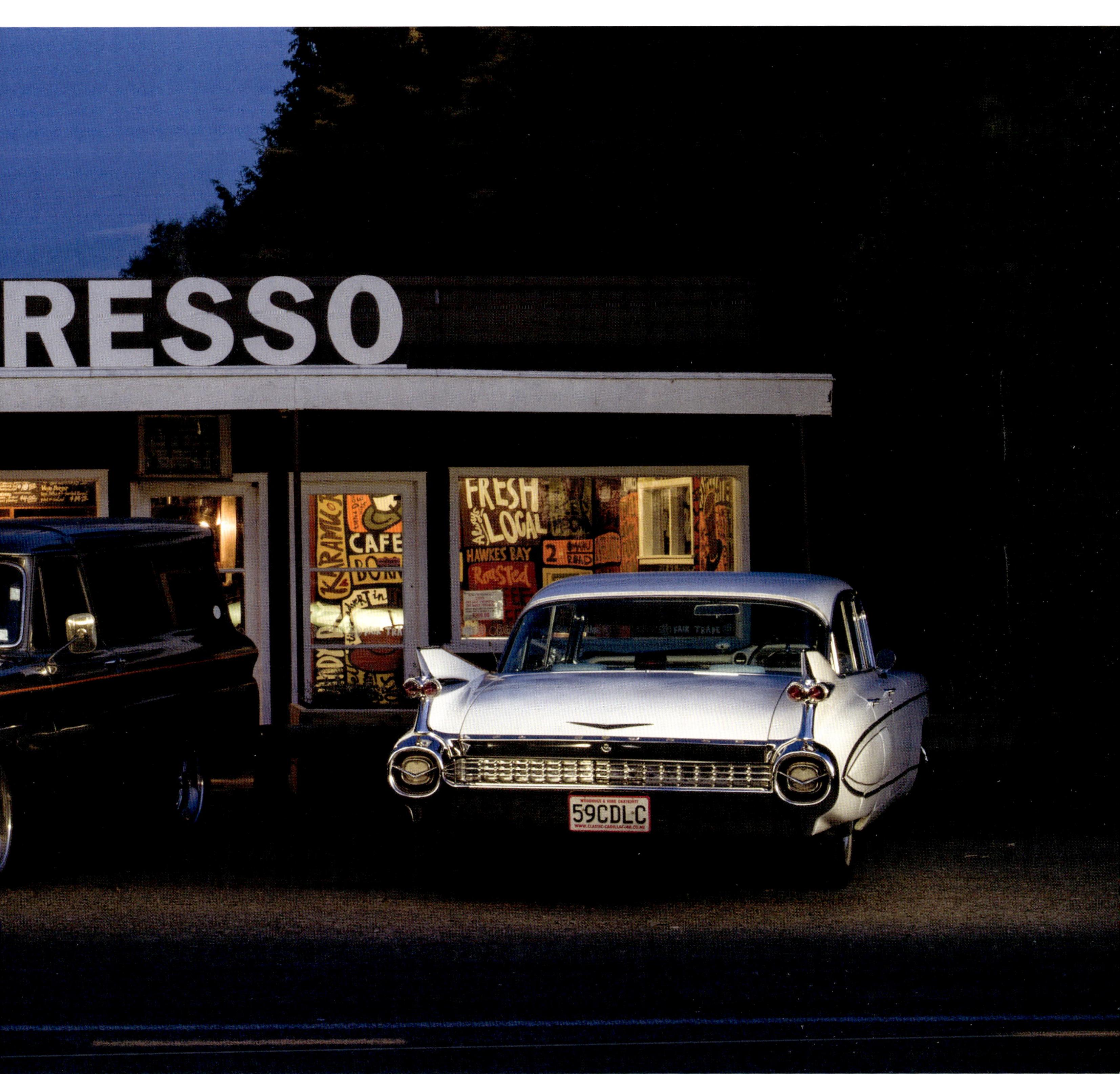

Bay Espresso, Karamu Road, Hastings

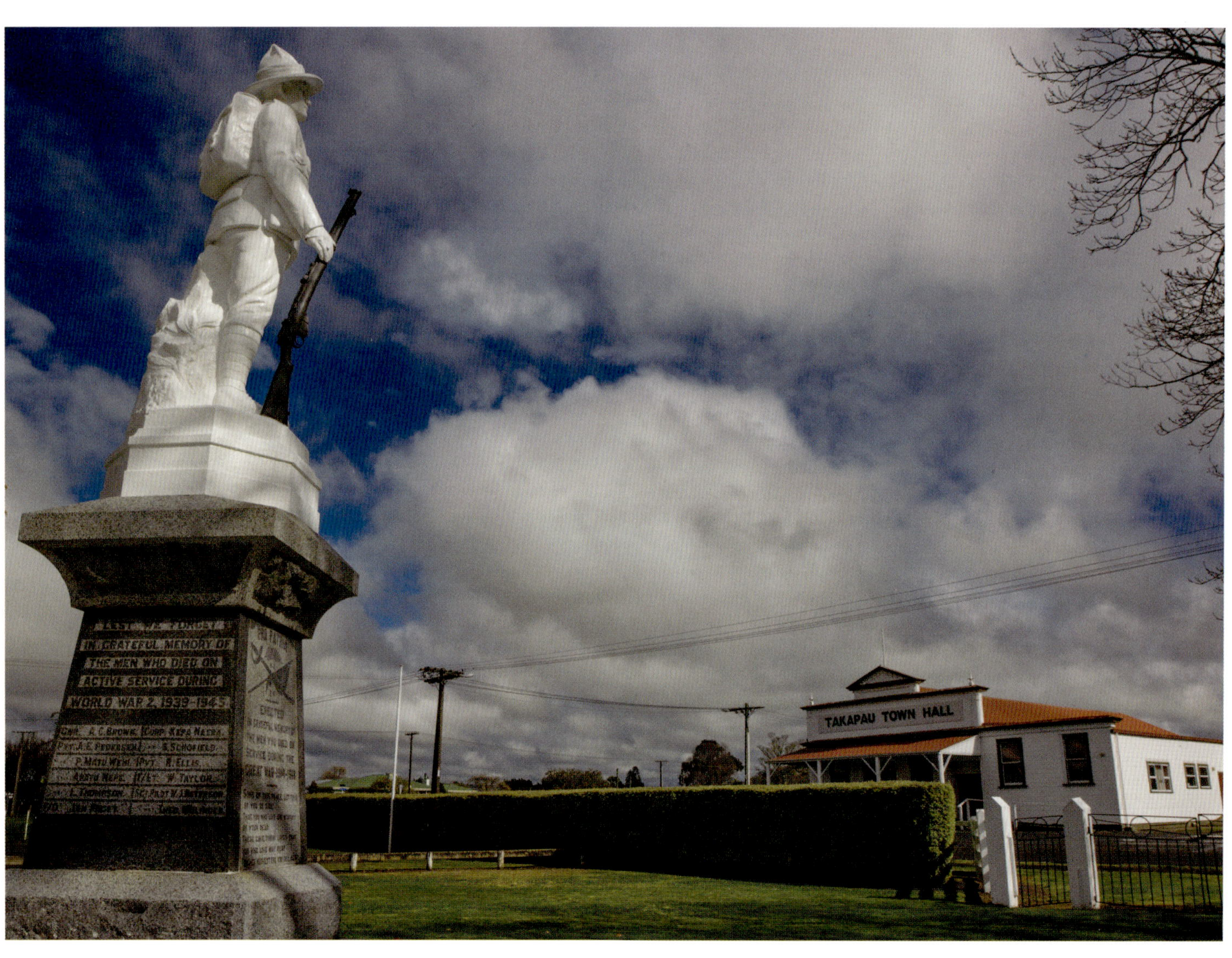

 Takapau War Memorial and Town Hall, Takapau, Central Hawke's Bay

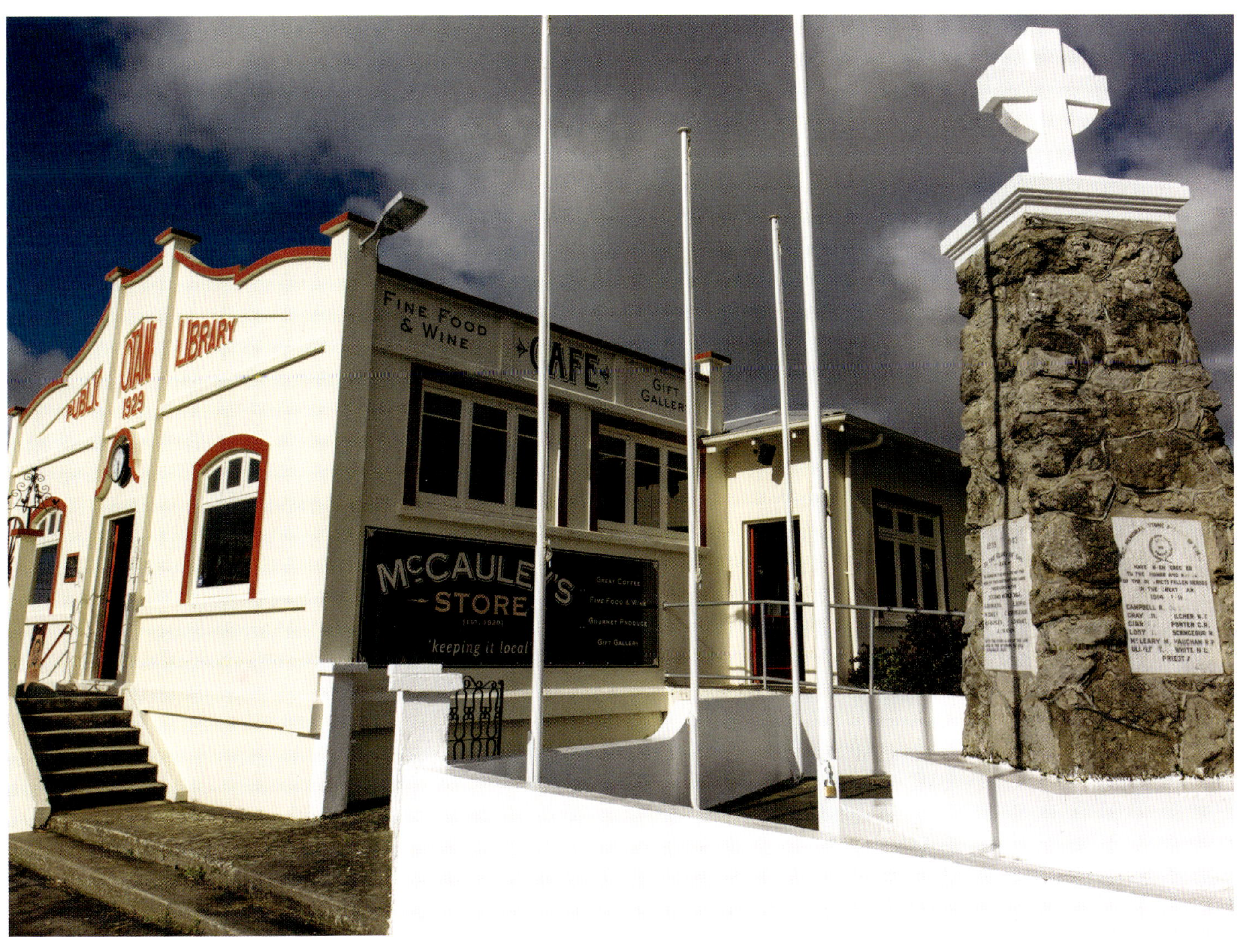

McCauley's Store & Café, Otane, Central Hawke's Bay

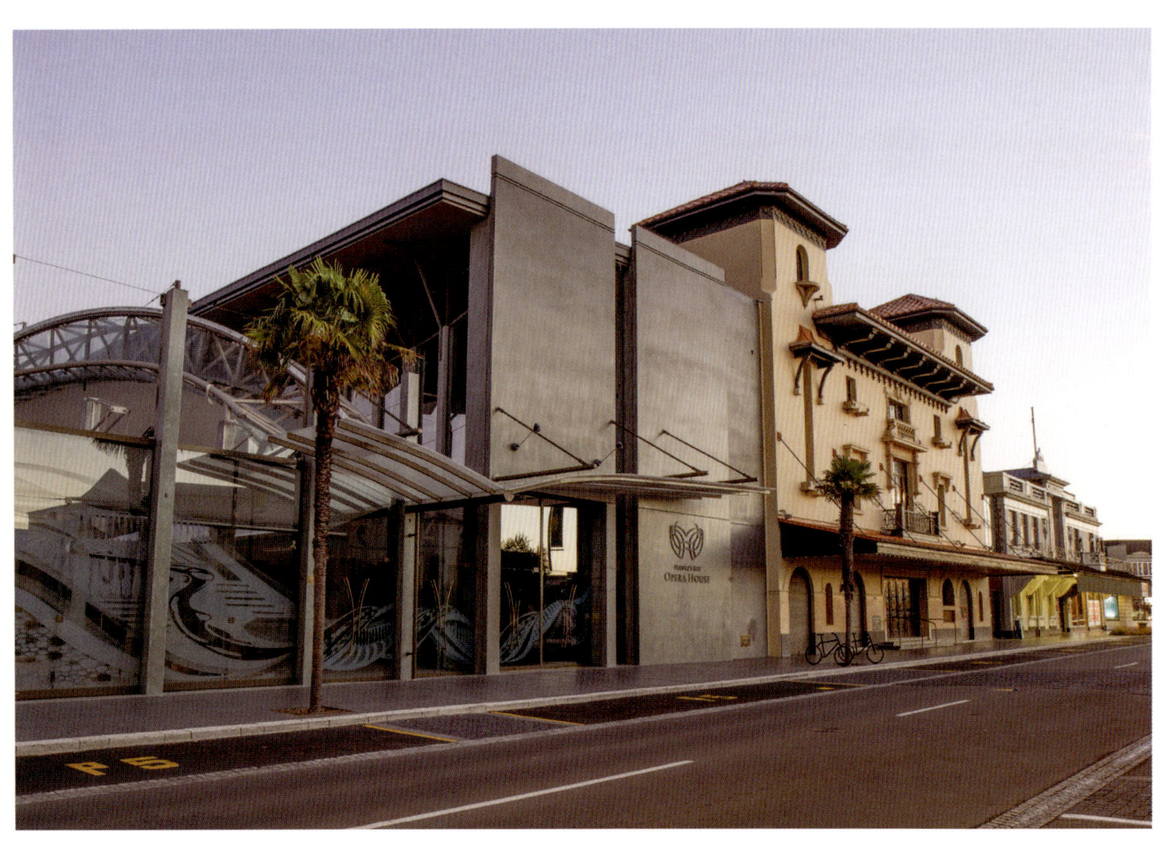

94 Hawke's Bay Opera House, Hastings Street, Hastings

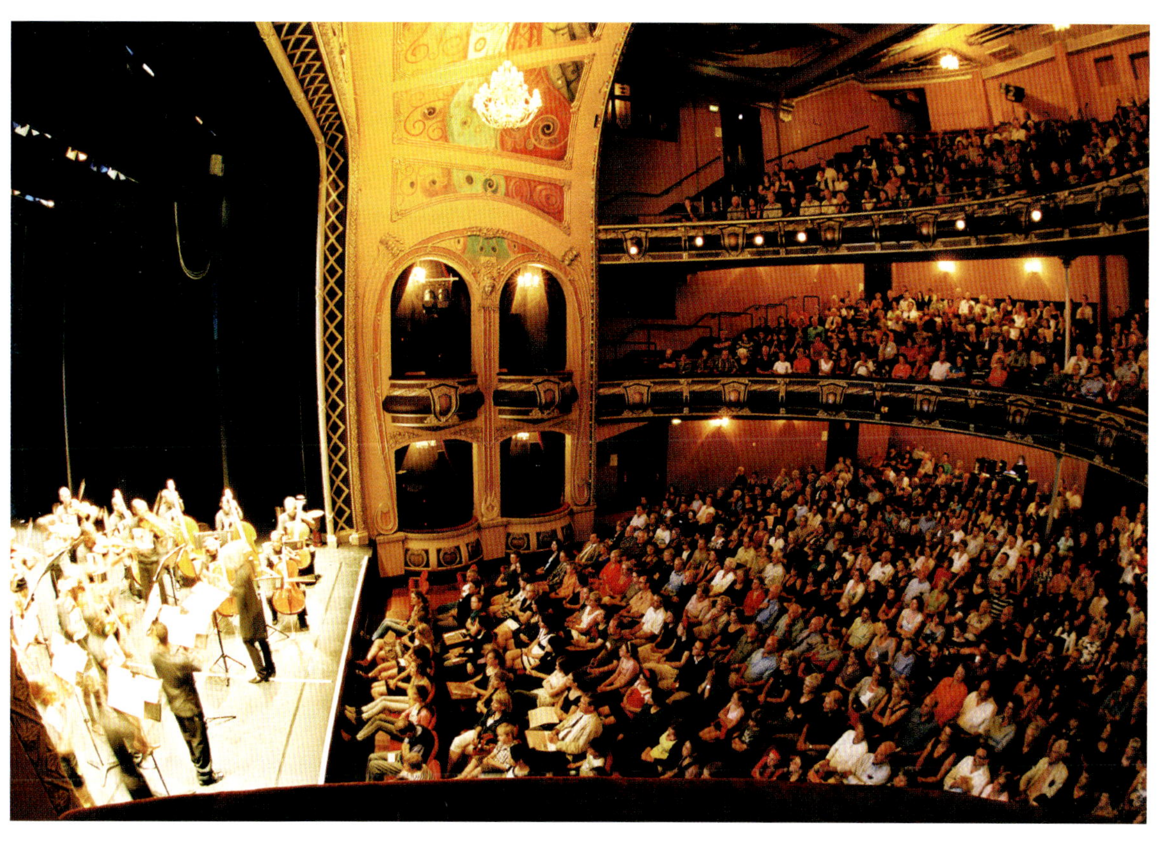

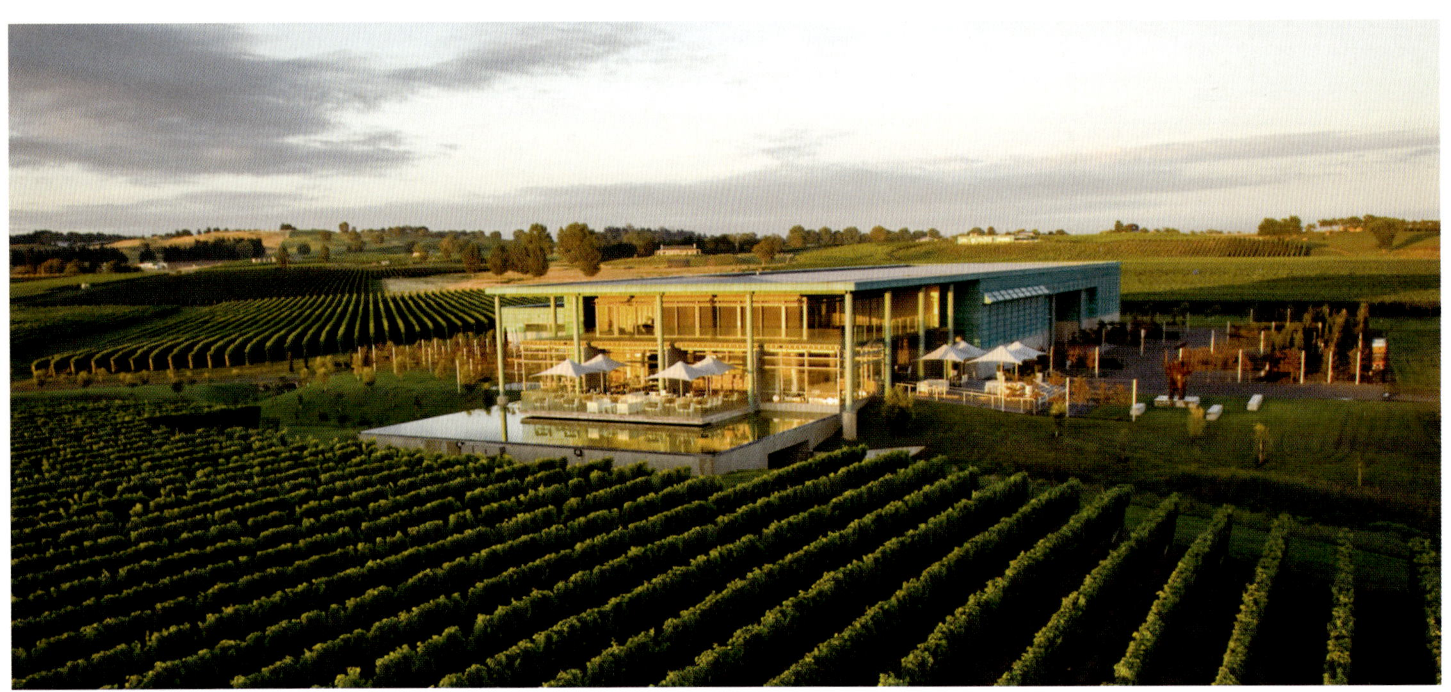

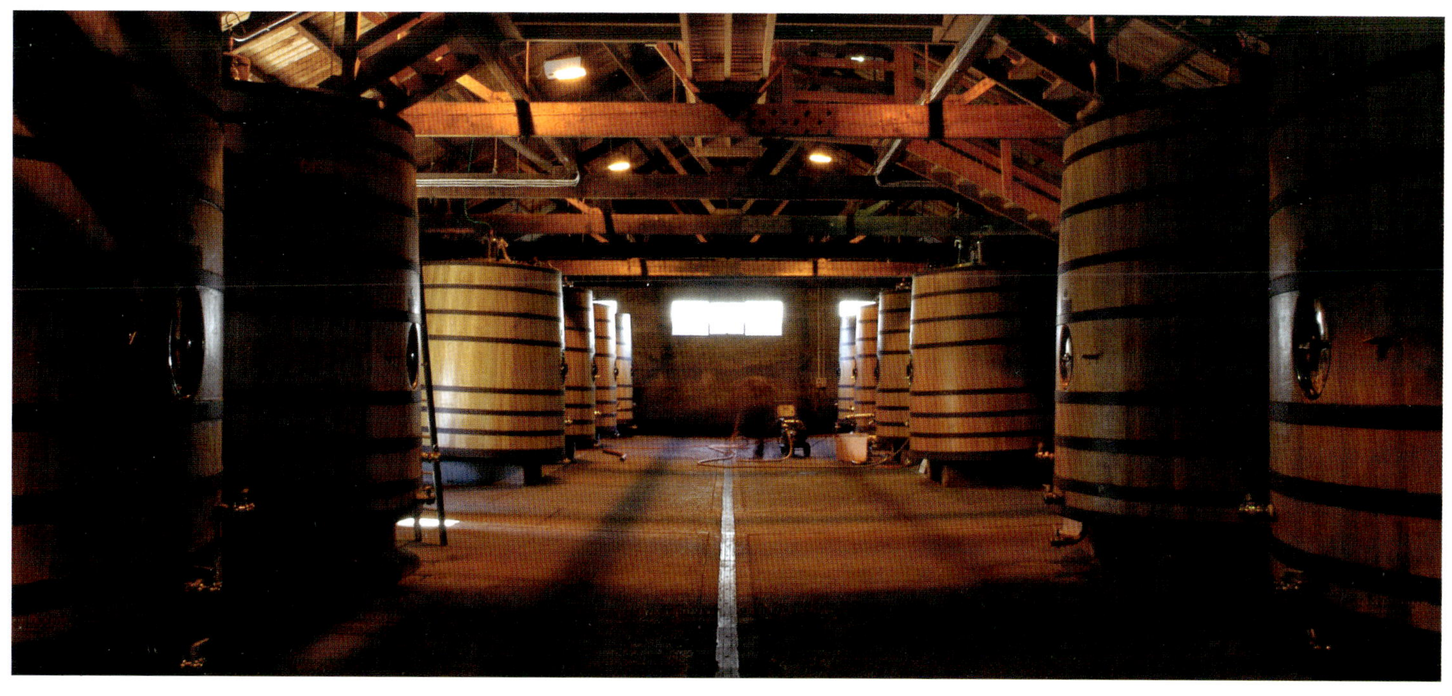

The Cuvee Room, Church Road Winery, Taradale

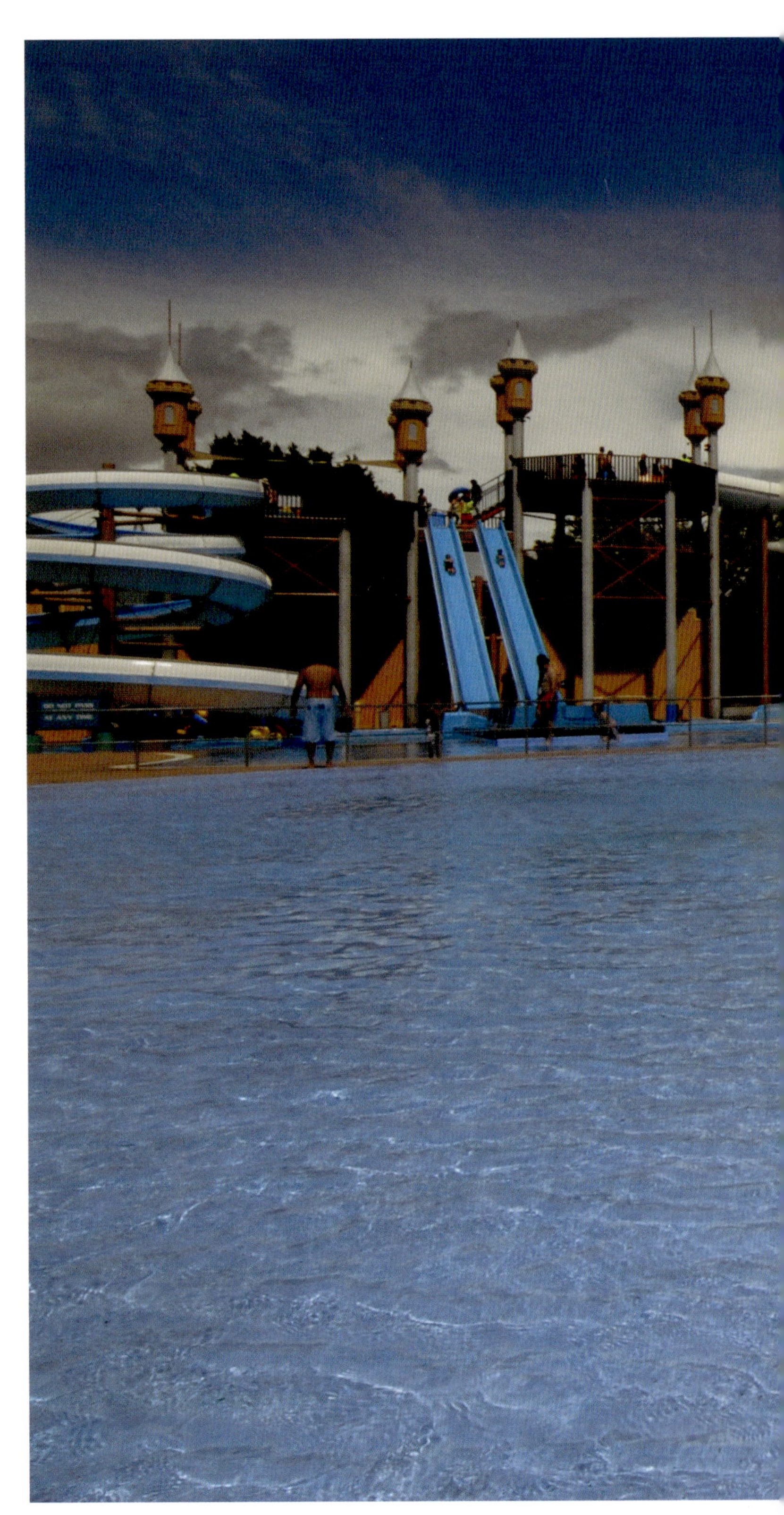

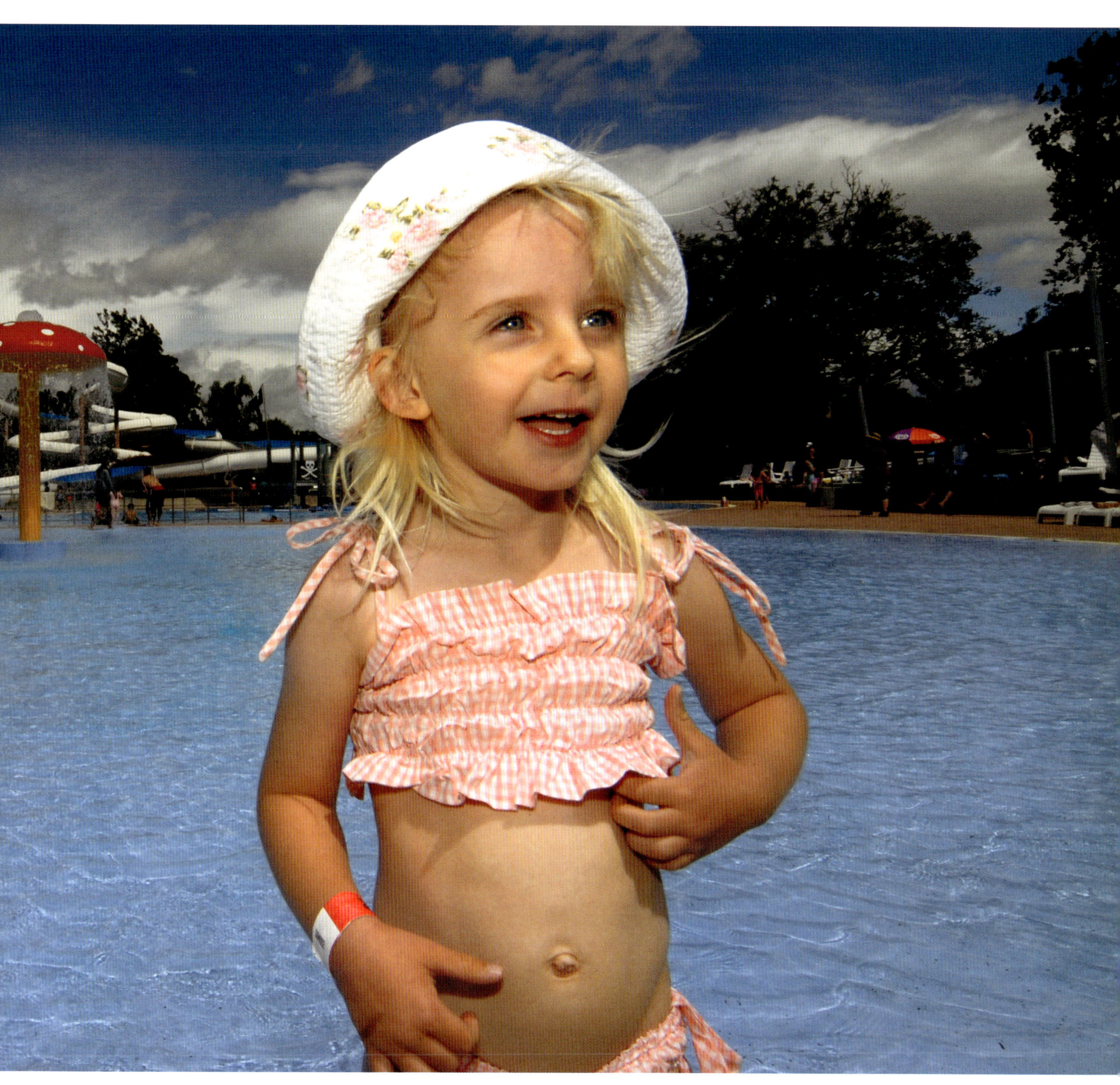

Poppy Hoskin at Splash Planet, Hastings

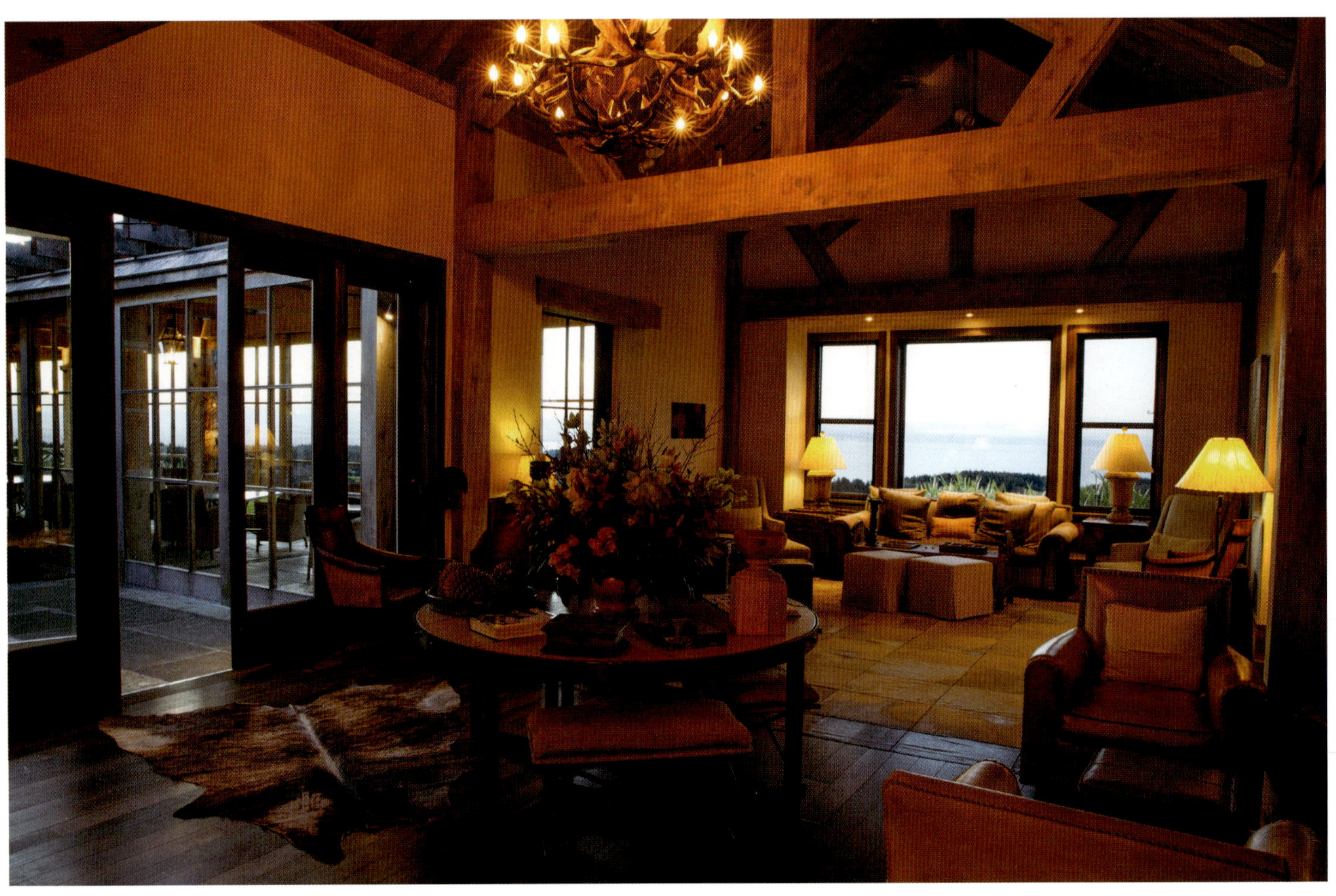

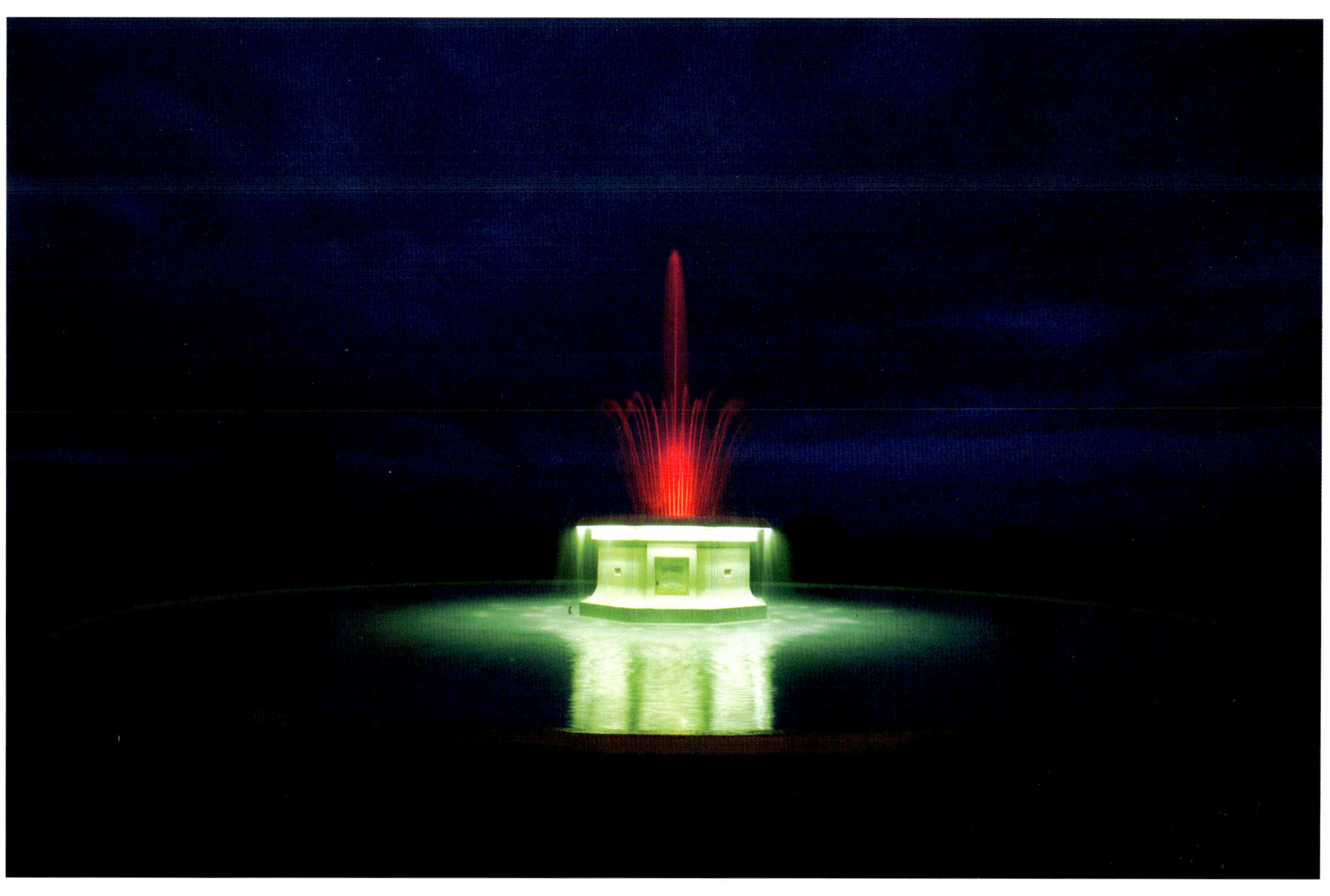

The Tom Parker Fountain, Marine Parade, Napier

KO TE WAI TE ORA O NGĀ MEA KATOA.

WATER IS THE LIFE GIVER OF ALL THINGS.

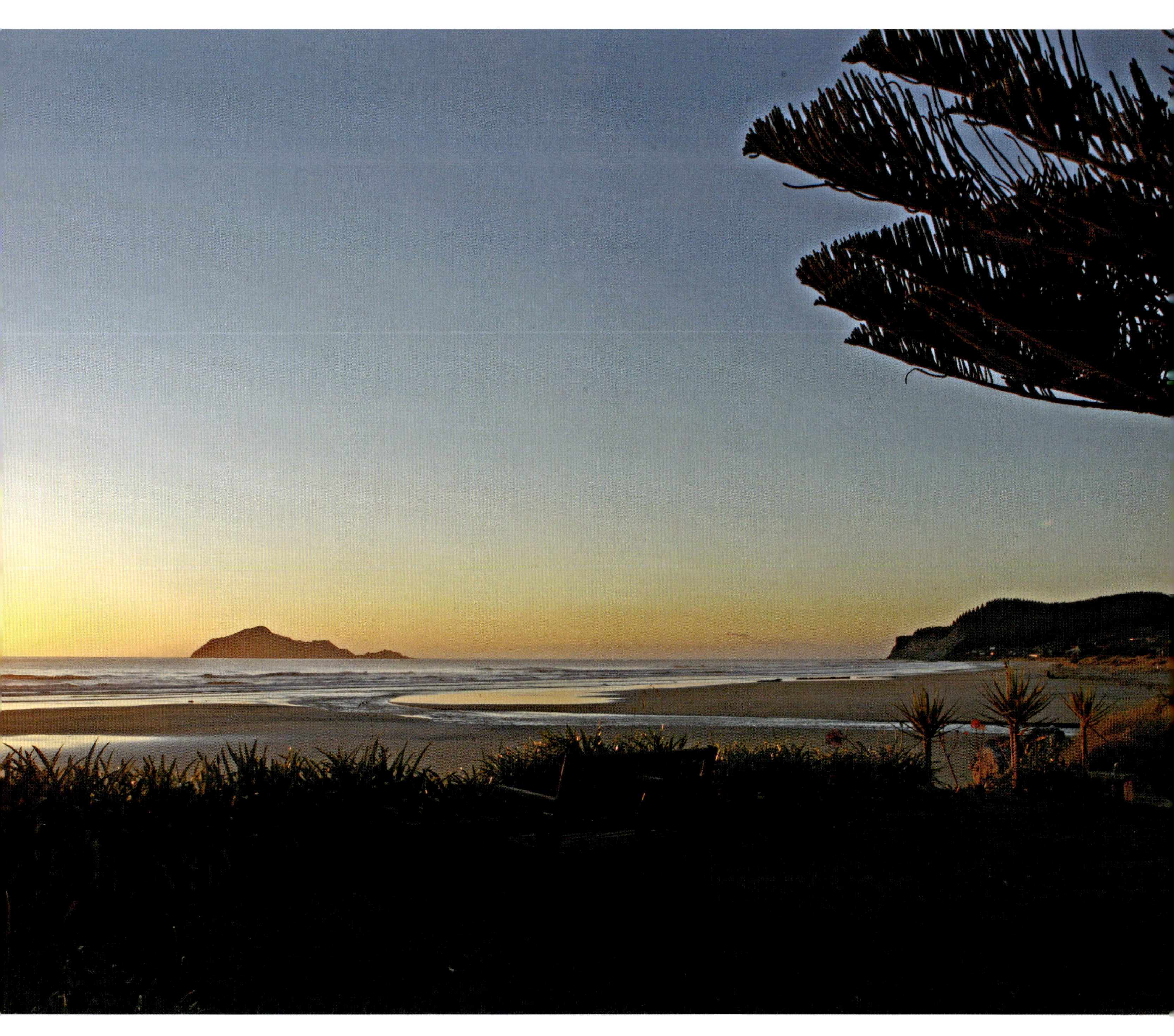

PORTRAIT OF OUR WATER

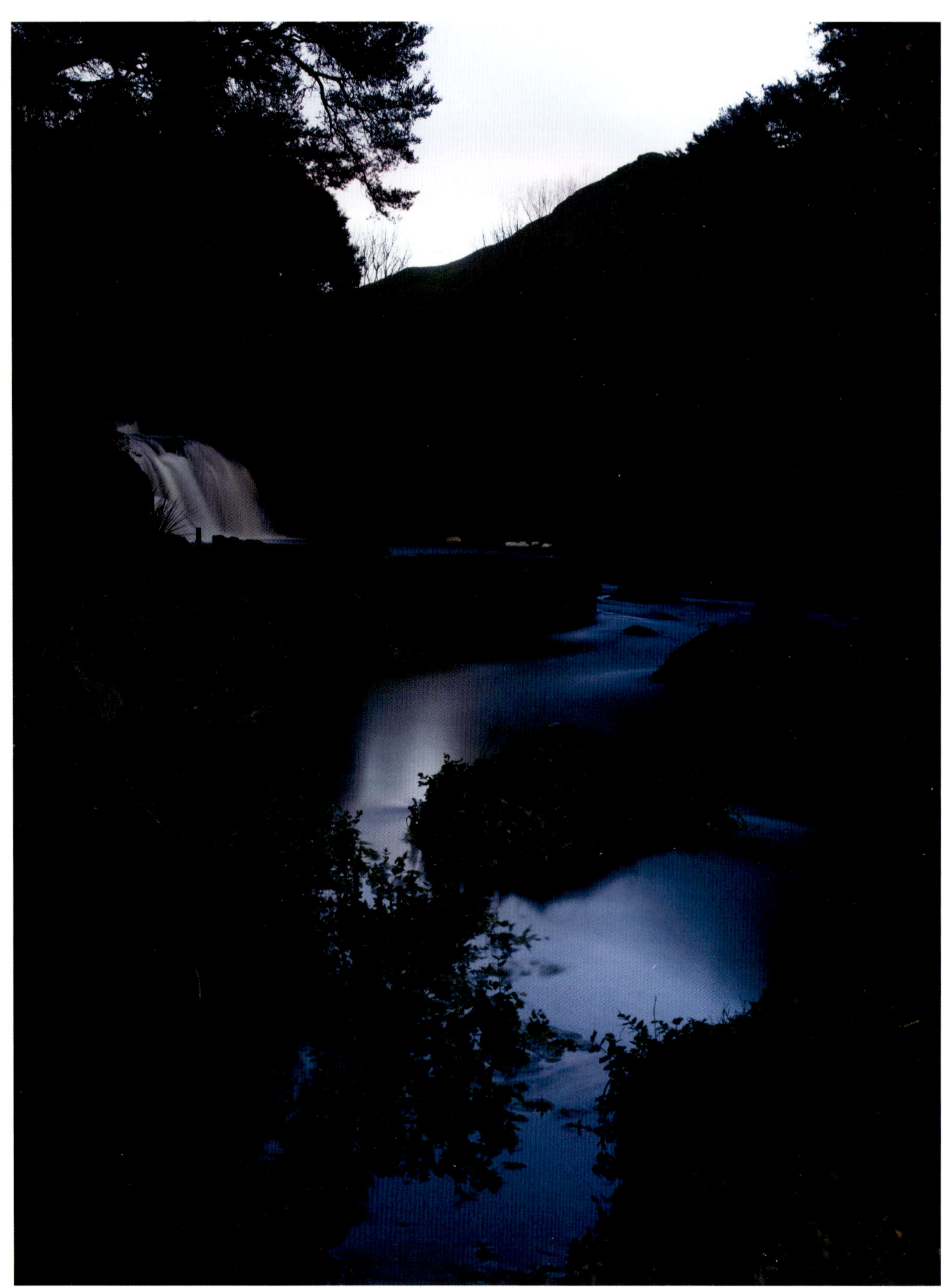

104 Maraetotara Falls, Maraetotara Valley, Hawke's Bay

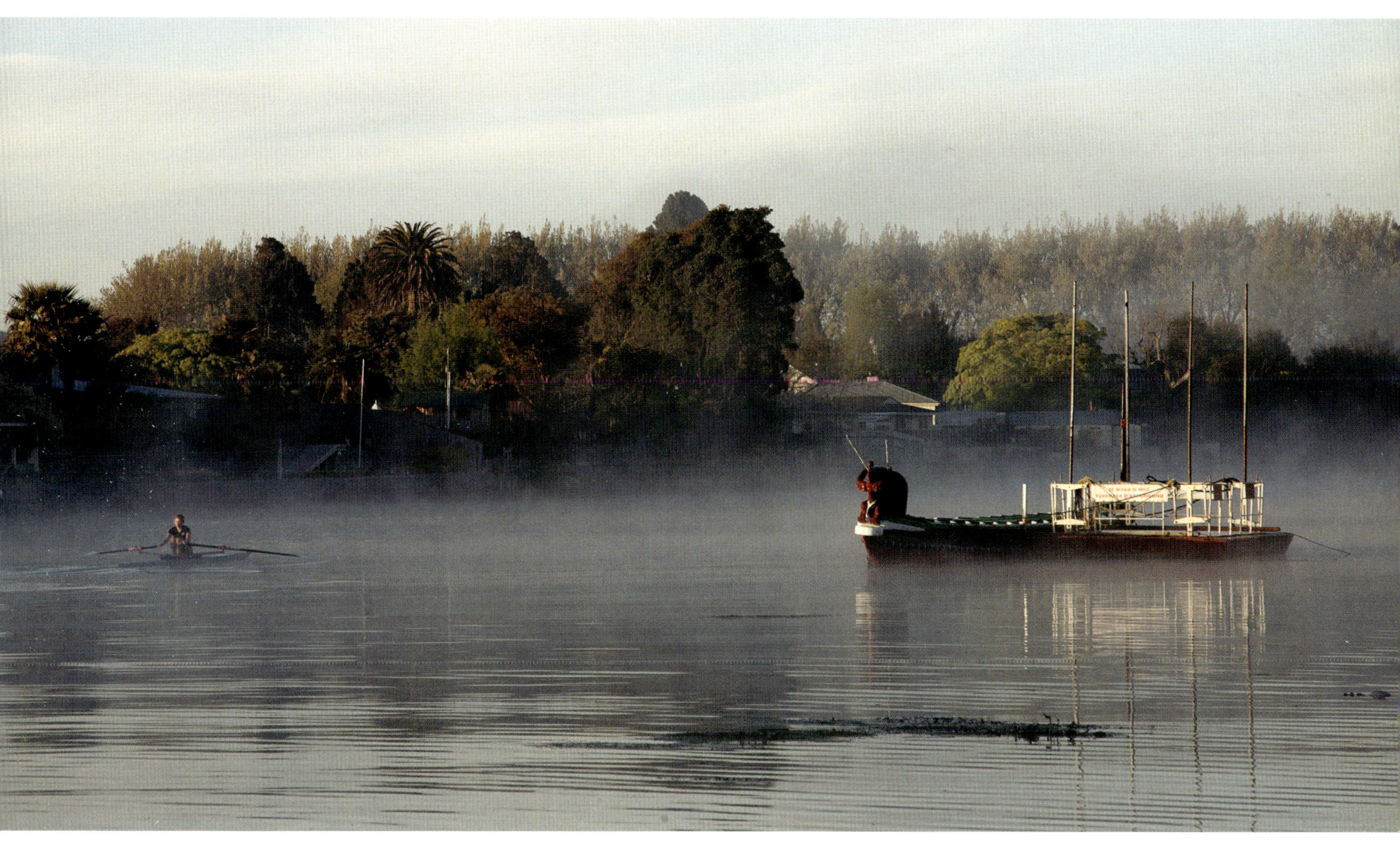

Early morning rower on the Clive River, Clive

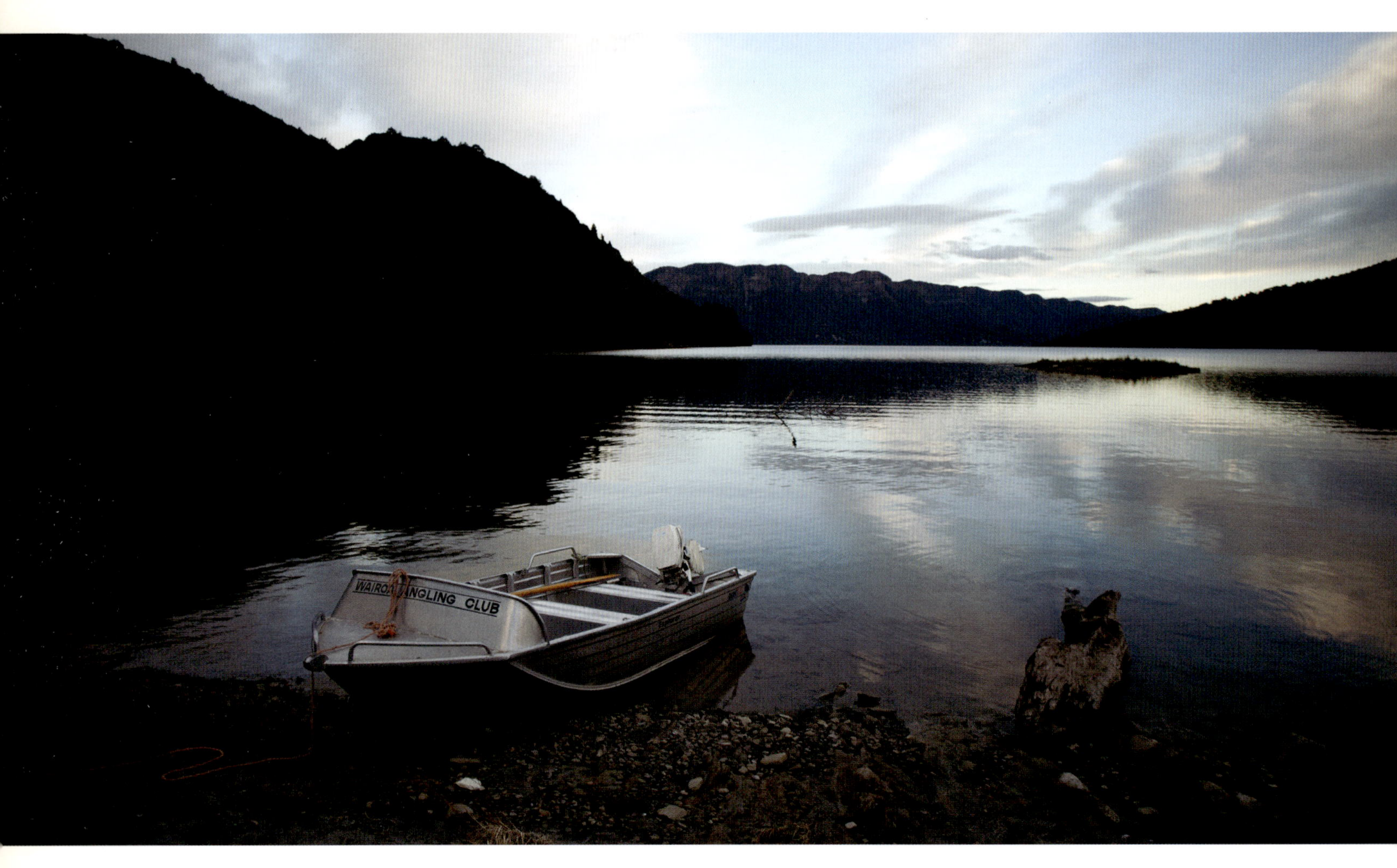

 Wairoa Angling Club dinghy, Lake Waikaremoana, Northern Hawke's Bay

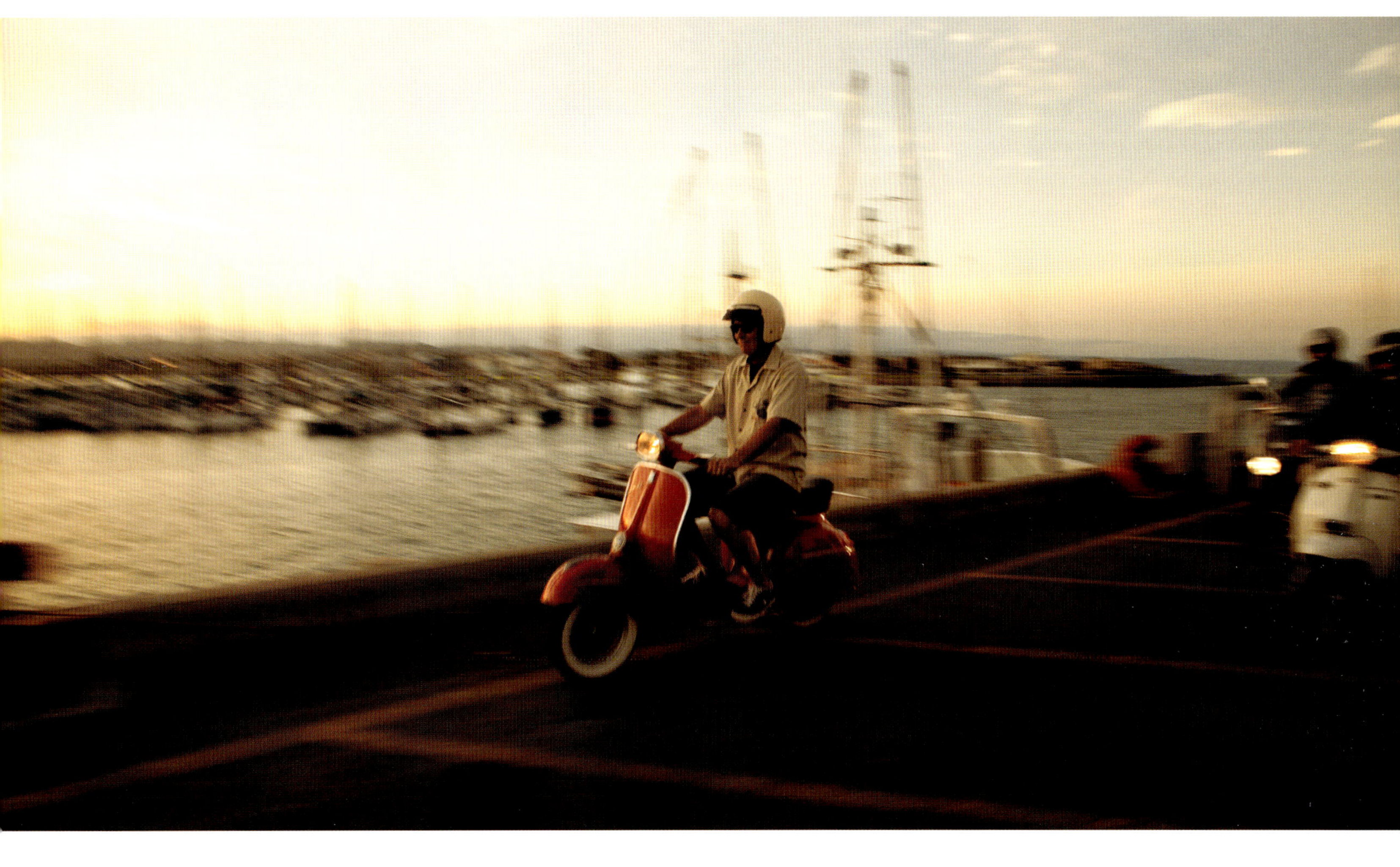

Ant Freeman riding his Vespa, Ahuriri, Napier

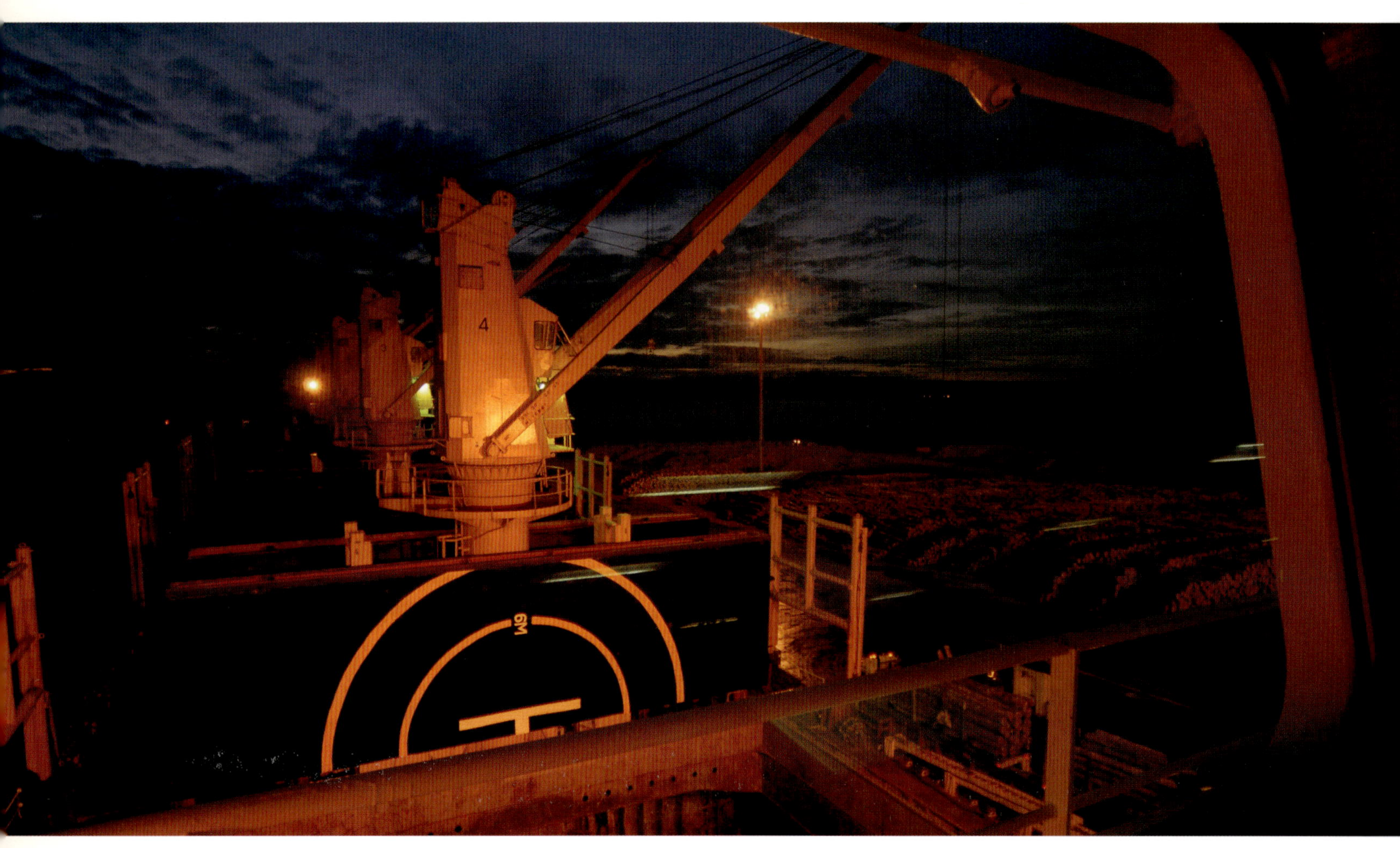

 Loading logs at Napier Port

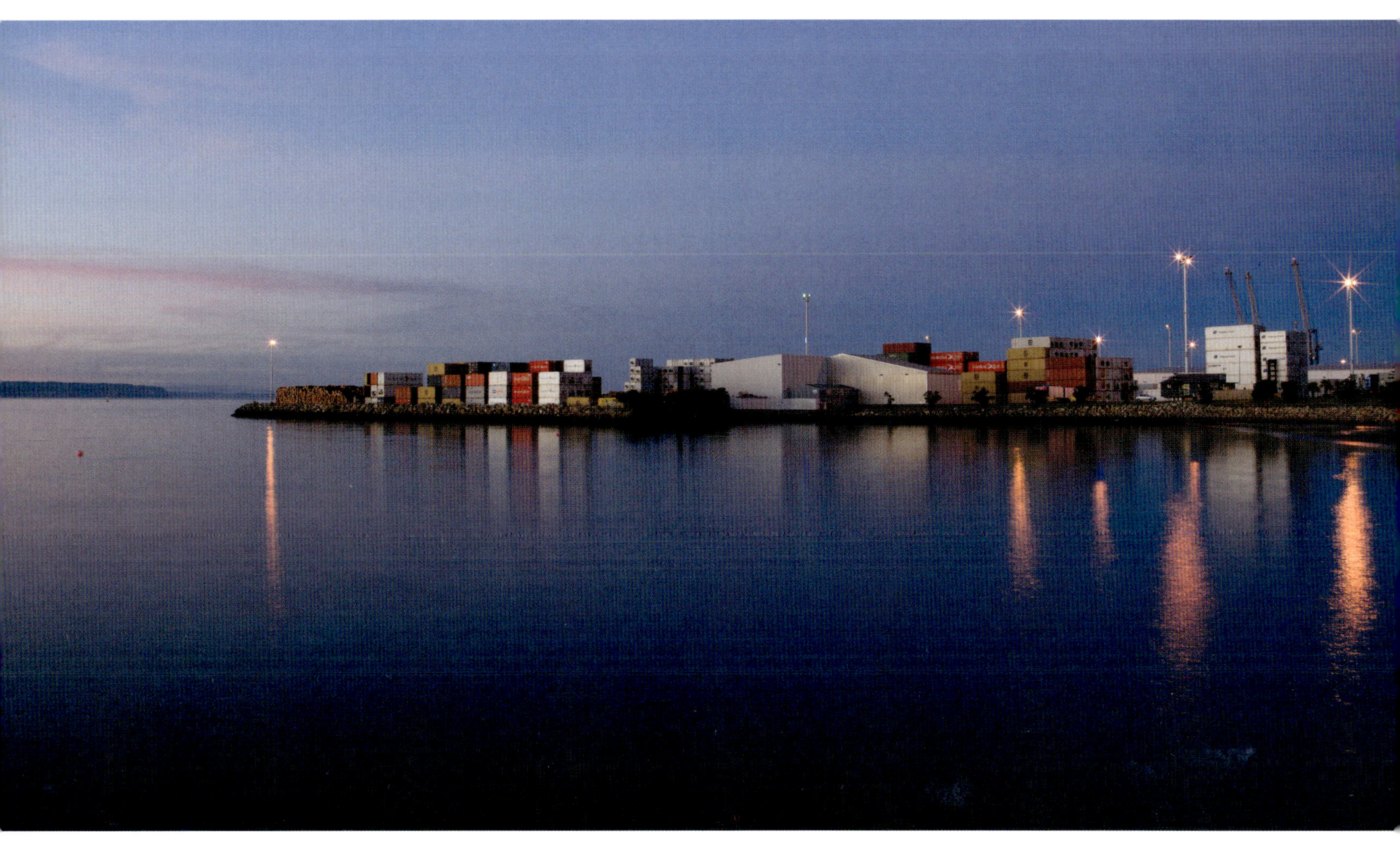

Early evening, Napier Port

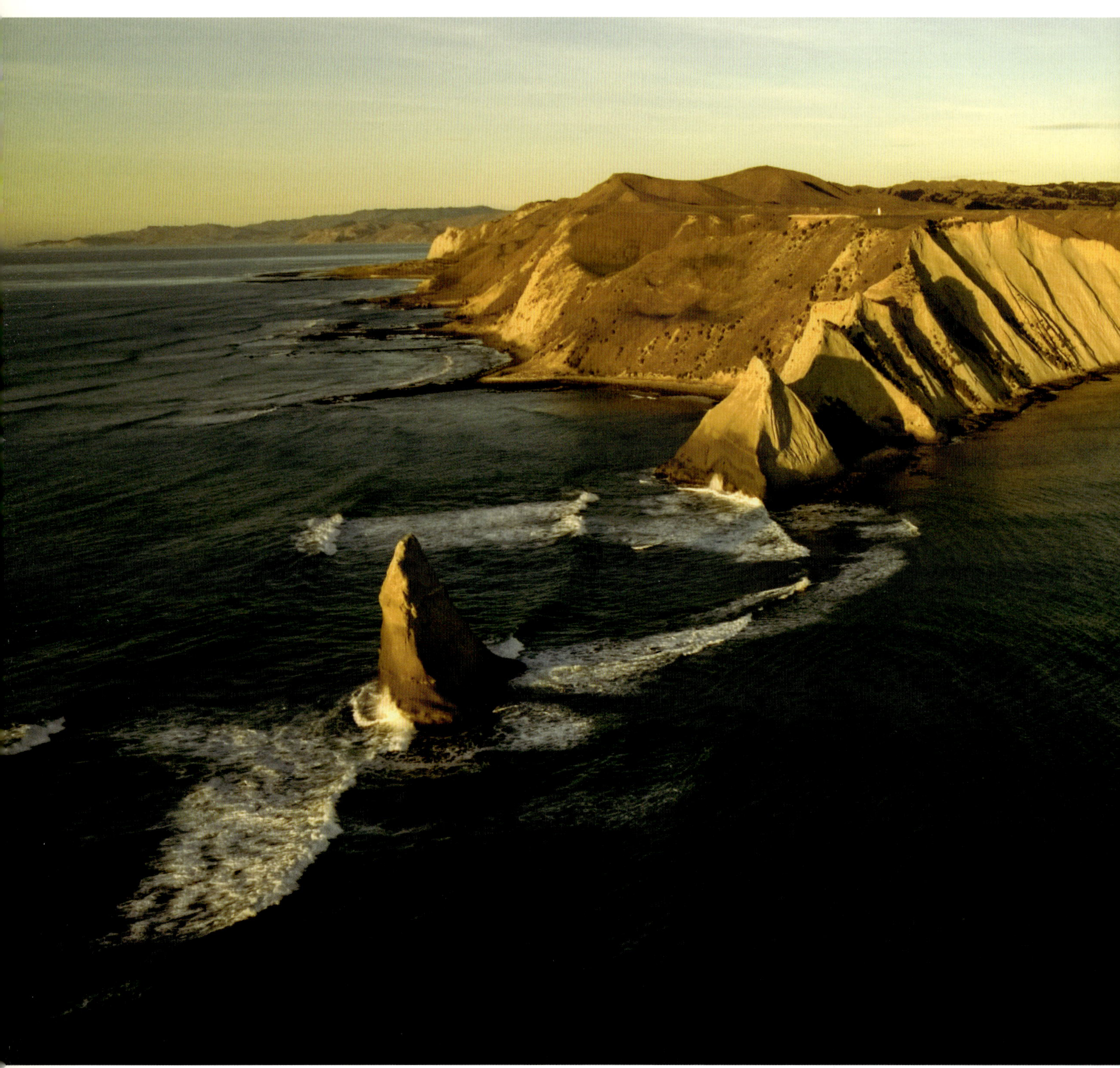

 Aerial view of Cape Kidnappers

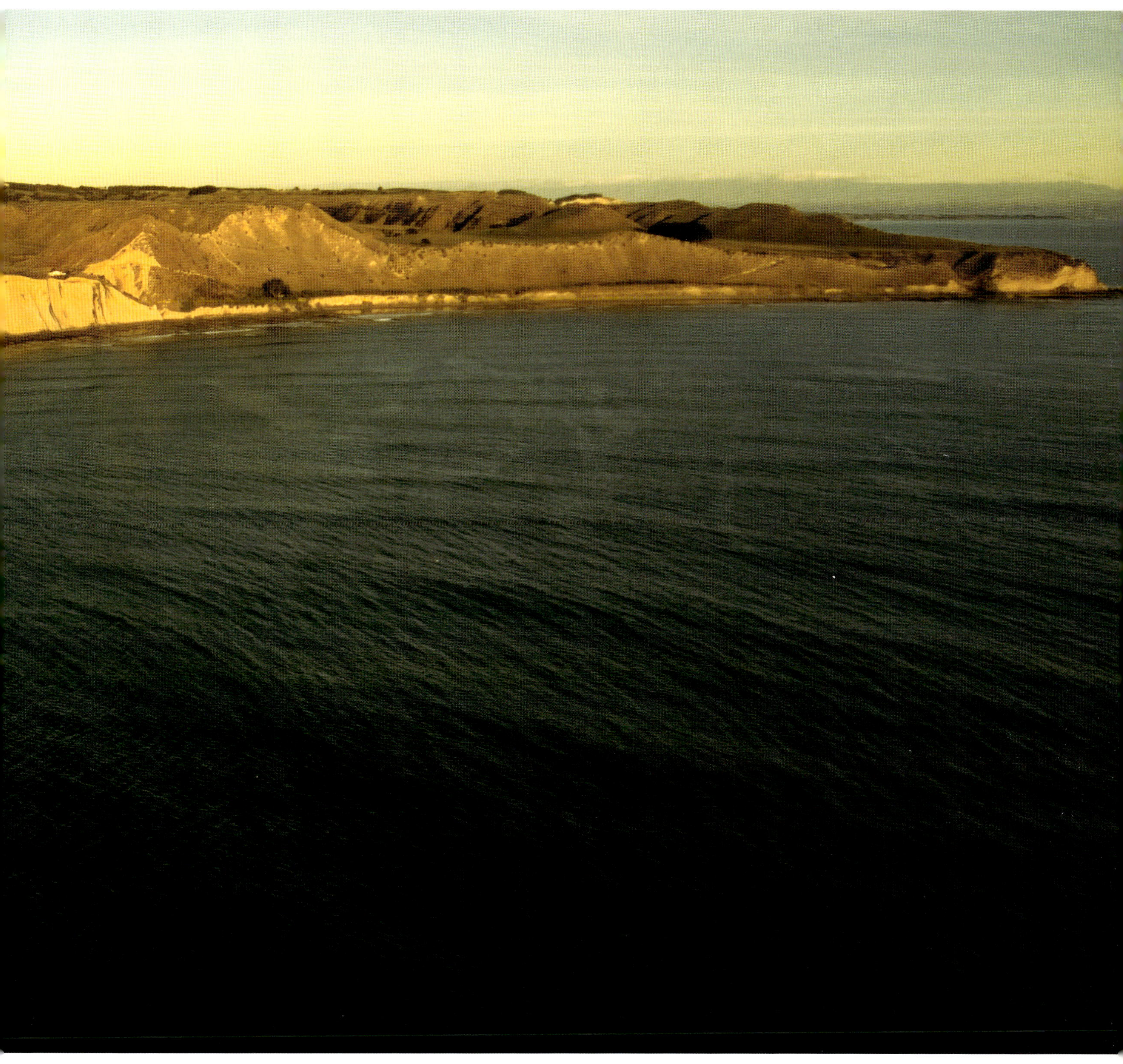

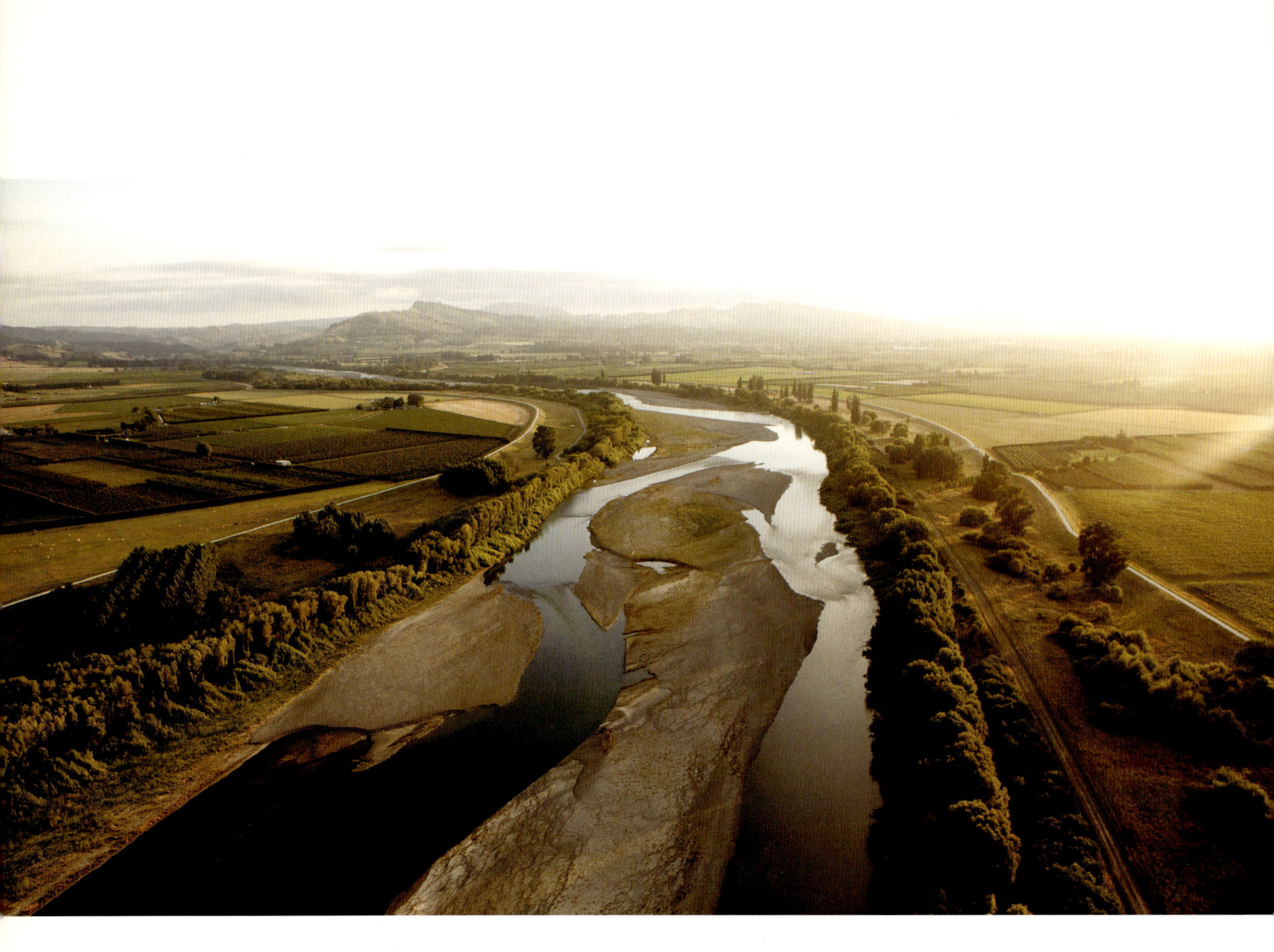

 Last light over the Tukituki River

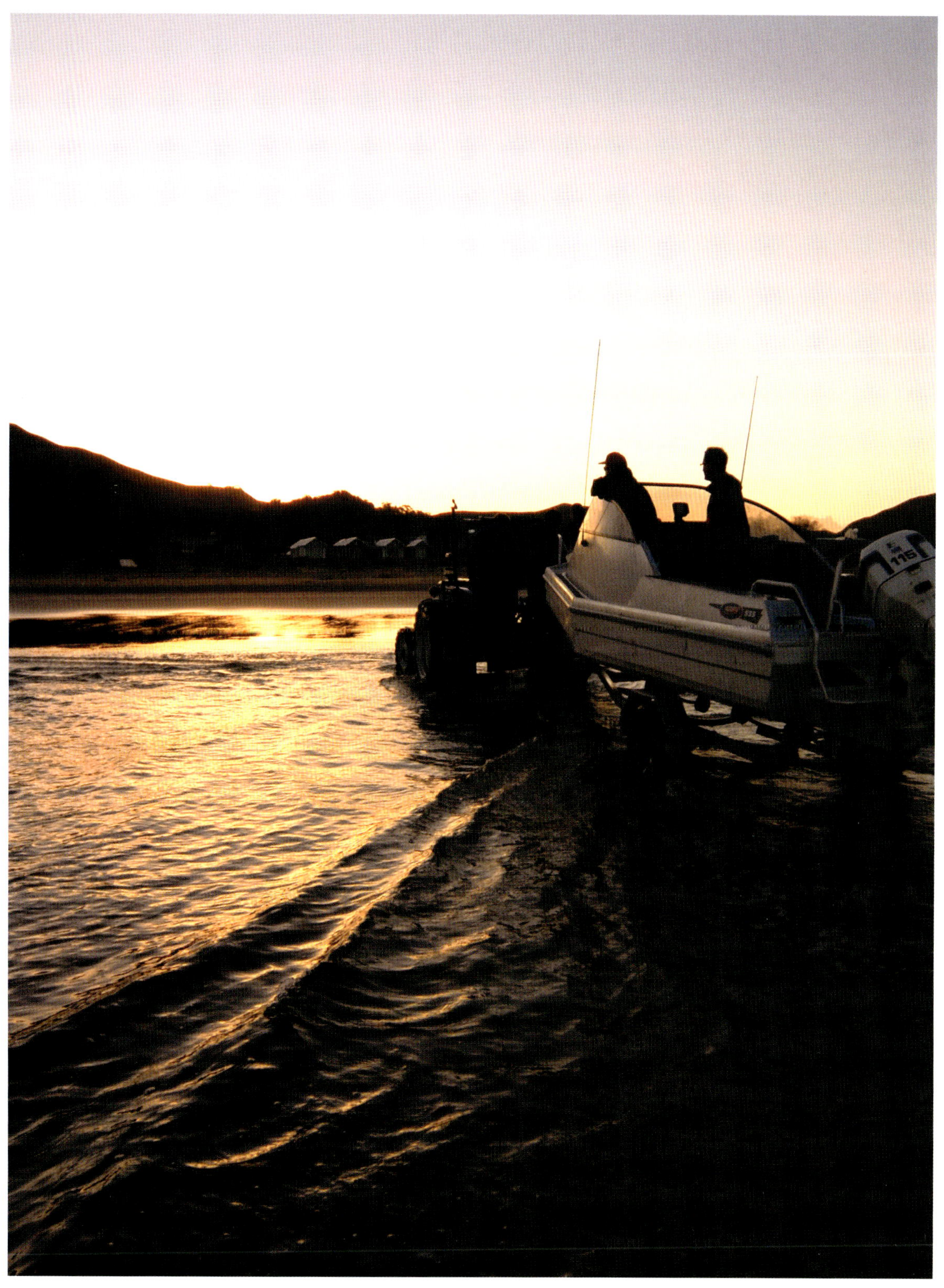

Fishing boat at Shoal Beach, Central Hawke's Bay

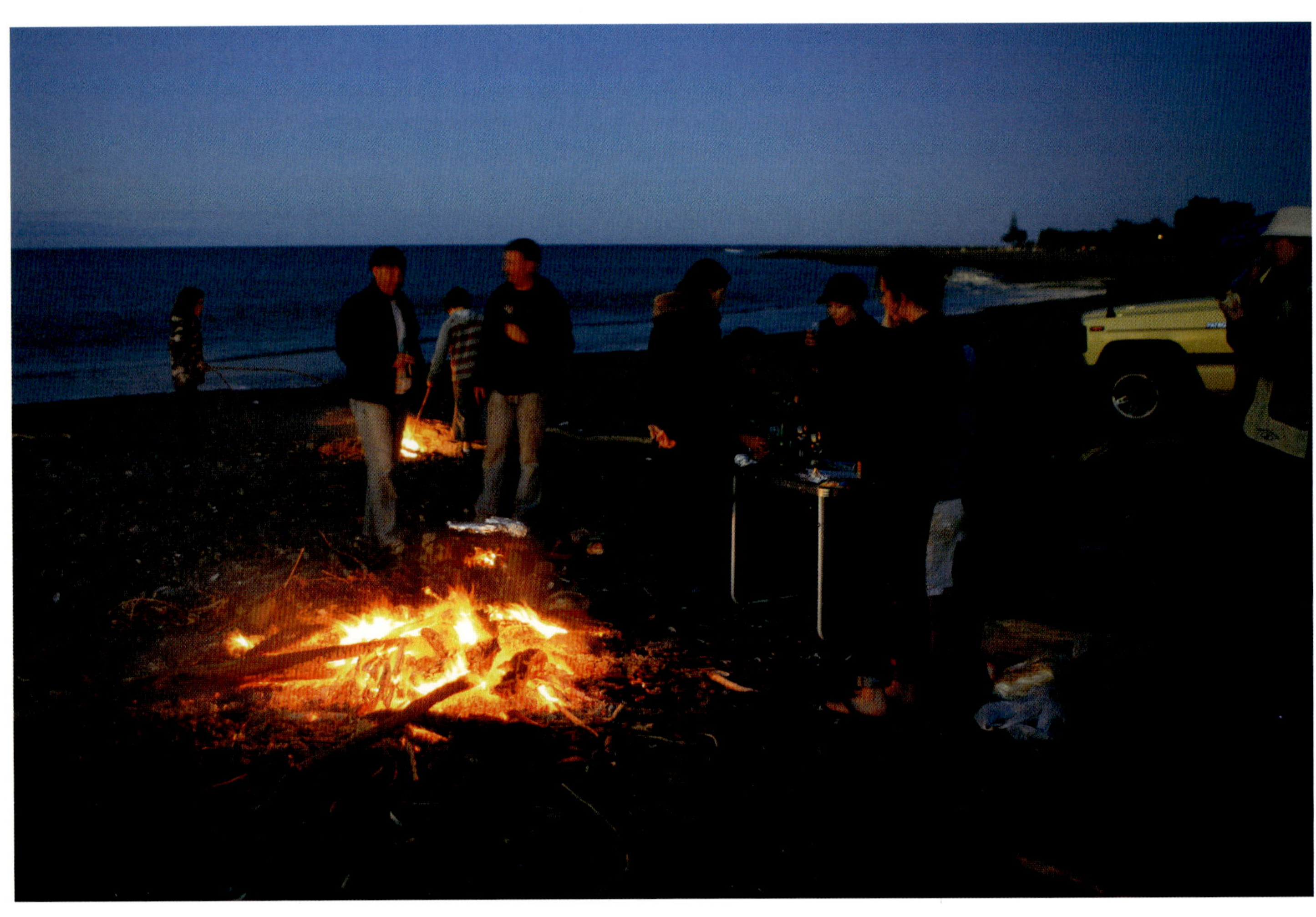

 Winter bonfire at Te Awanga Beach

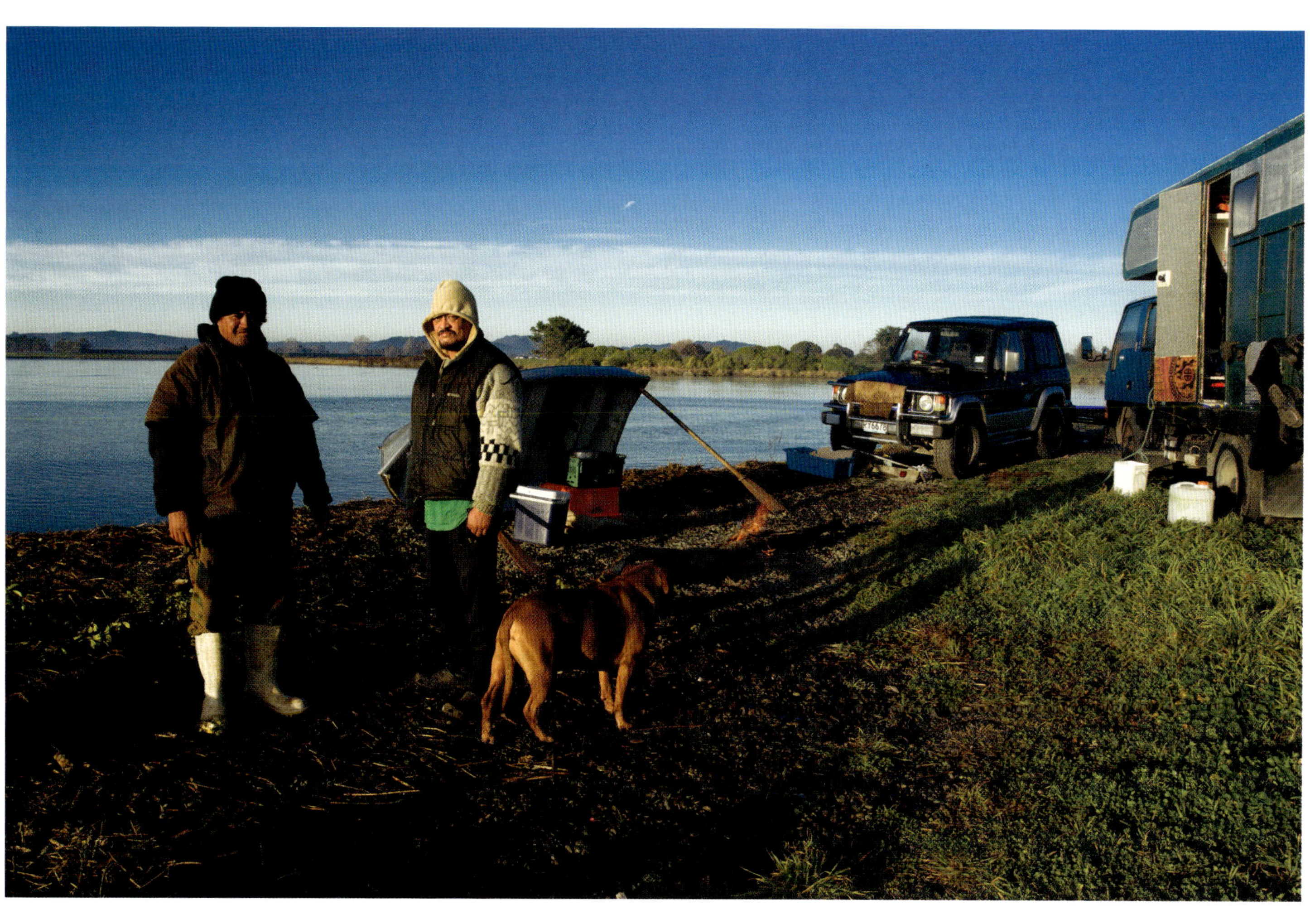

Fishermen at river mouth, Awatoto

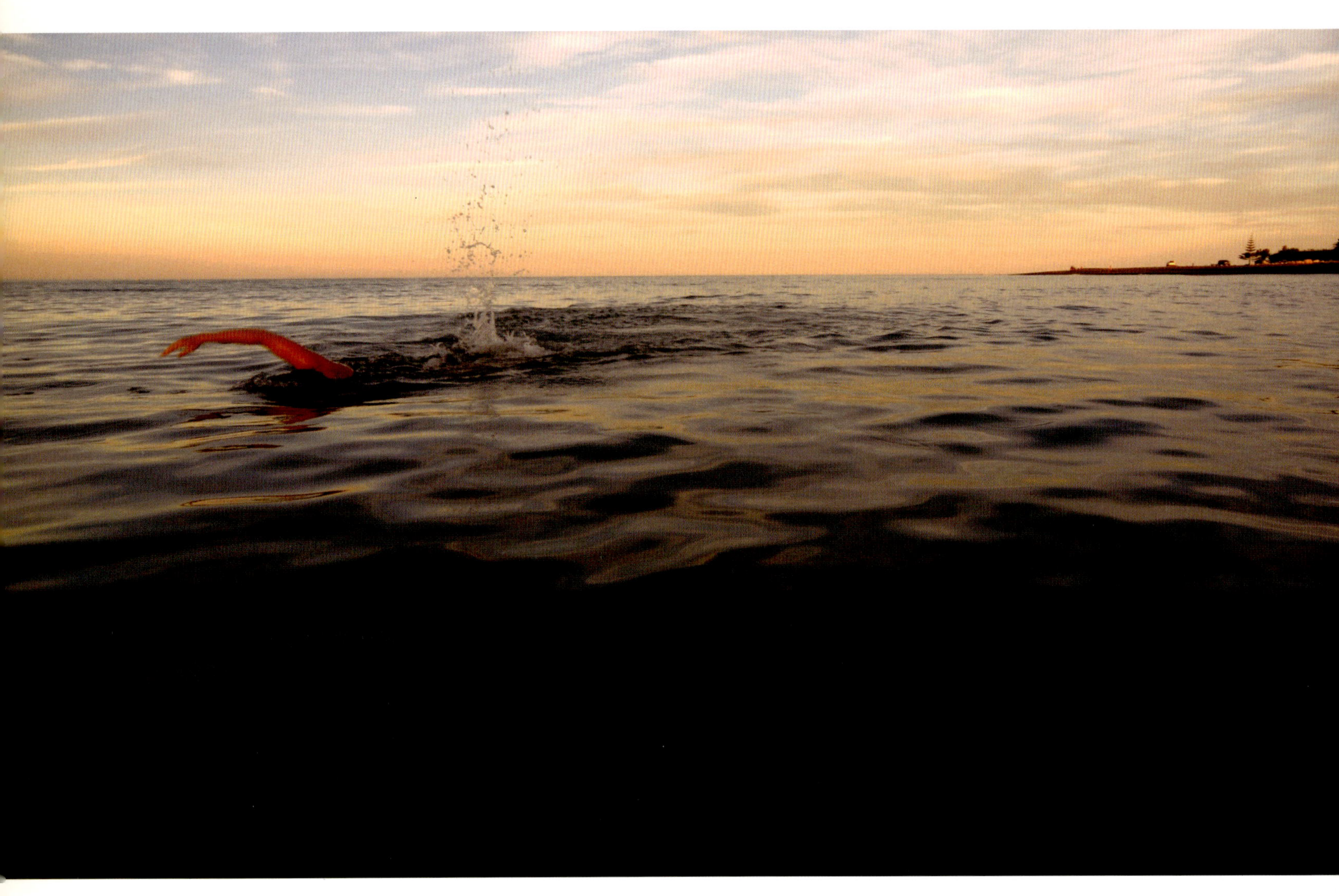

116 Early morning swimmer, Te Awanga

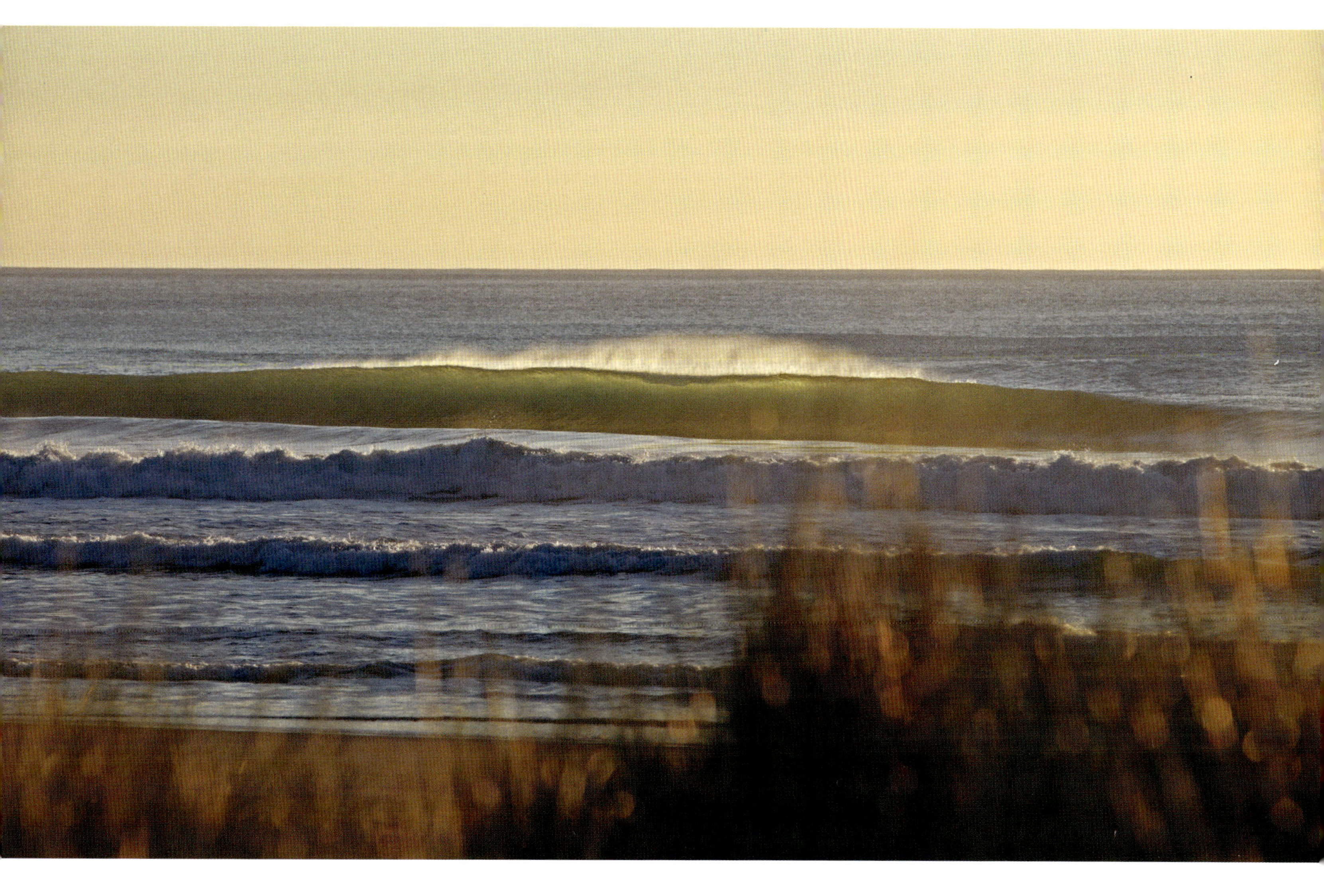

Surf breaking at Ocean Beach

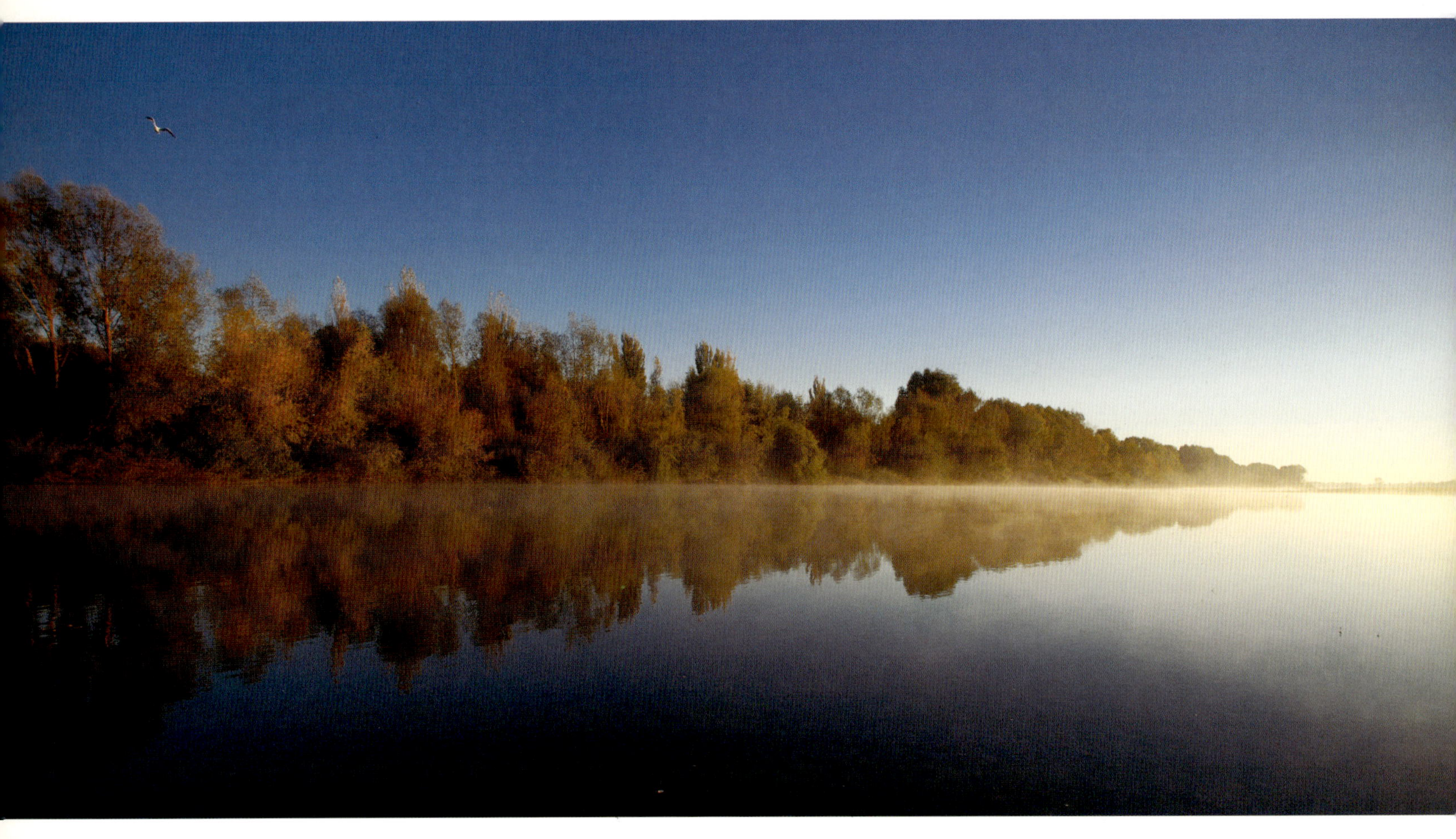

 Reflections, Tukituki River mouth, Haumoana

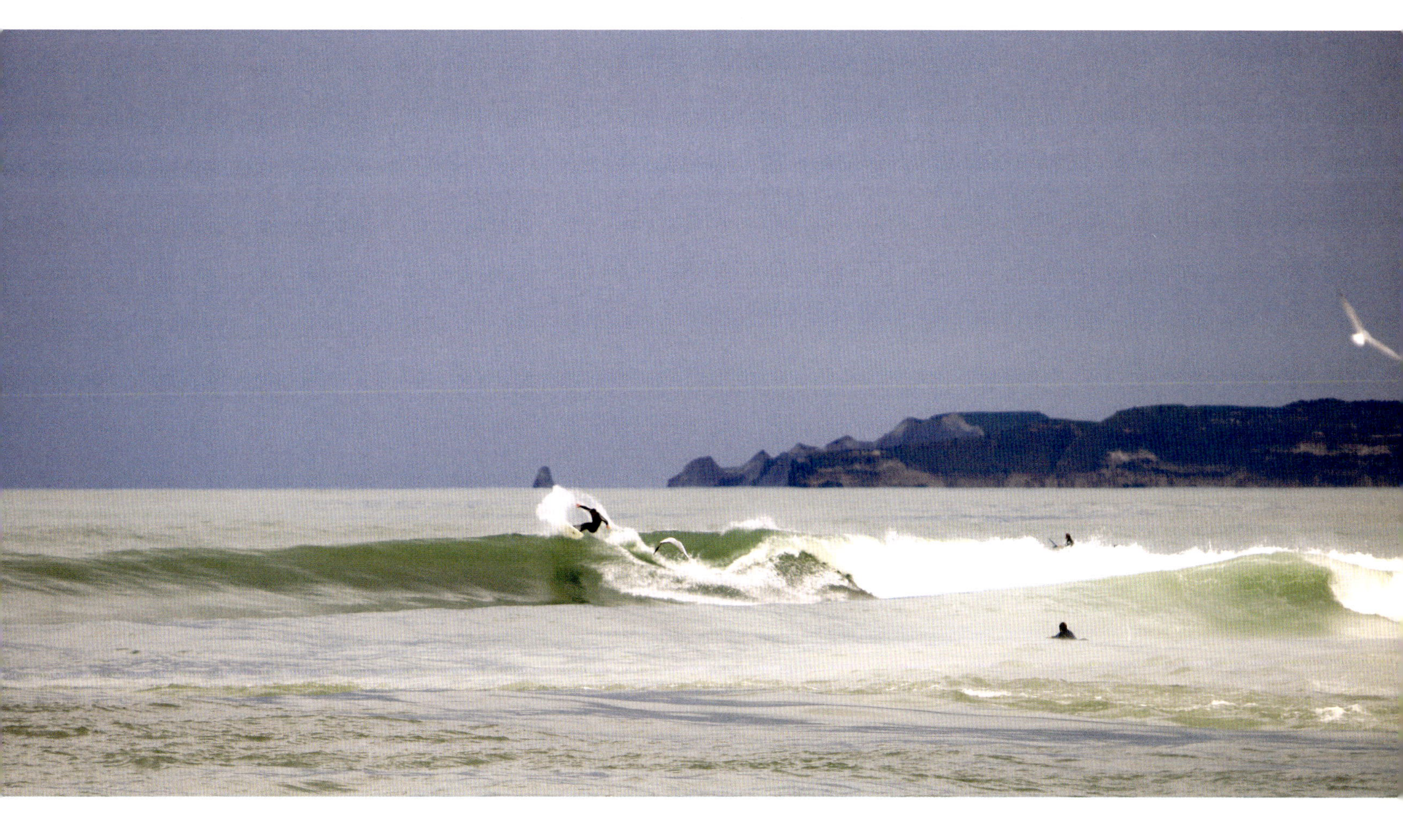

Surfers at river mouth, Awatoto

 Blacks Beach, Mahia, Northern Hawke's Bay

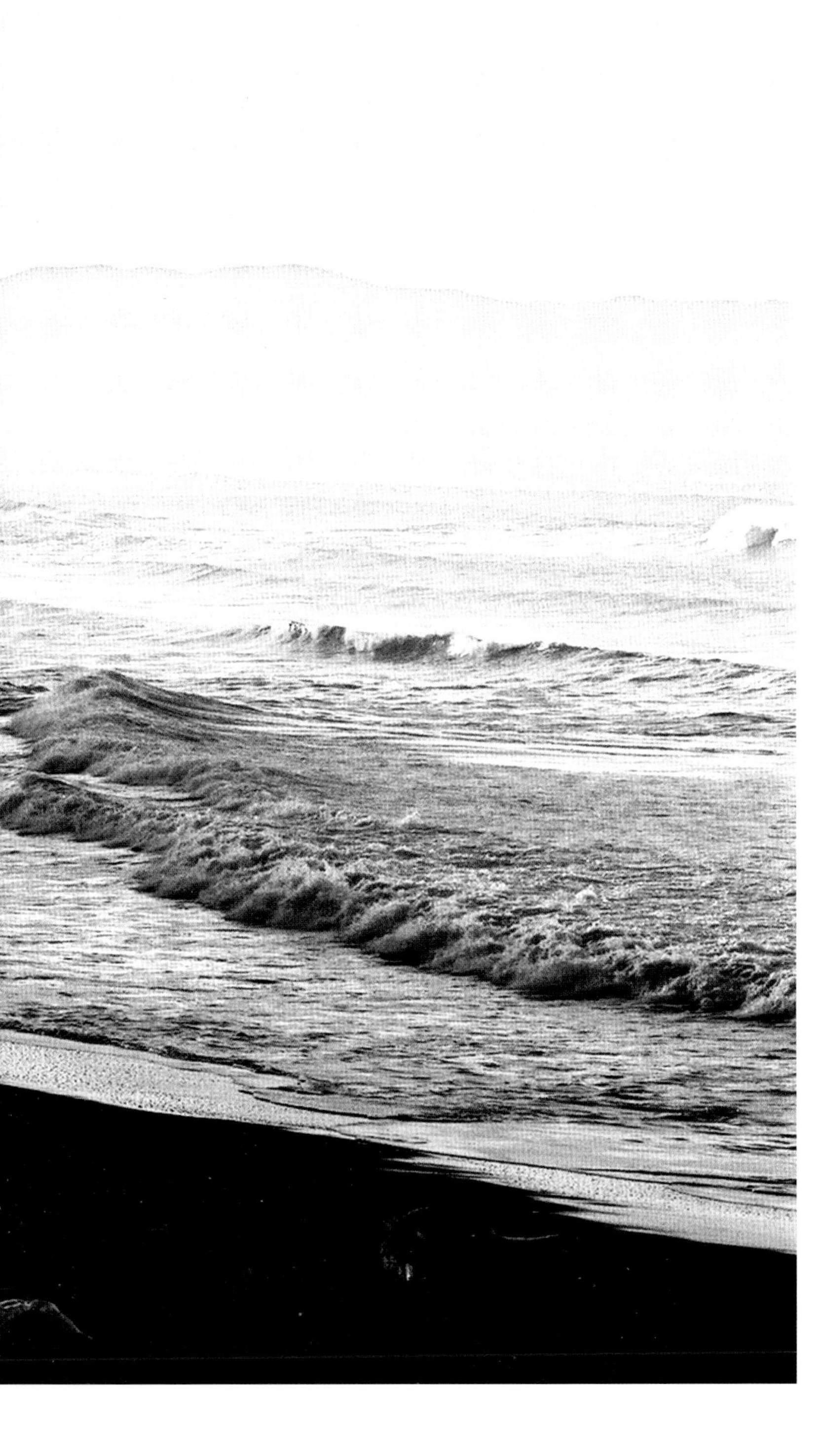

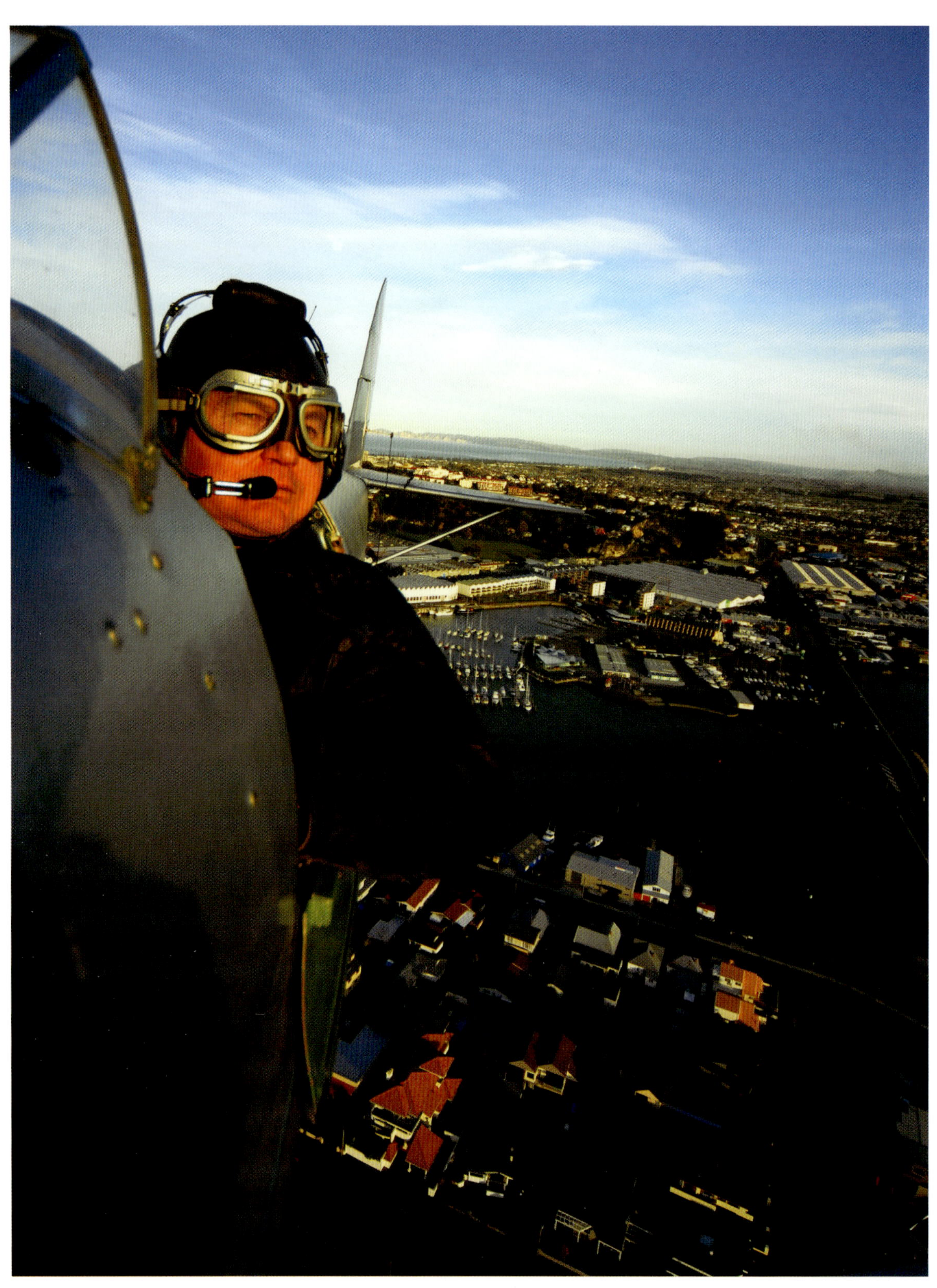

122 Bill Harris flying his Tiger Moth over Ahuriri, Napier

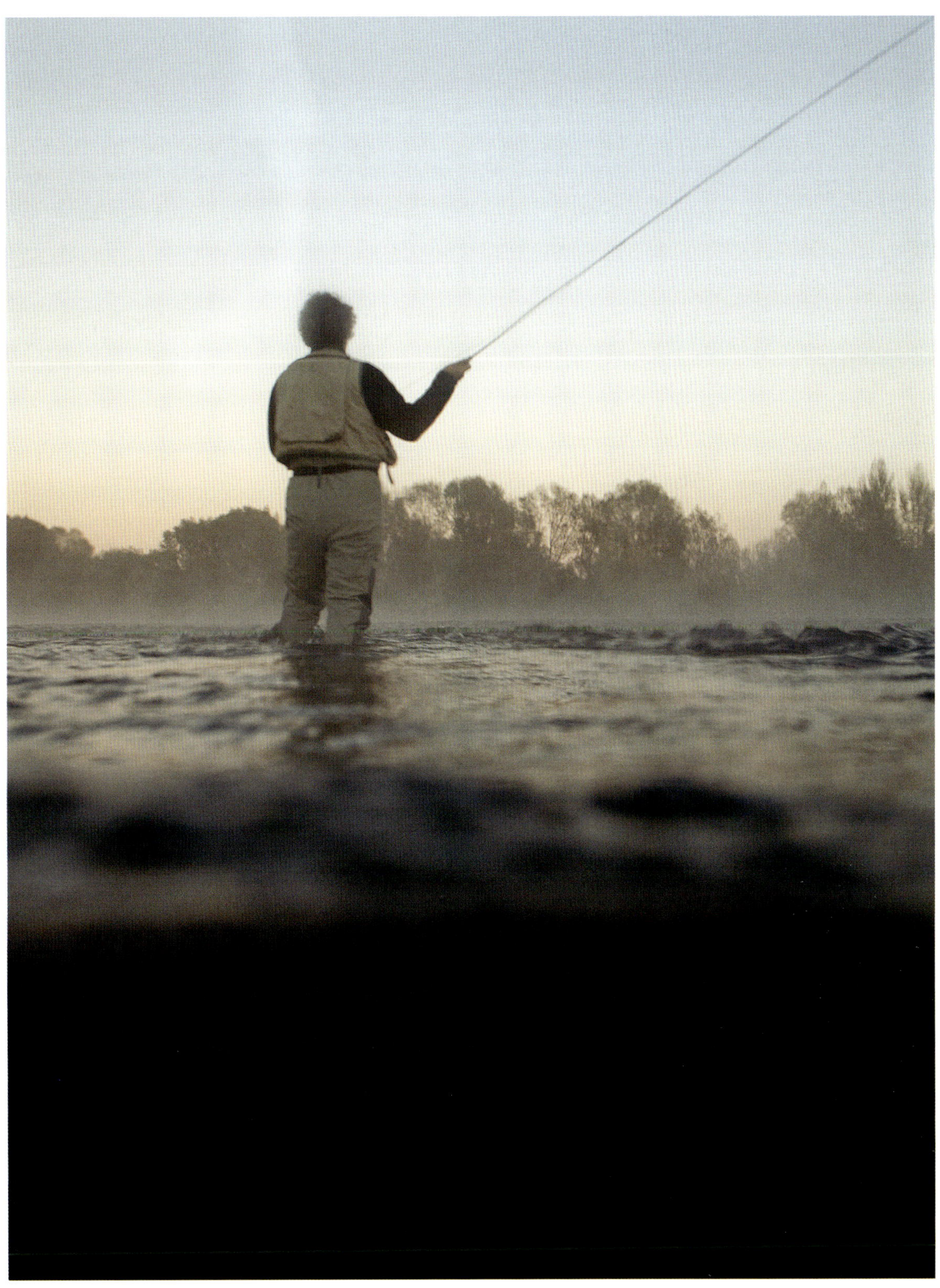

Local fly fisherman Andy King fishing in the Tukituki River

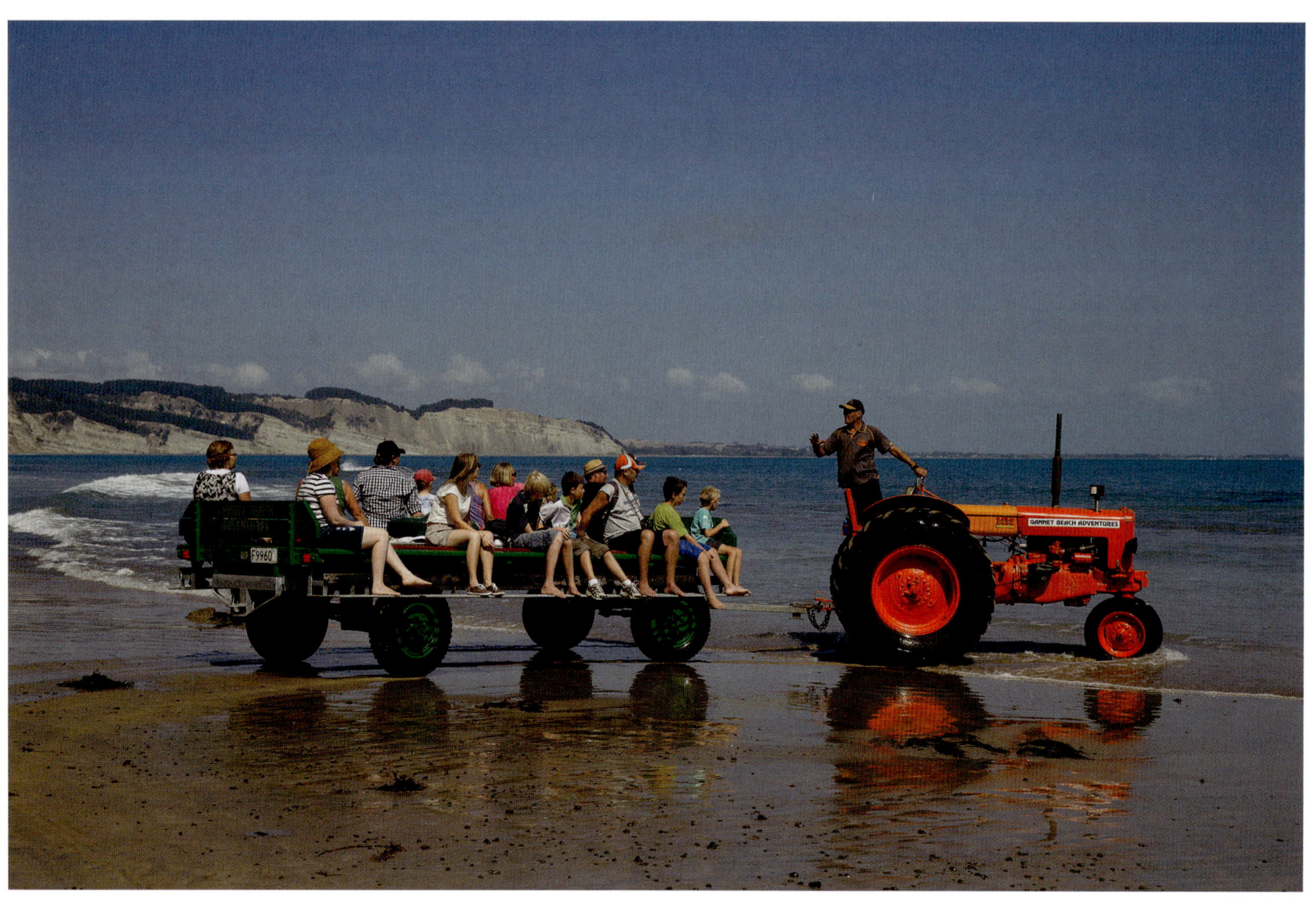

 Tractor safari with Gannet Beach Adventures to Cape Kidnappers

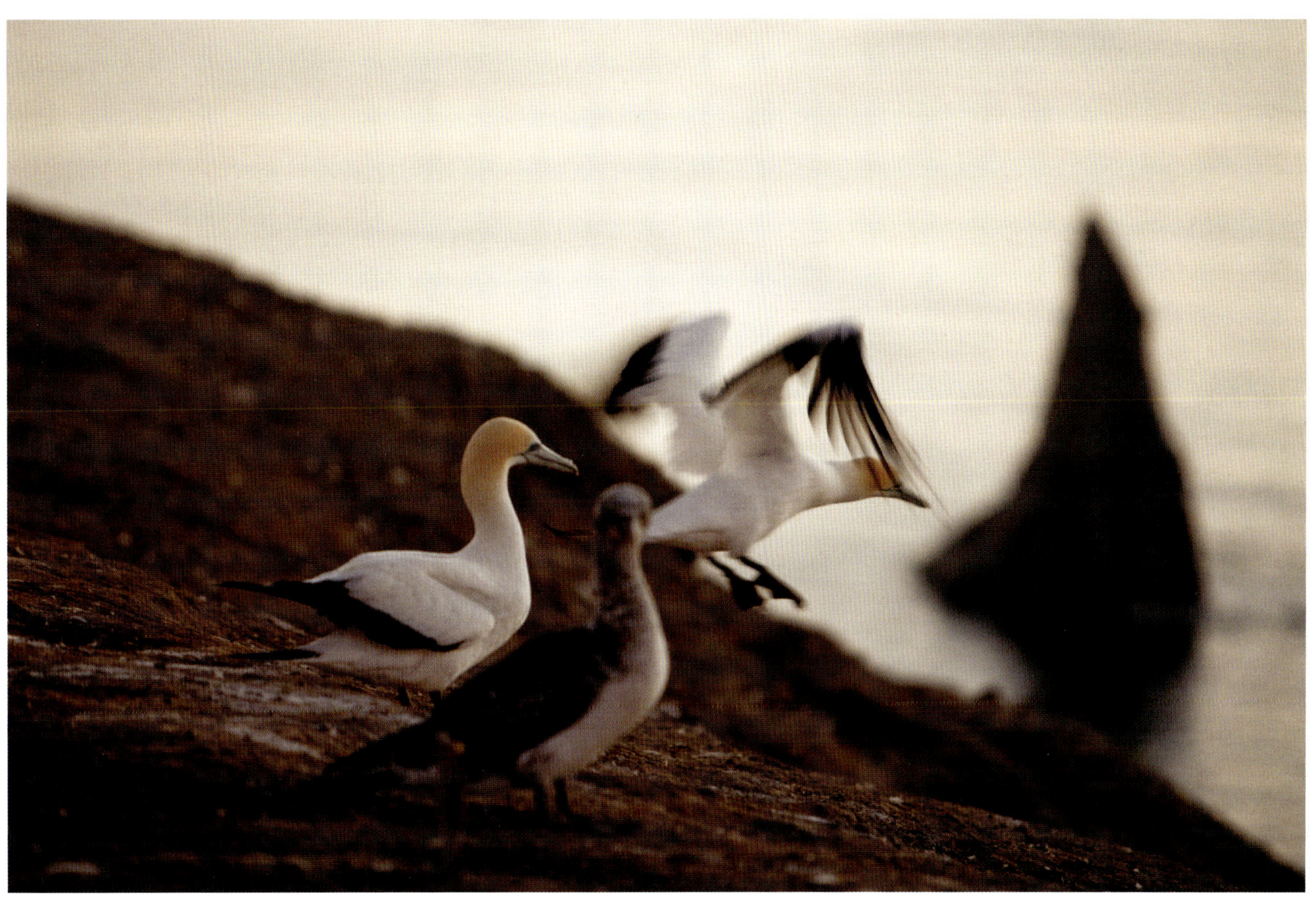

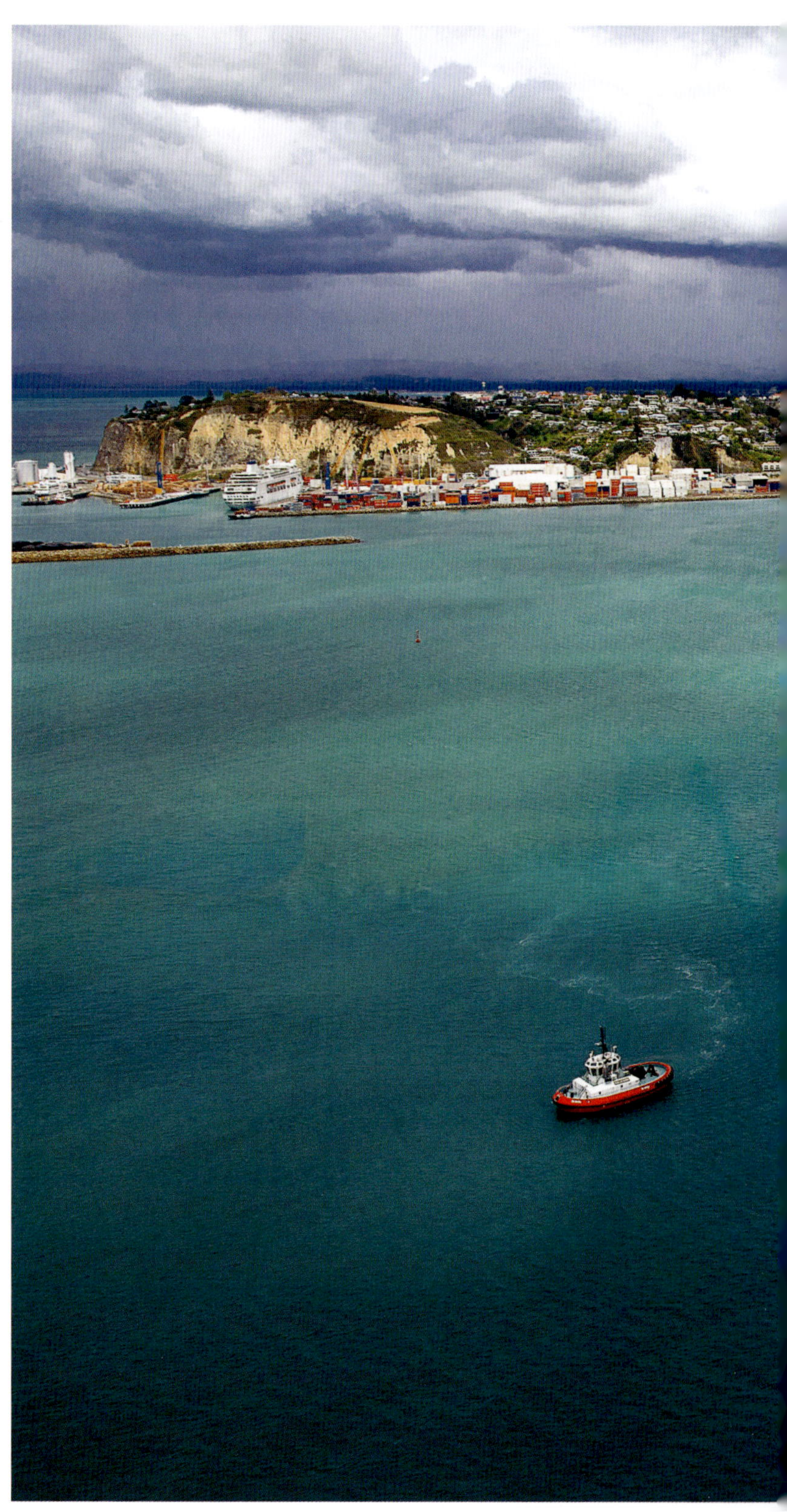

 Cruise ship preparing to berth, Napier Port

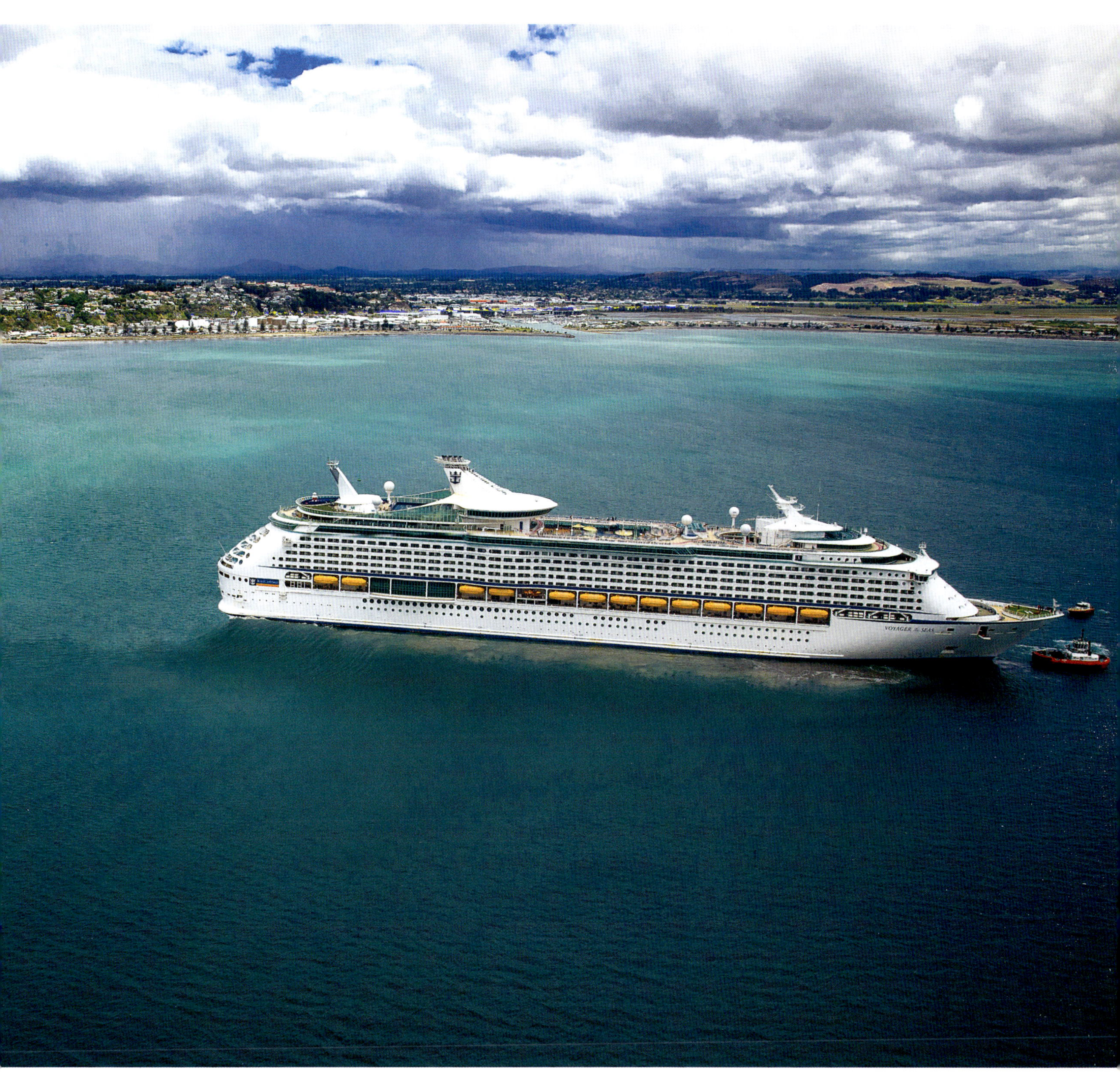
VOYAGER SEAS

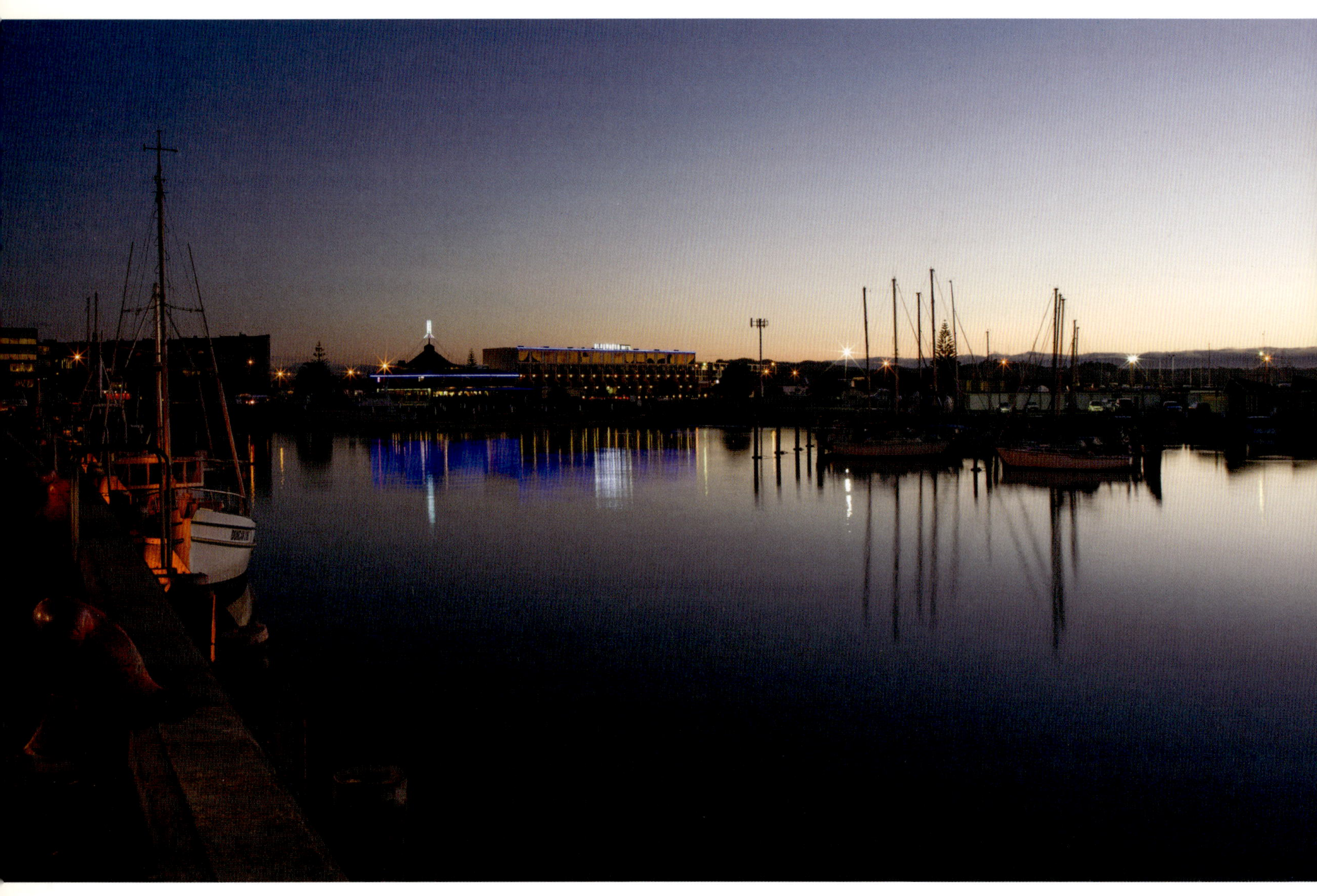

 Sunset at the 'Iron Pot', Ahuriri, Napier

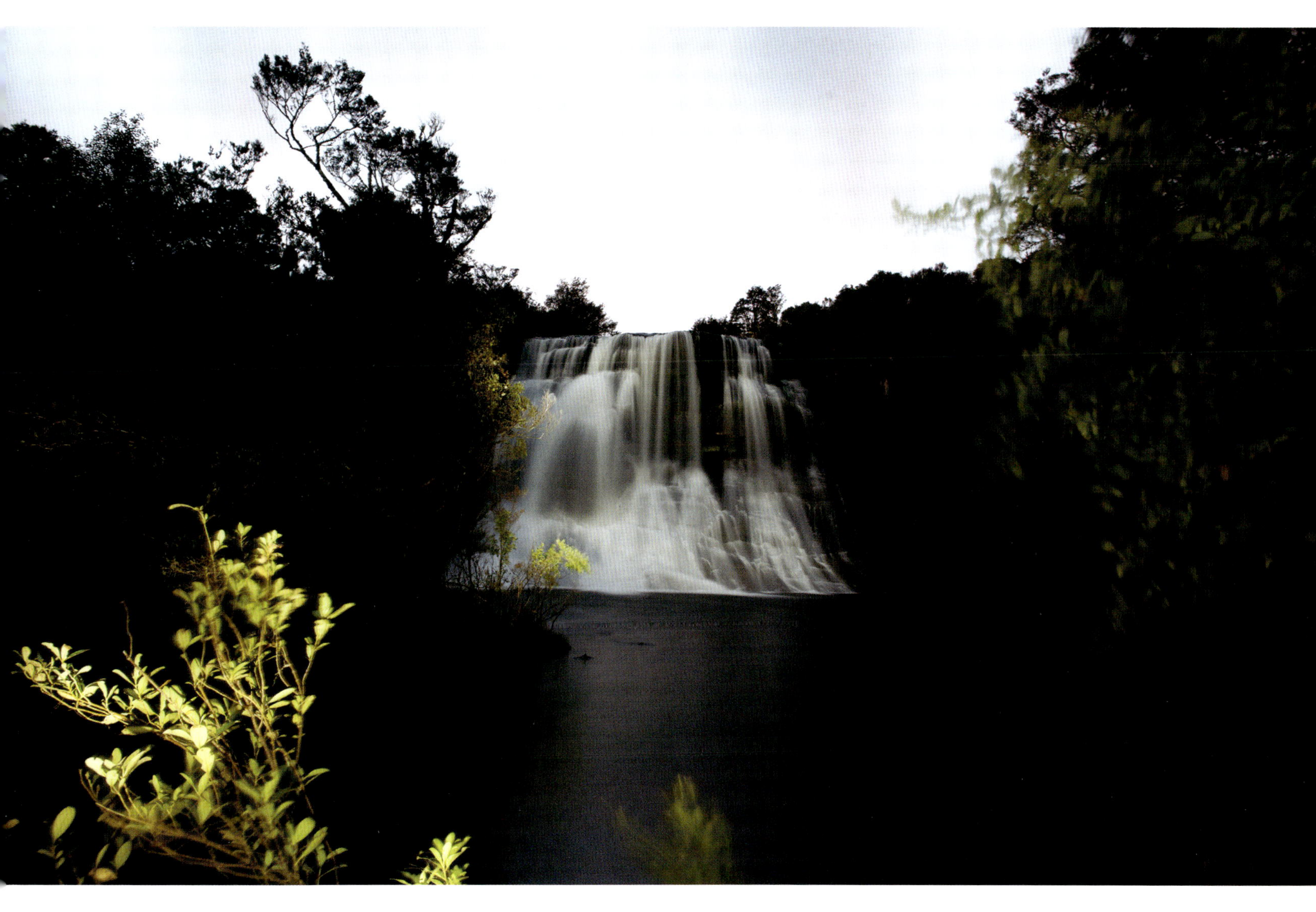

Papakorito Falls, Lake Waikaremoana, Northern Hawke's Bay

RAUHĪ MAI NGĀ HUI HUINGA TANGATA O TE AO.

COME, ASSEMBLE PEOPLE OF THE WORLD.

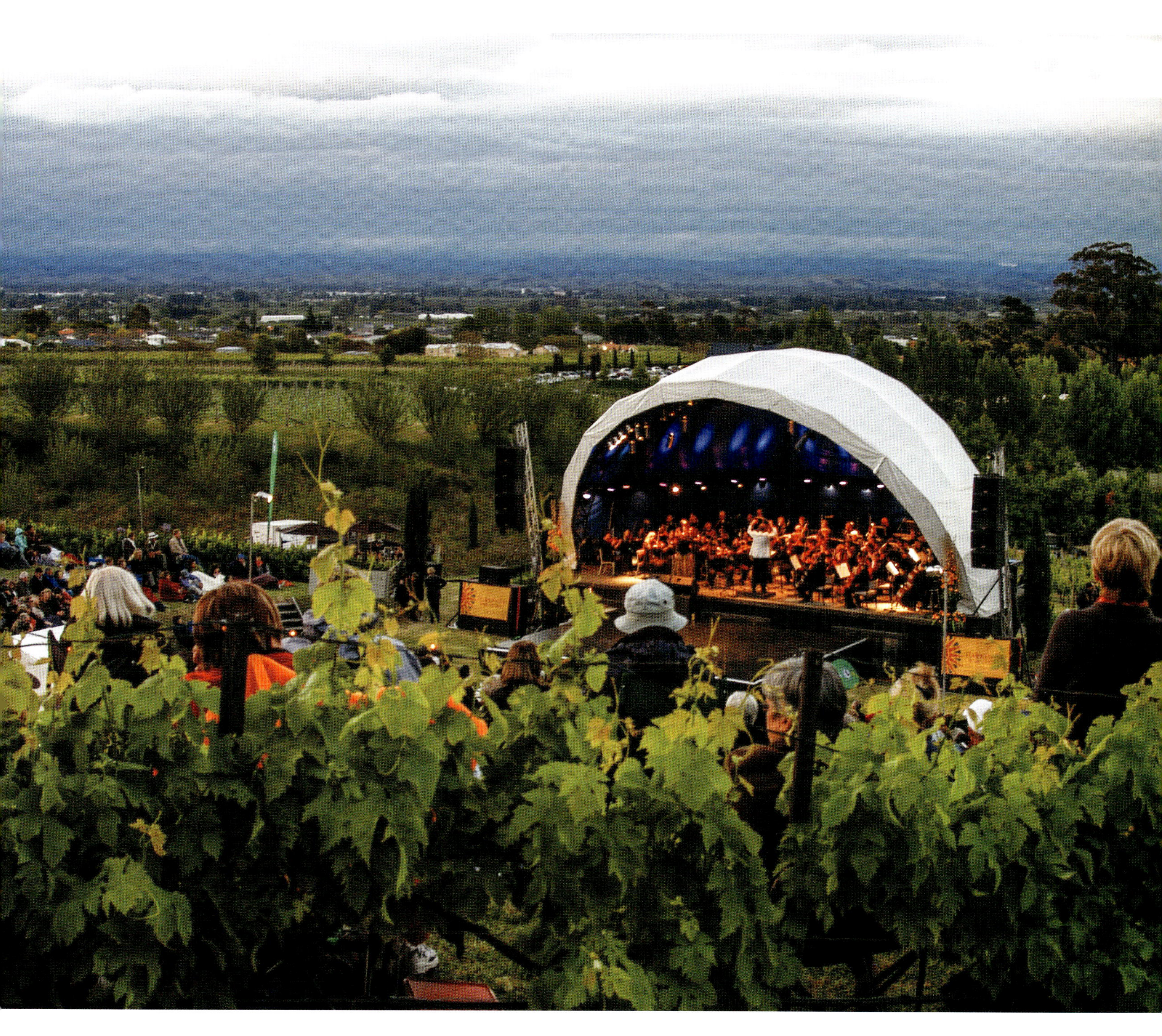

PORTRAIT OF OUR GATHERINGS

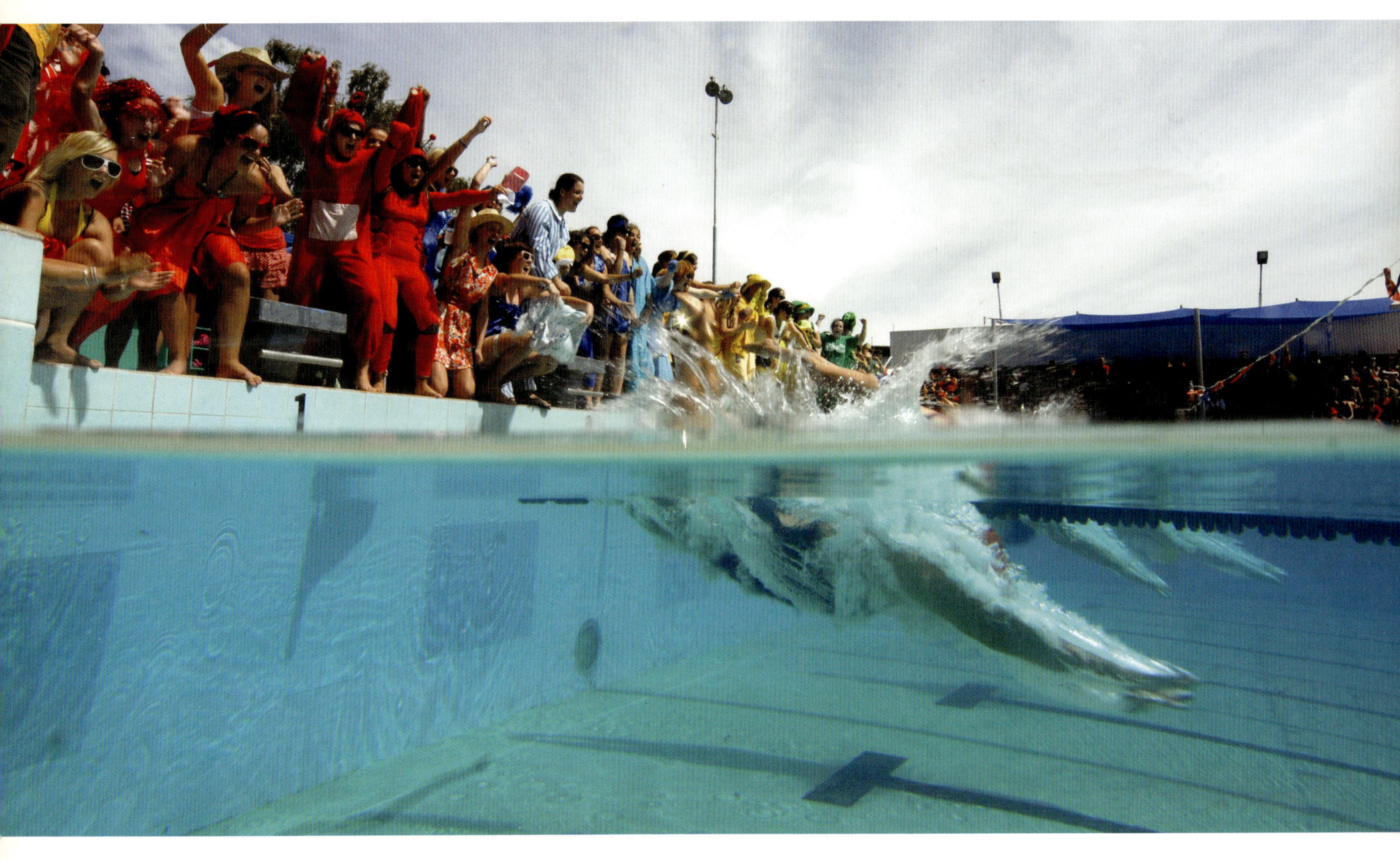

 Swimming sports, Napier Girls' High School

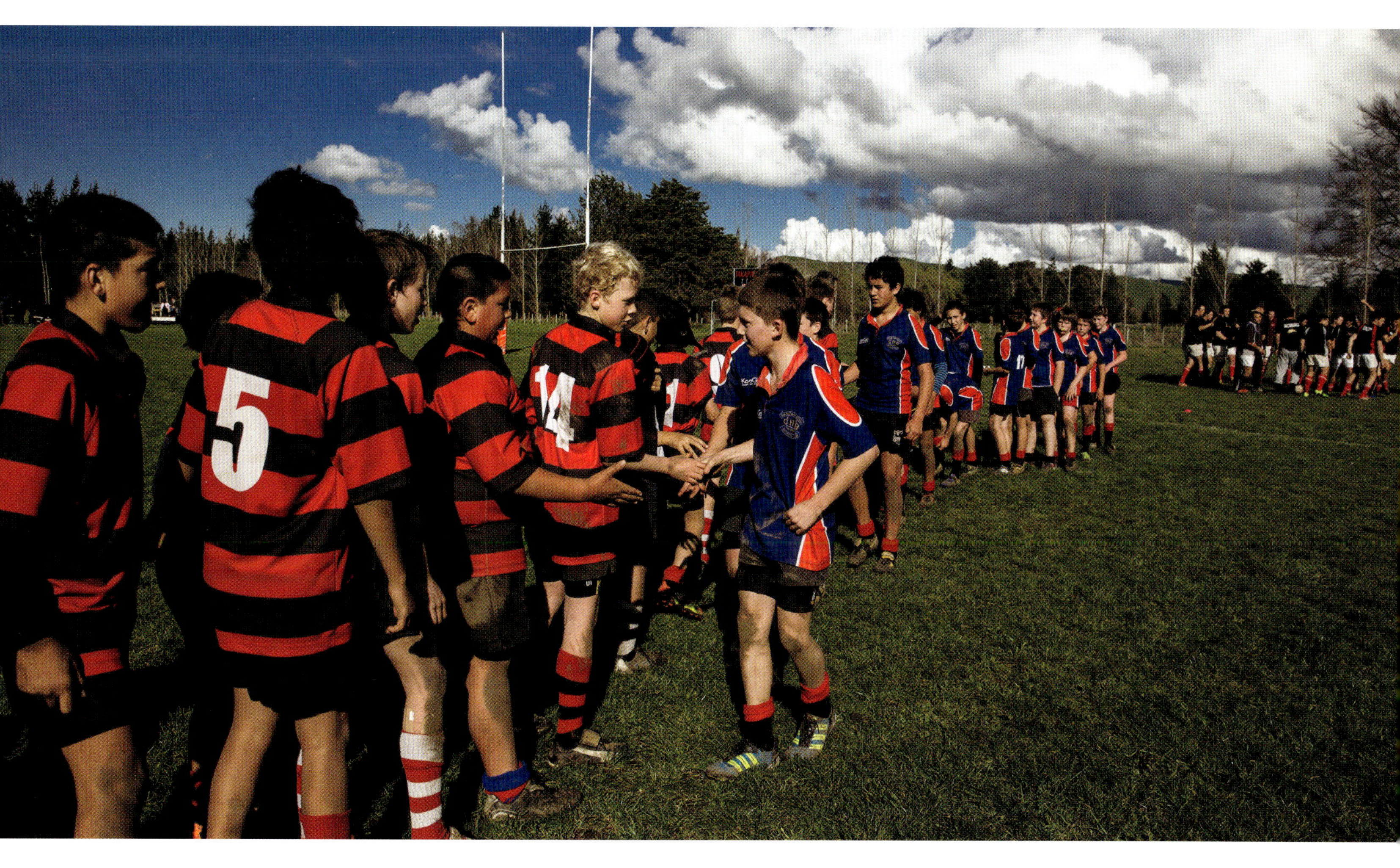

Grass roots rugby, Takapau, Central Hawke's Bay

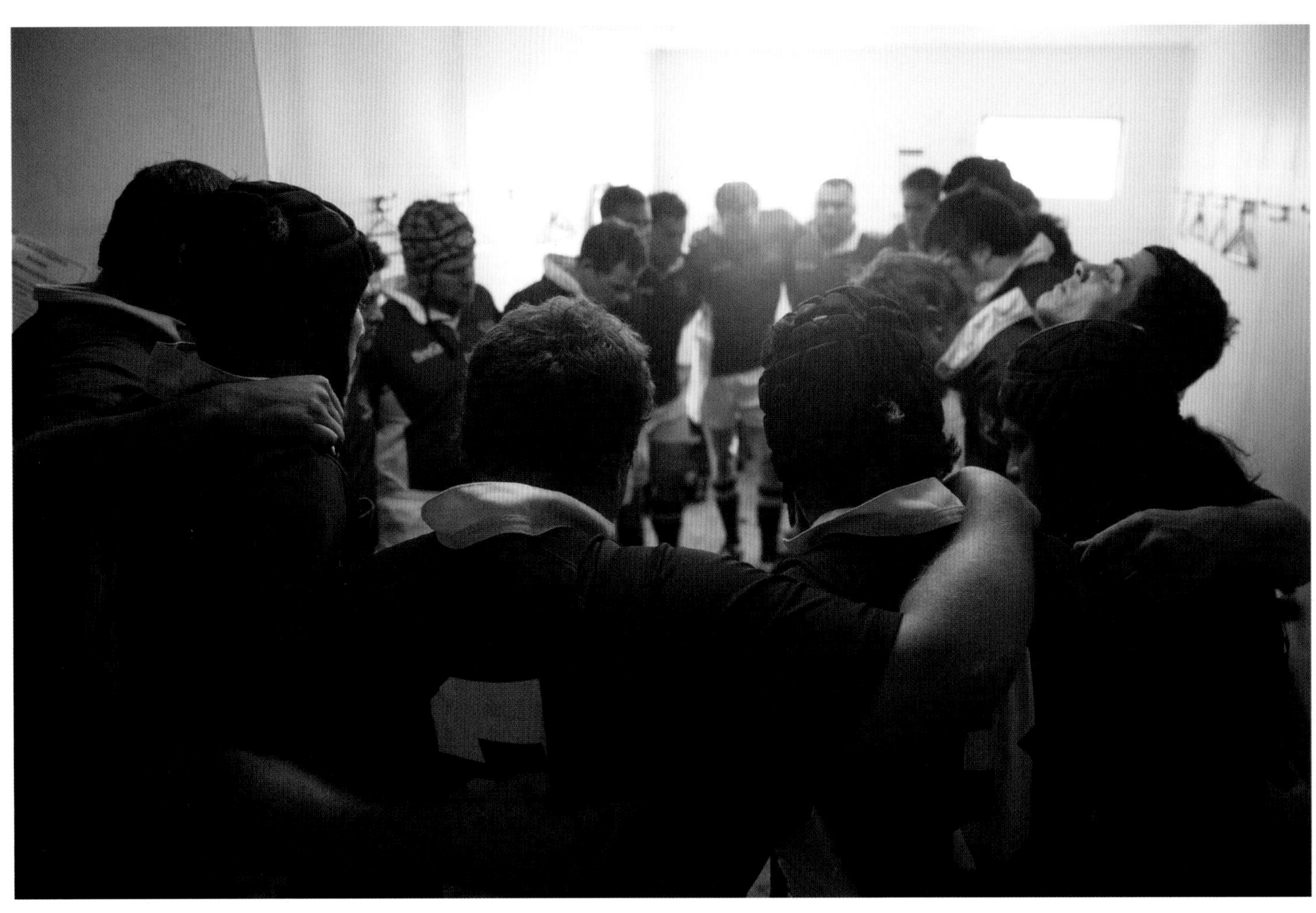

 Pre-game team talk, Takapau, Central Hawke's Bay

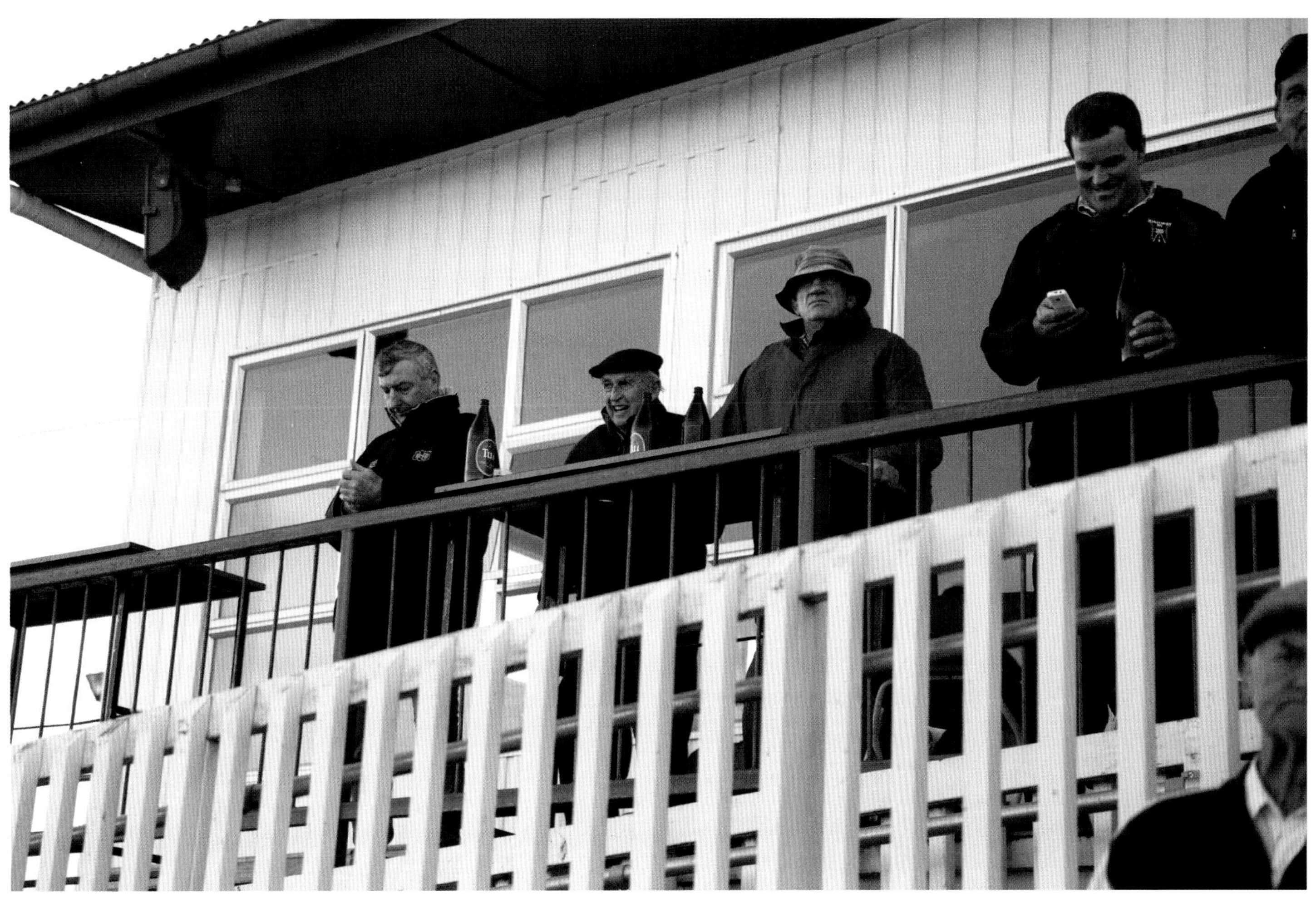

Supporters, Takapau Rugby Club, Central Hawke's Bay

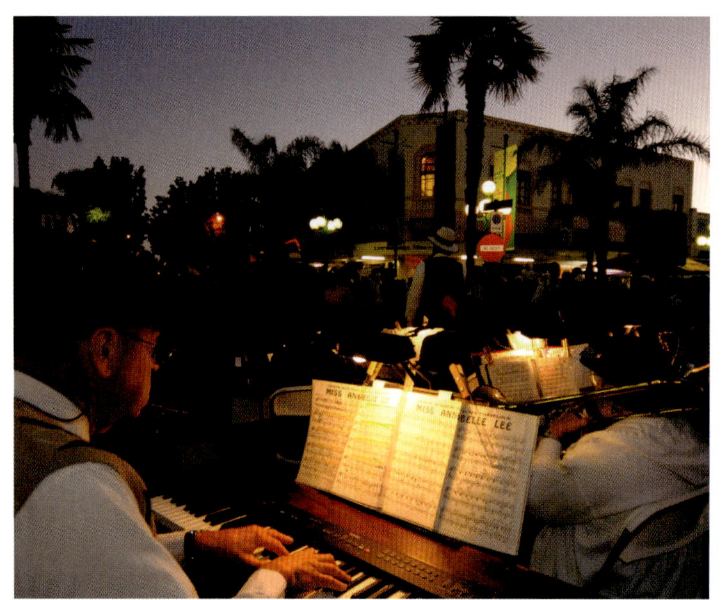

 Art Deco celebration, Marine Parade, Napier

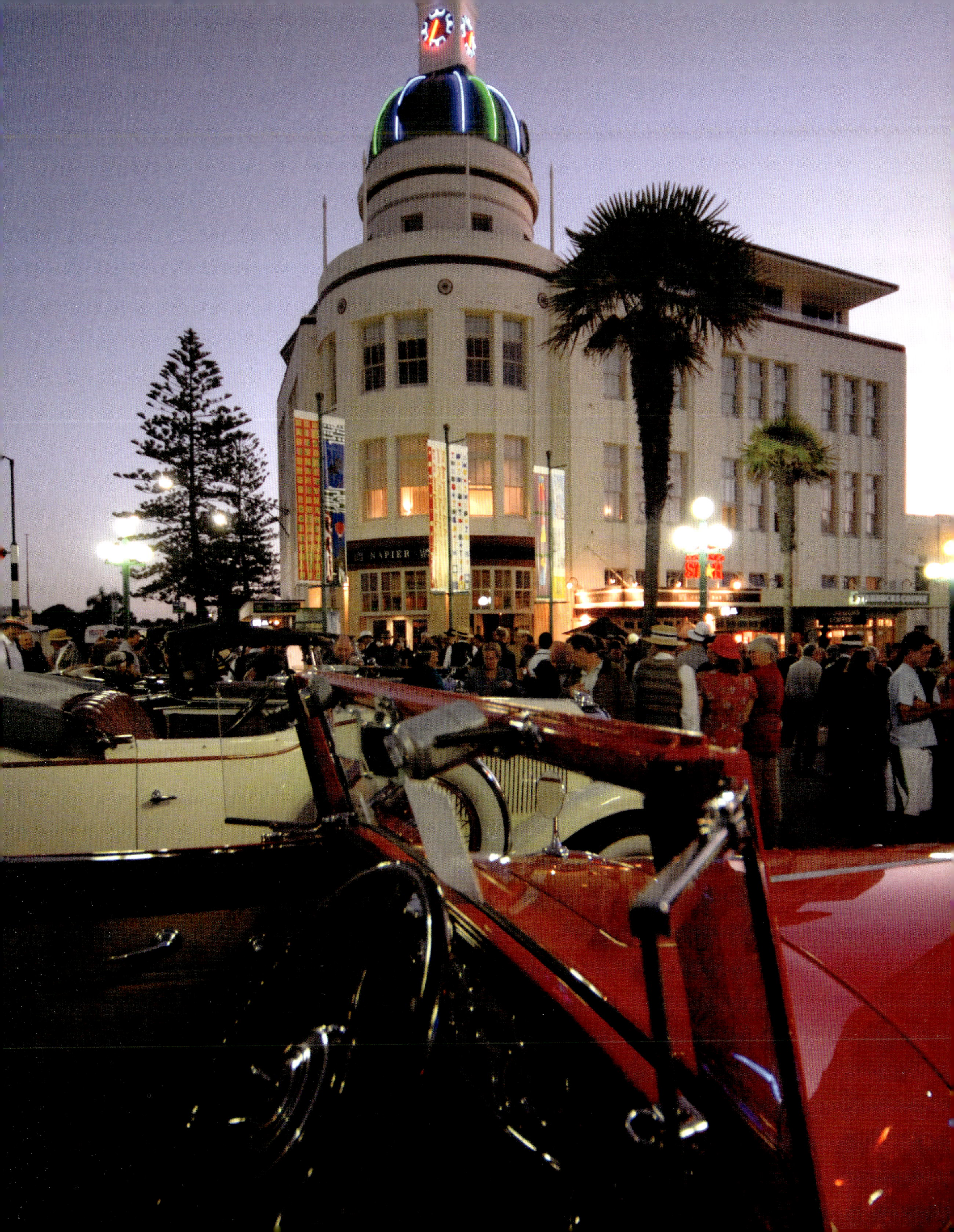
NAPIER

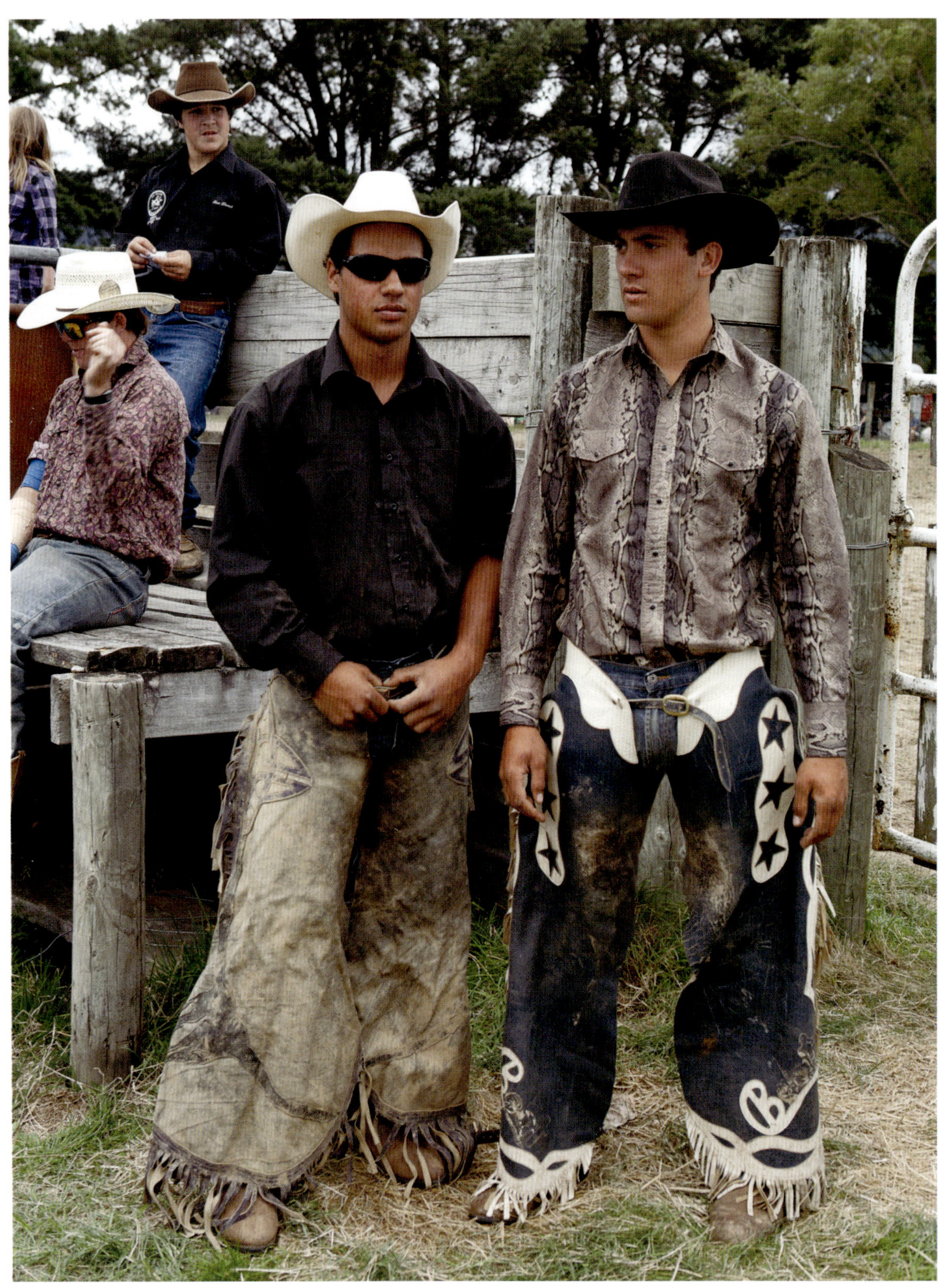

 Cowboys, Mohaka Rodeo, Northern Hawke's Bay

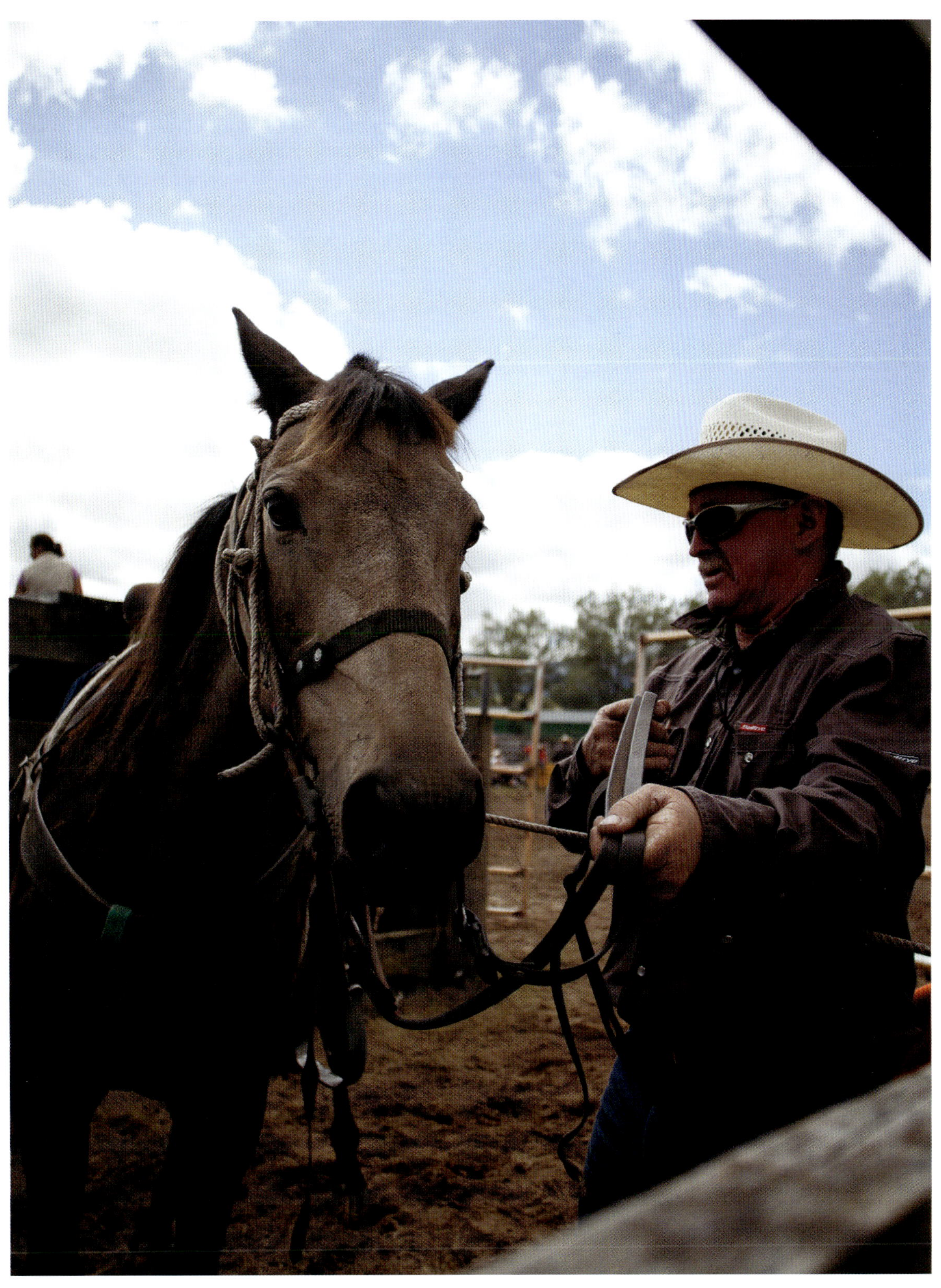

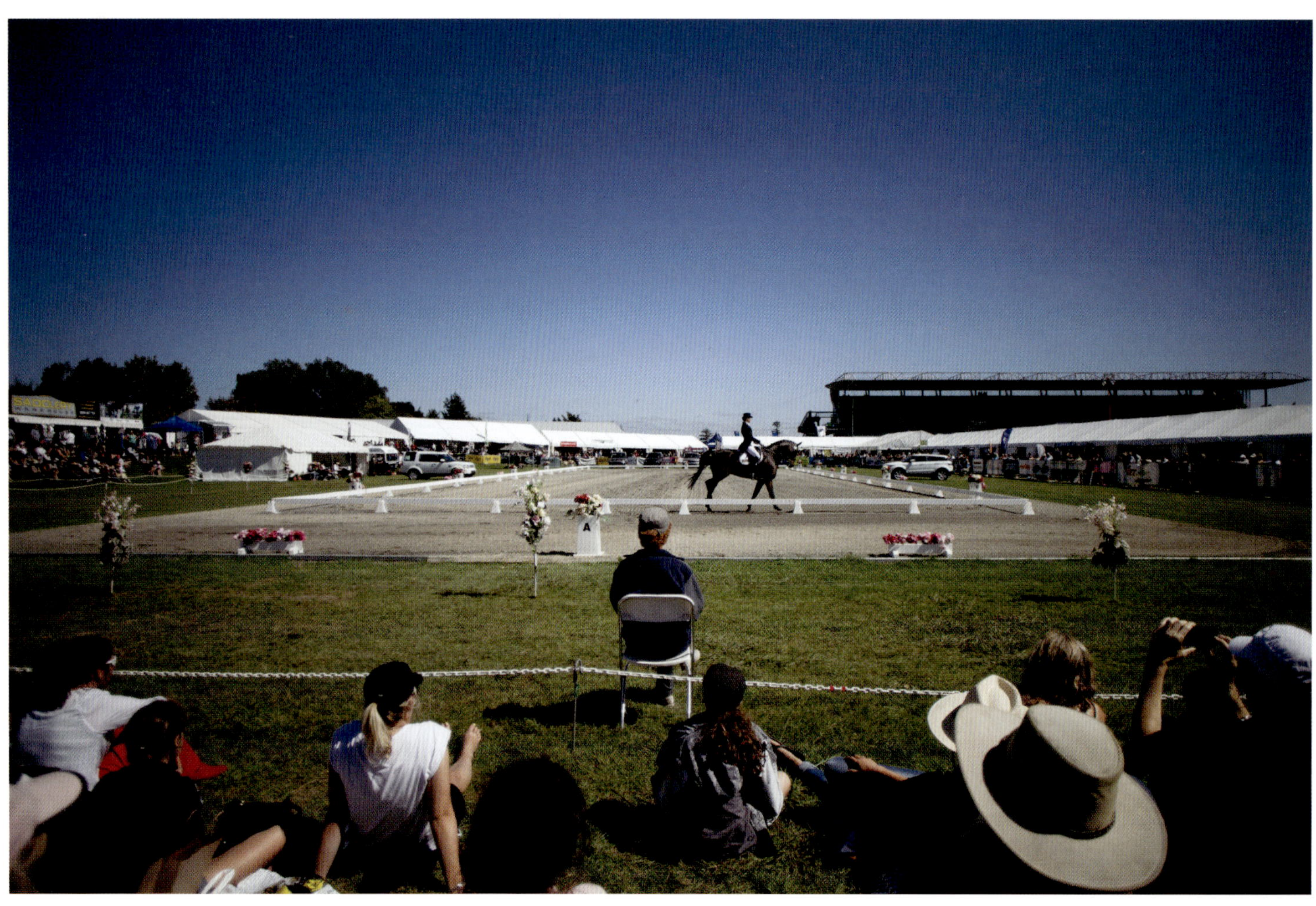

 Competing at Horse of the Year, Showgrounds Hawke's Bay, Hastings

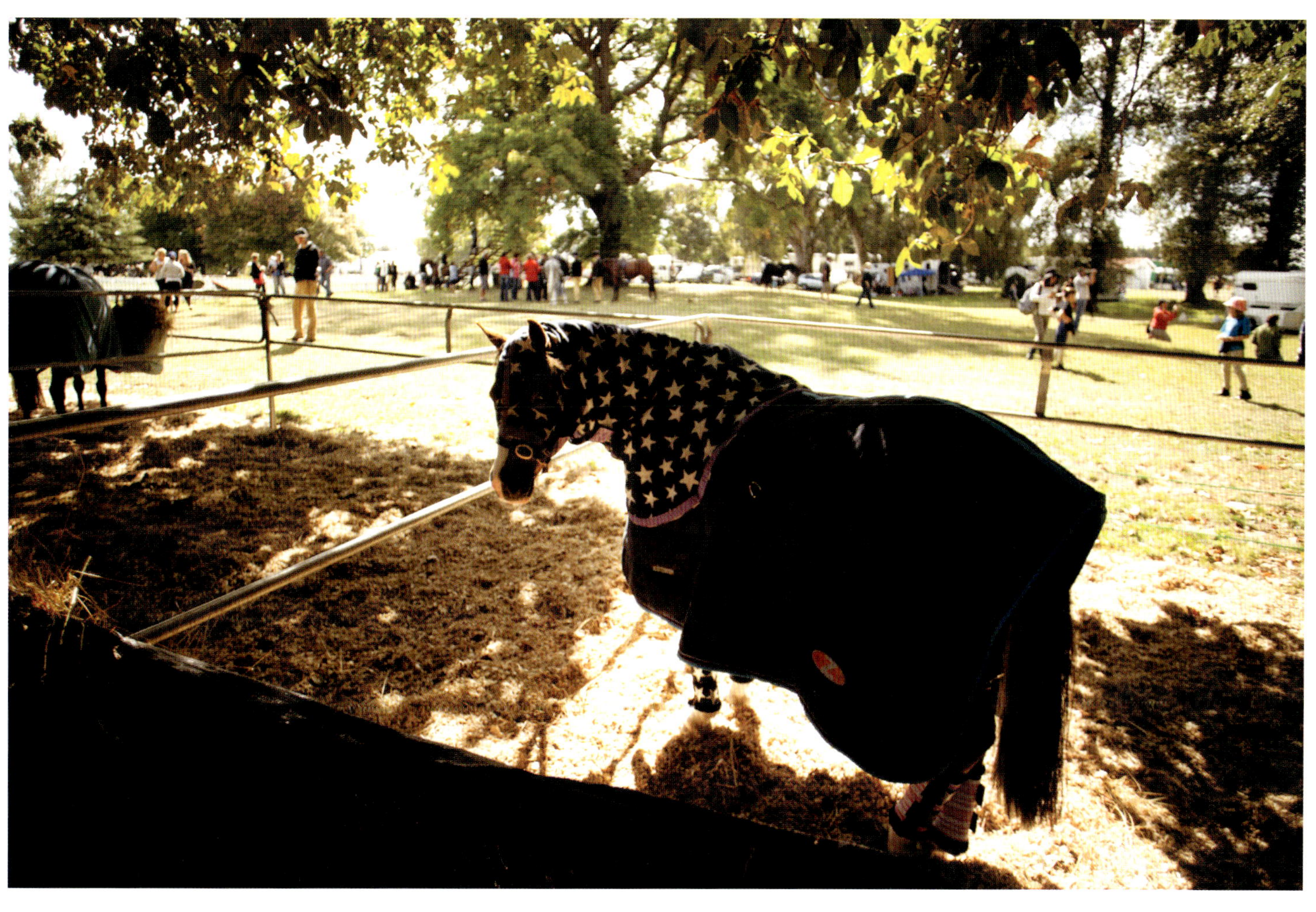

Resting, Horse of the Year, Showgrounds Hawke's Bay, Hastings

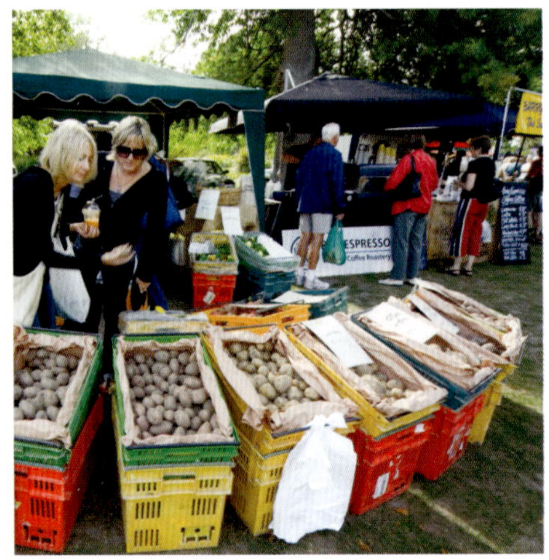
ESPRESSO

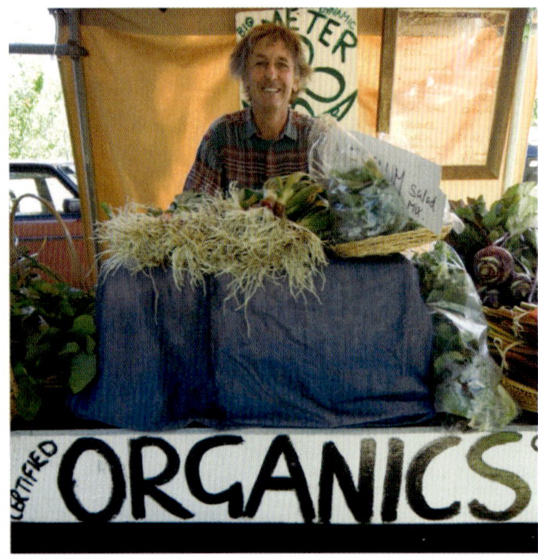
ORGANICS

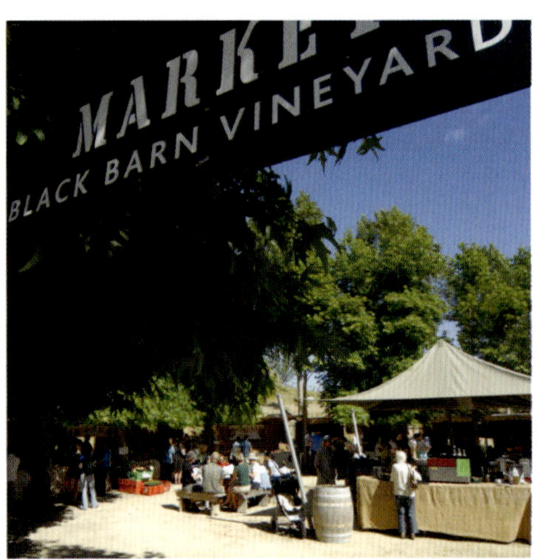
BLACK BARN VINEYARD

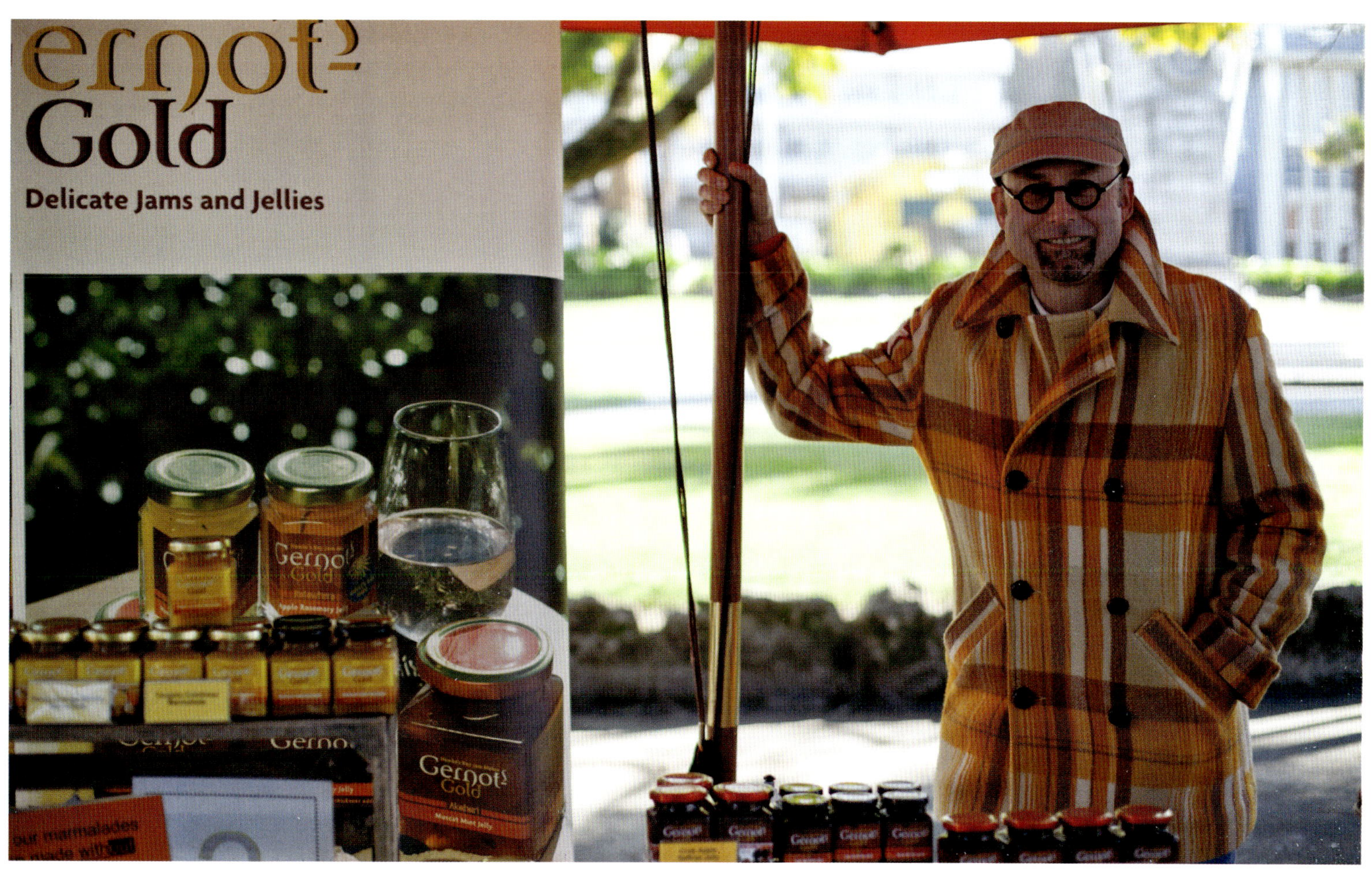

Gernot Göex, Napier Urban Street Market, Clive Square, Napier

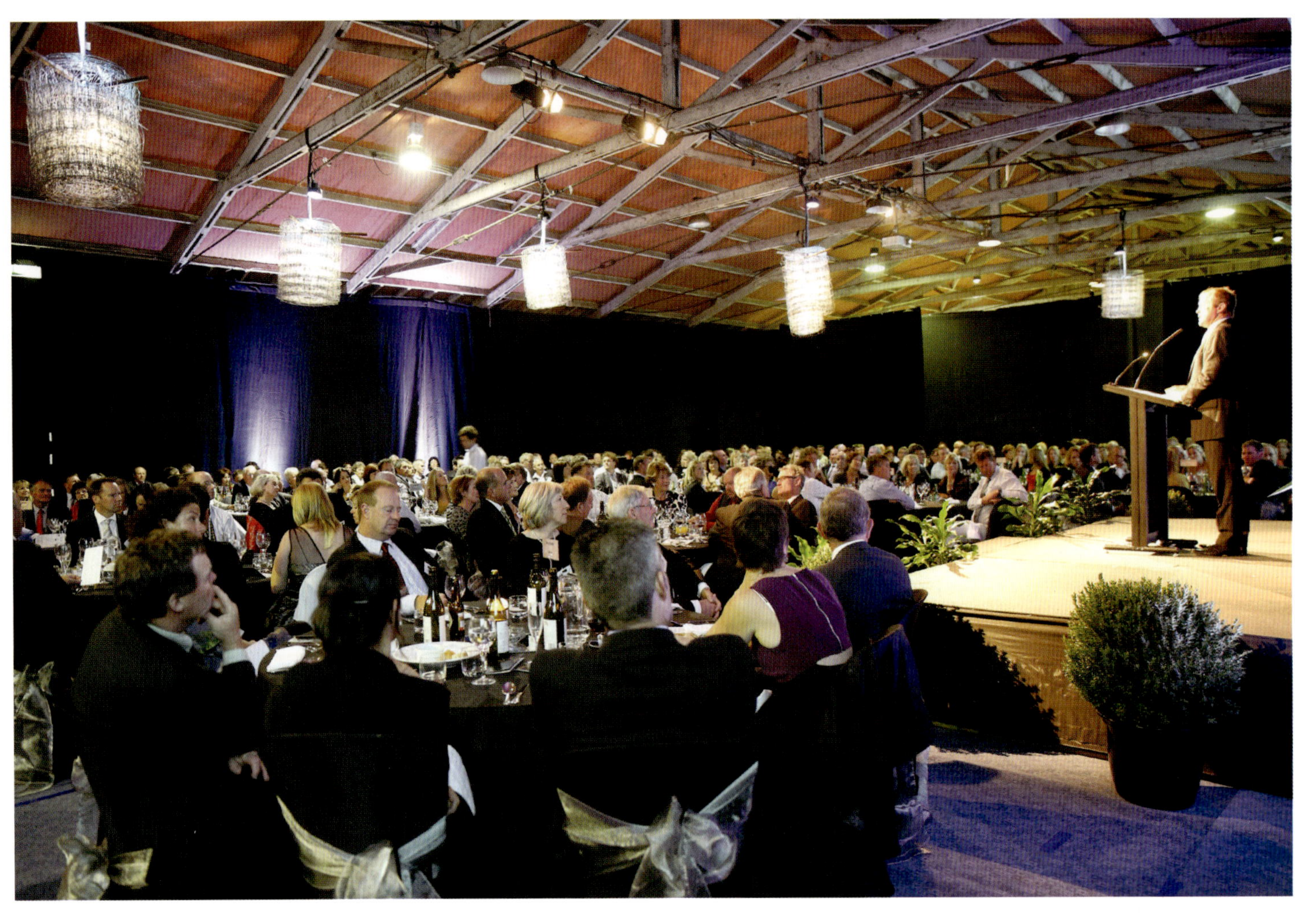

 Hawke's Bay Farmer of the Year Gala Awards Dinner, Showgrounds Hawke's Bay, Hastings

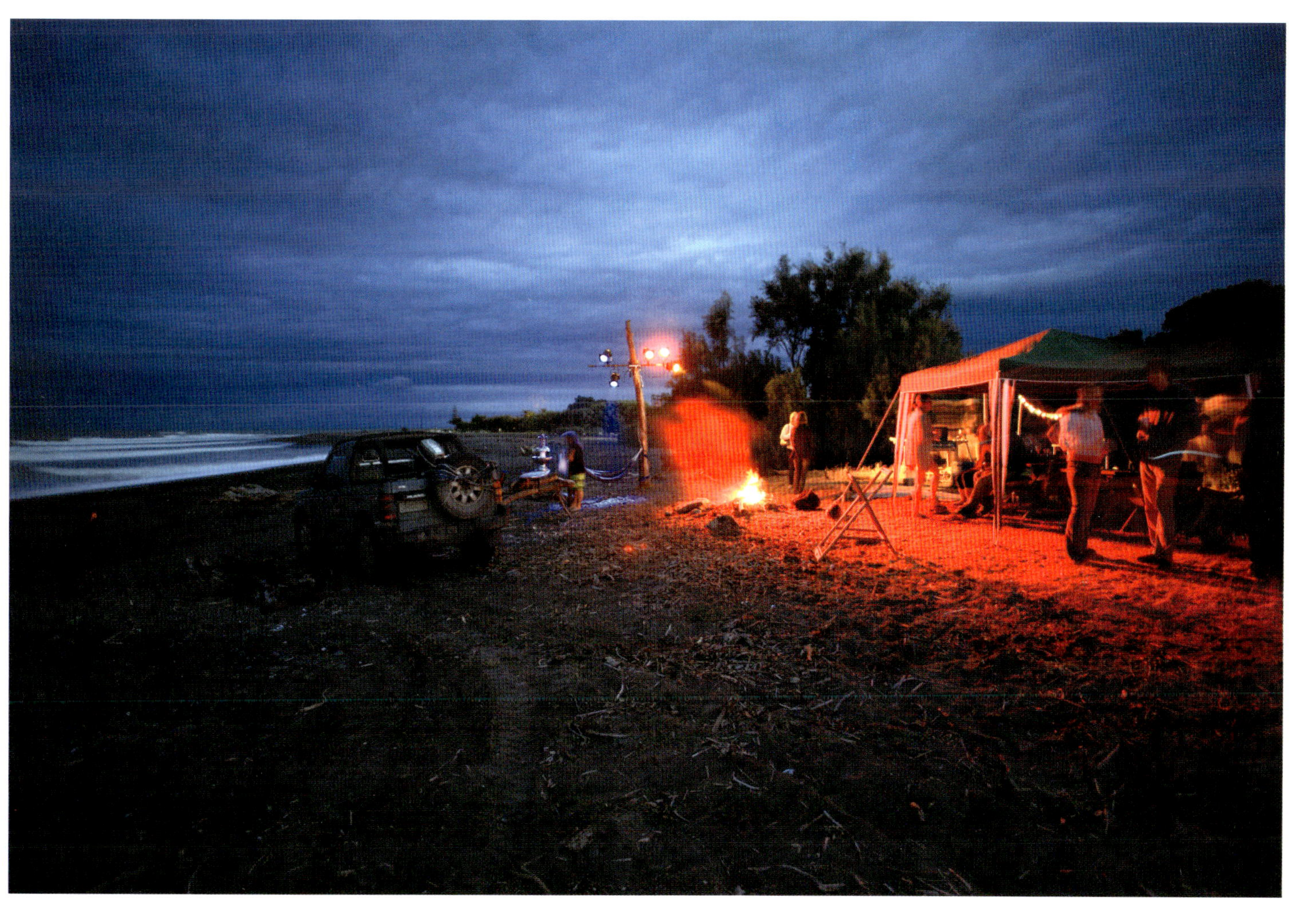

Issac McCormick's annual Christmas Eve beach party, Te Awanga

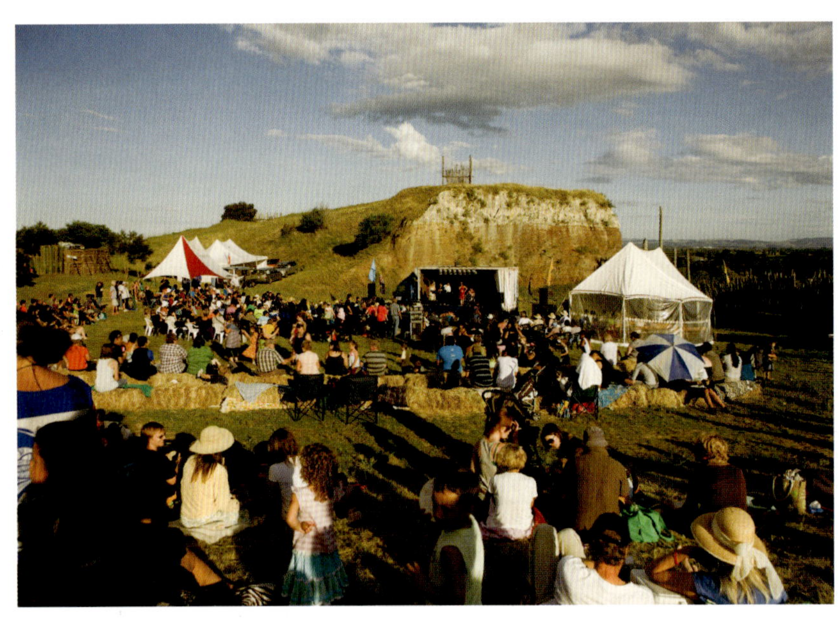

 Māori Motown, Ngati Paarau entertain at Te Atamira Otatara, Waiohiki, Taradale

Facing Page: Crowds enjoying the annual Mission Concert 2012, Mission Estate Winery, Taradale

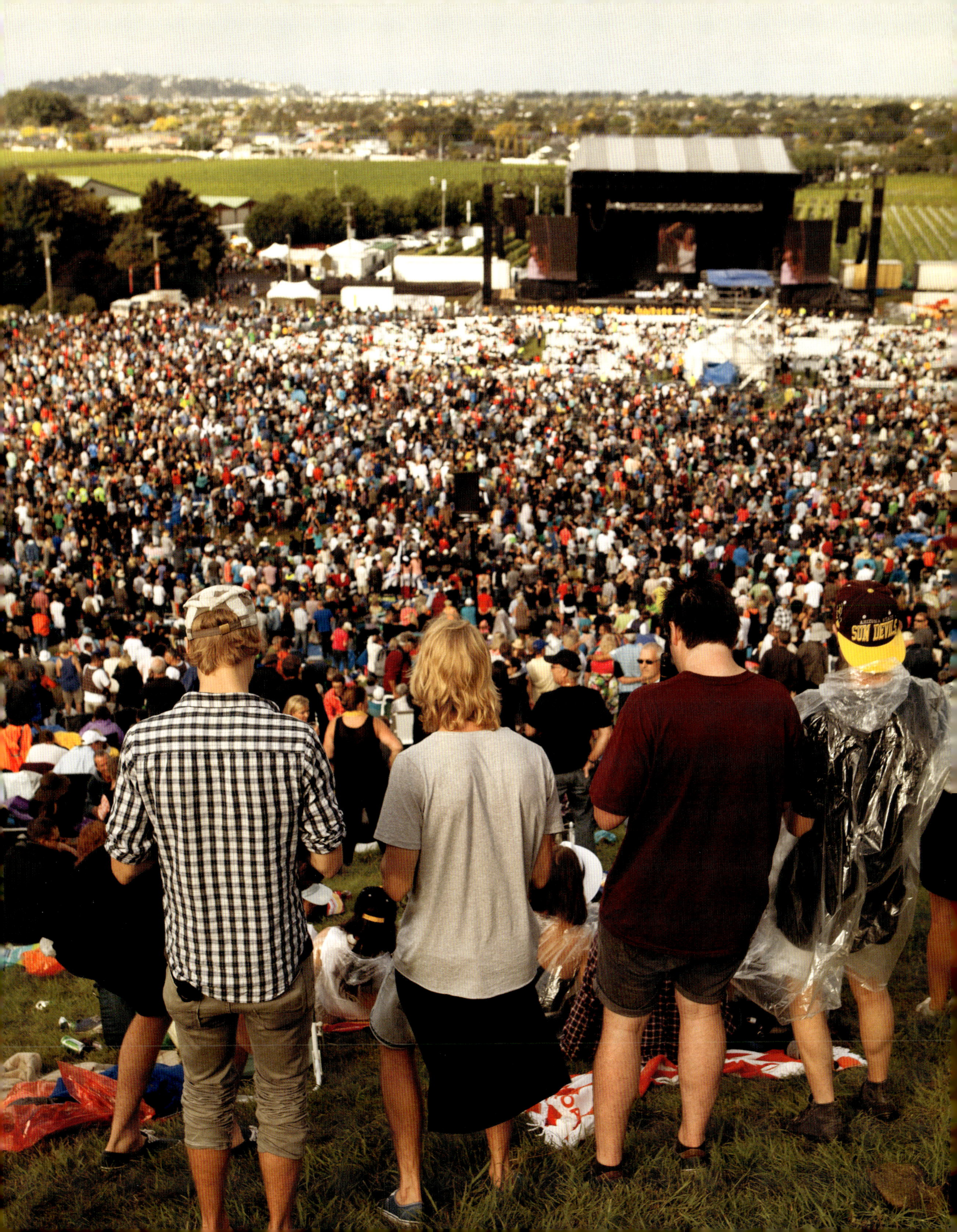
SUN DEVILS

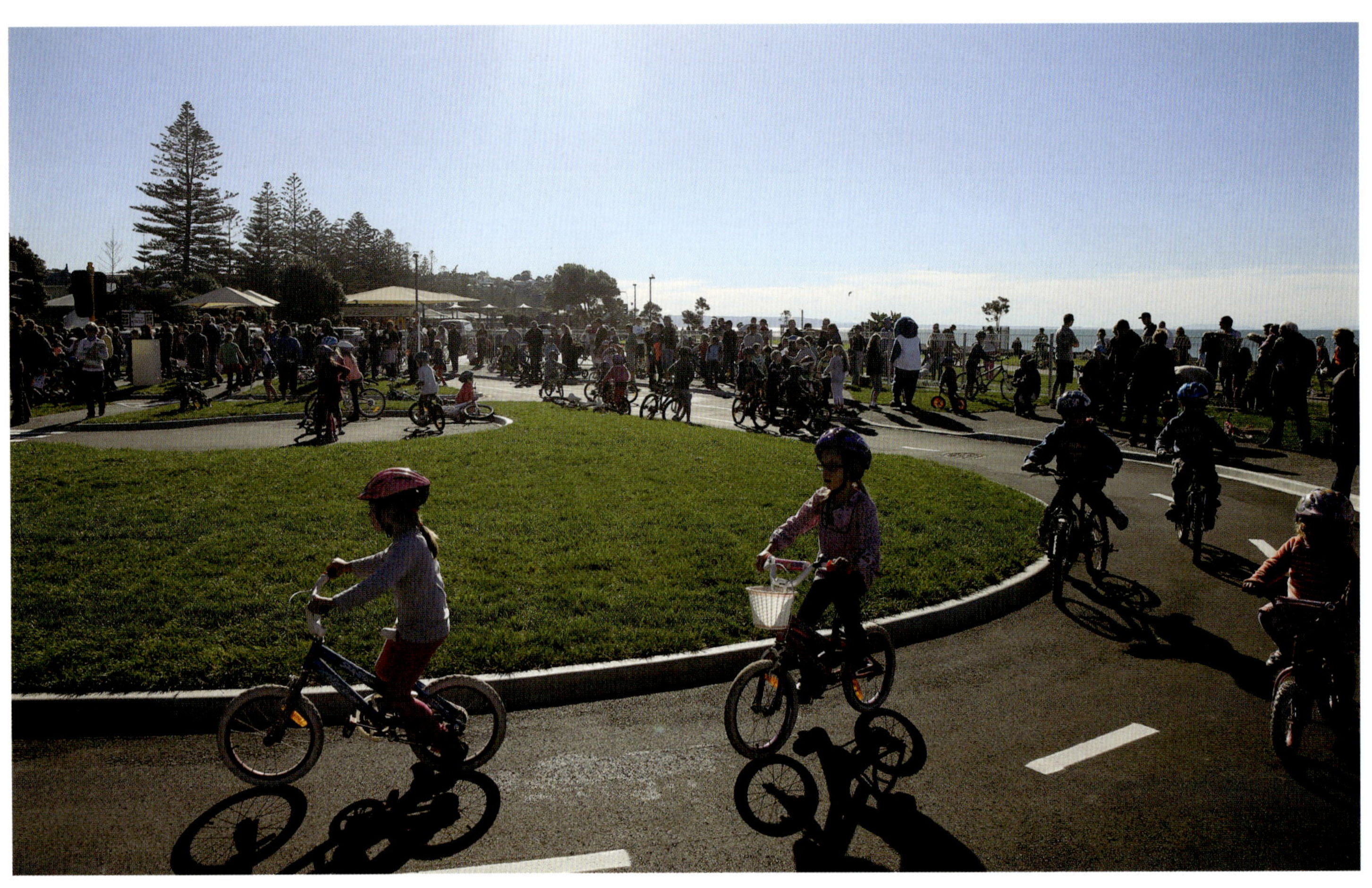

 Opening day at the Junior Bike Track, Marine Parade, Napier, 2013

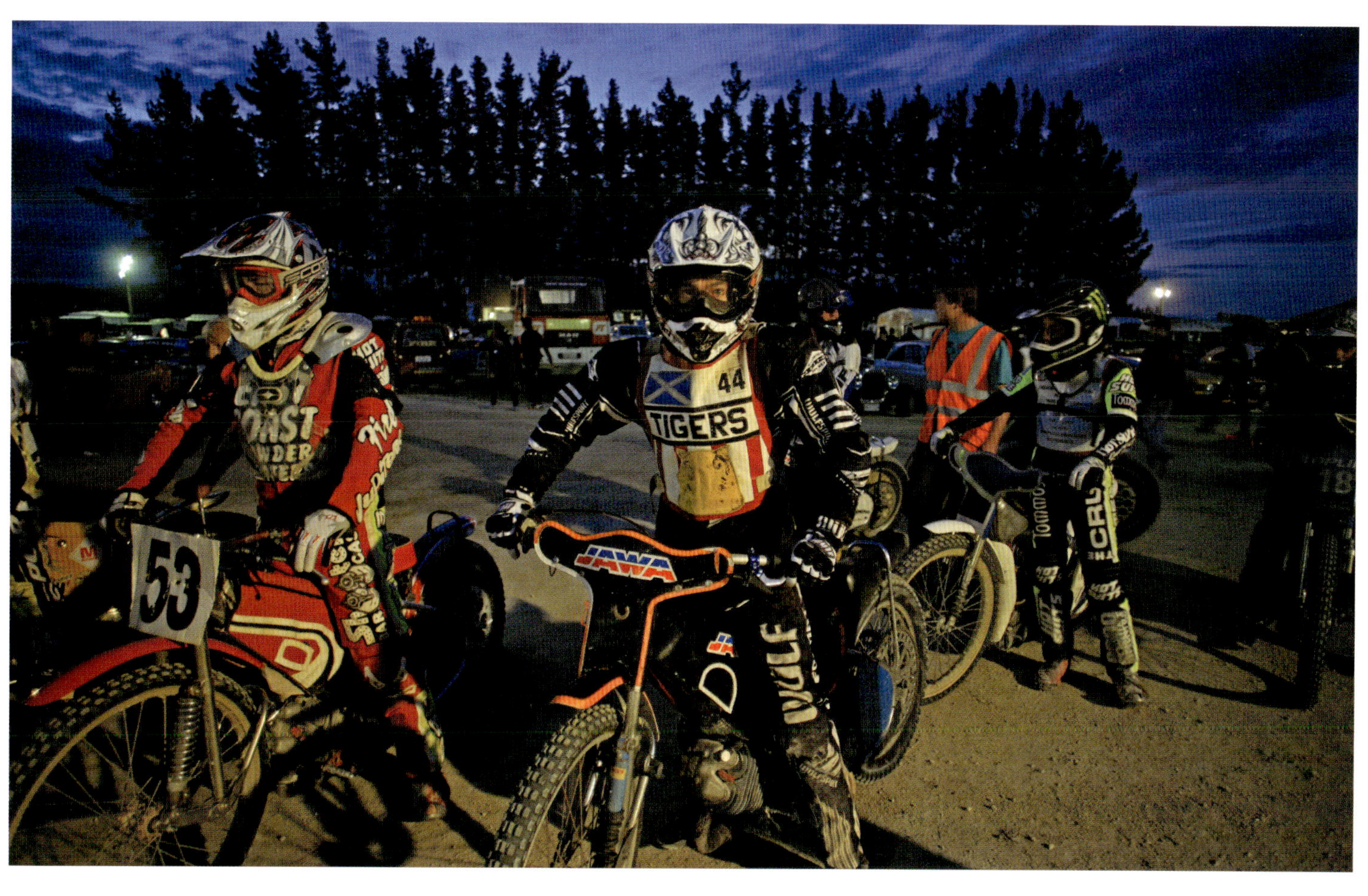

Speedway bikes at the Meeanee Speedway, Meeanee, Napier

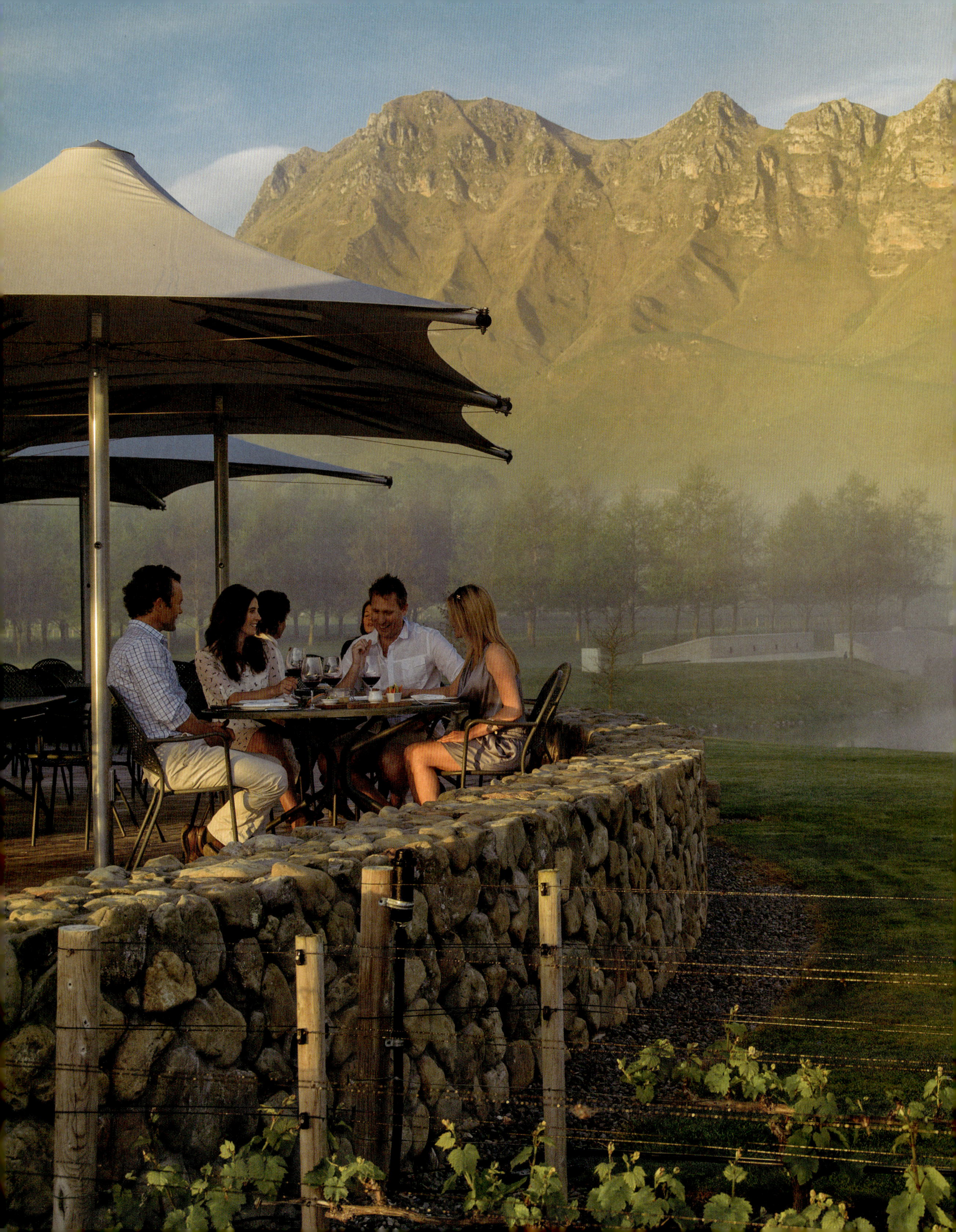

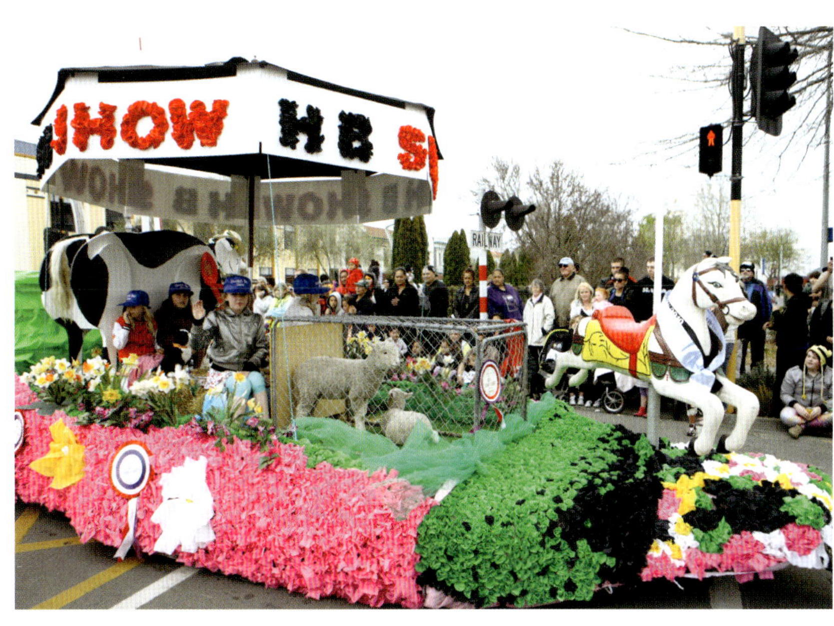

Annual Spring Blossom Parade, Hastings

Facing page: Outdoor dining Terrôir Restaurant, Craggy Range Winery, Havelock North

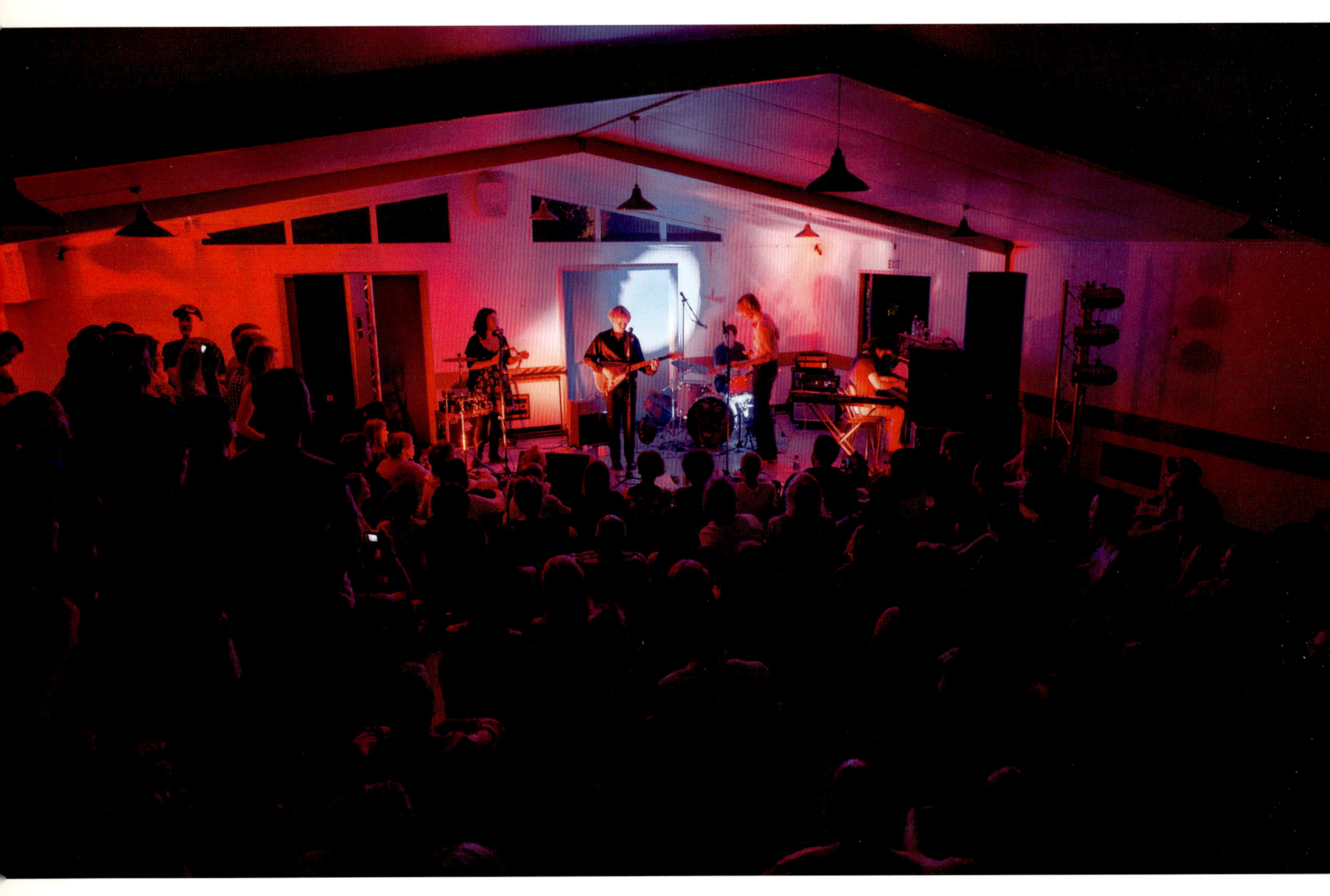

152 'BARB' performing at Te Awanga Hall

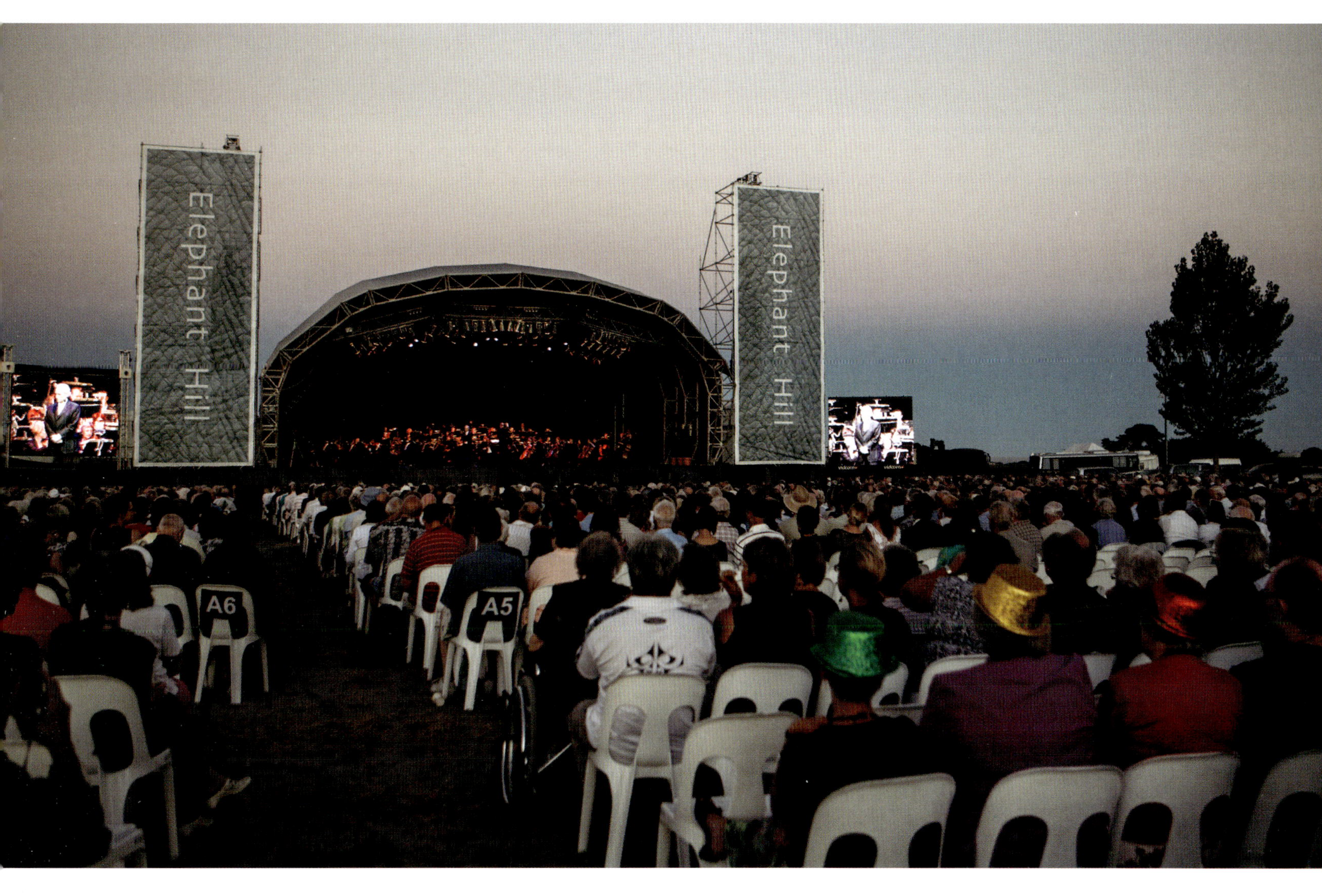

José Carreras performing at the opening of Elephant Hill Winery

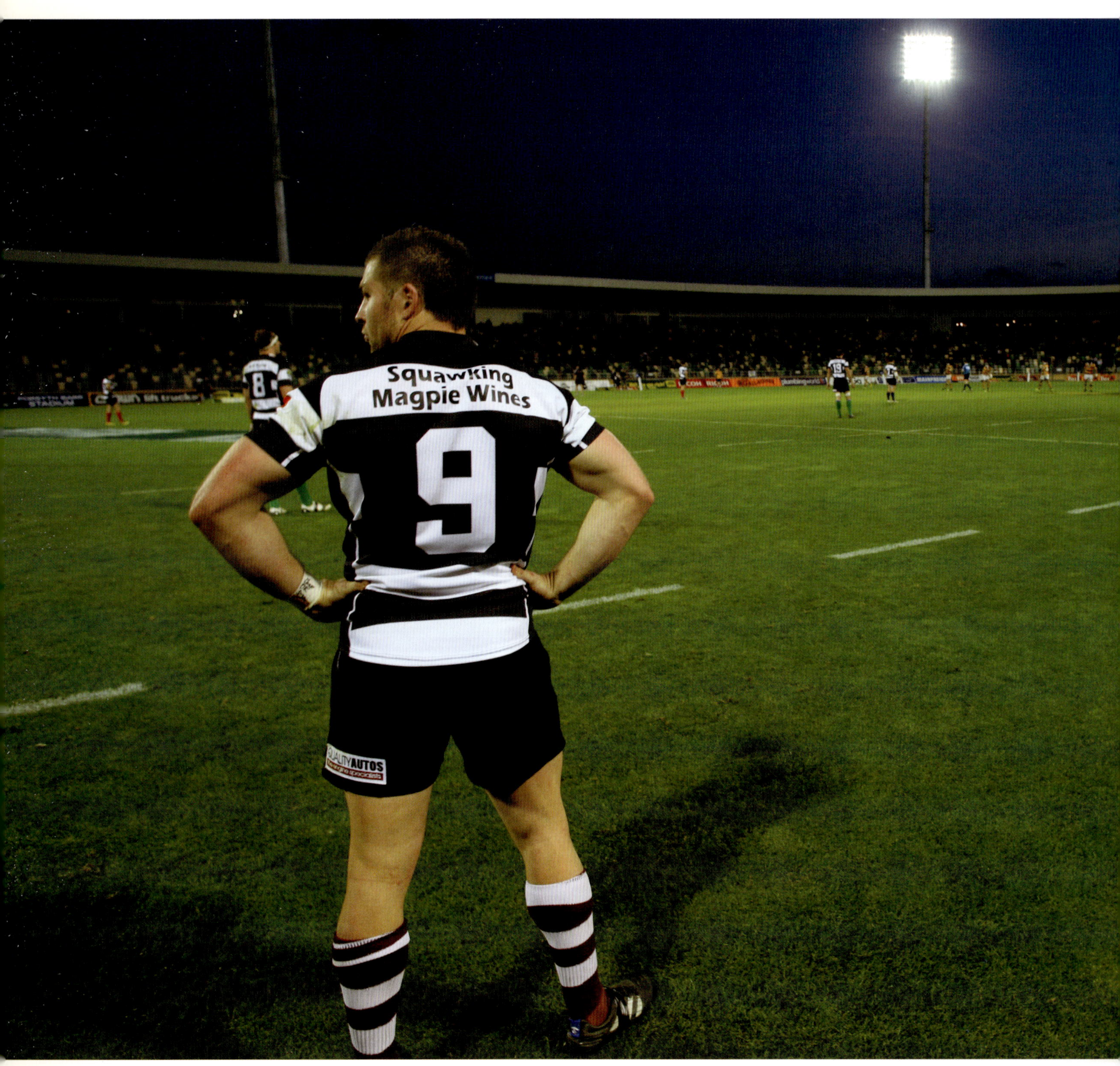

Hawke's Bay 'Magpies' playing rugby at McLean Park, Napier

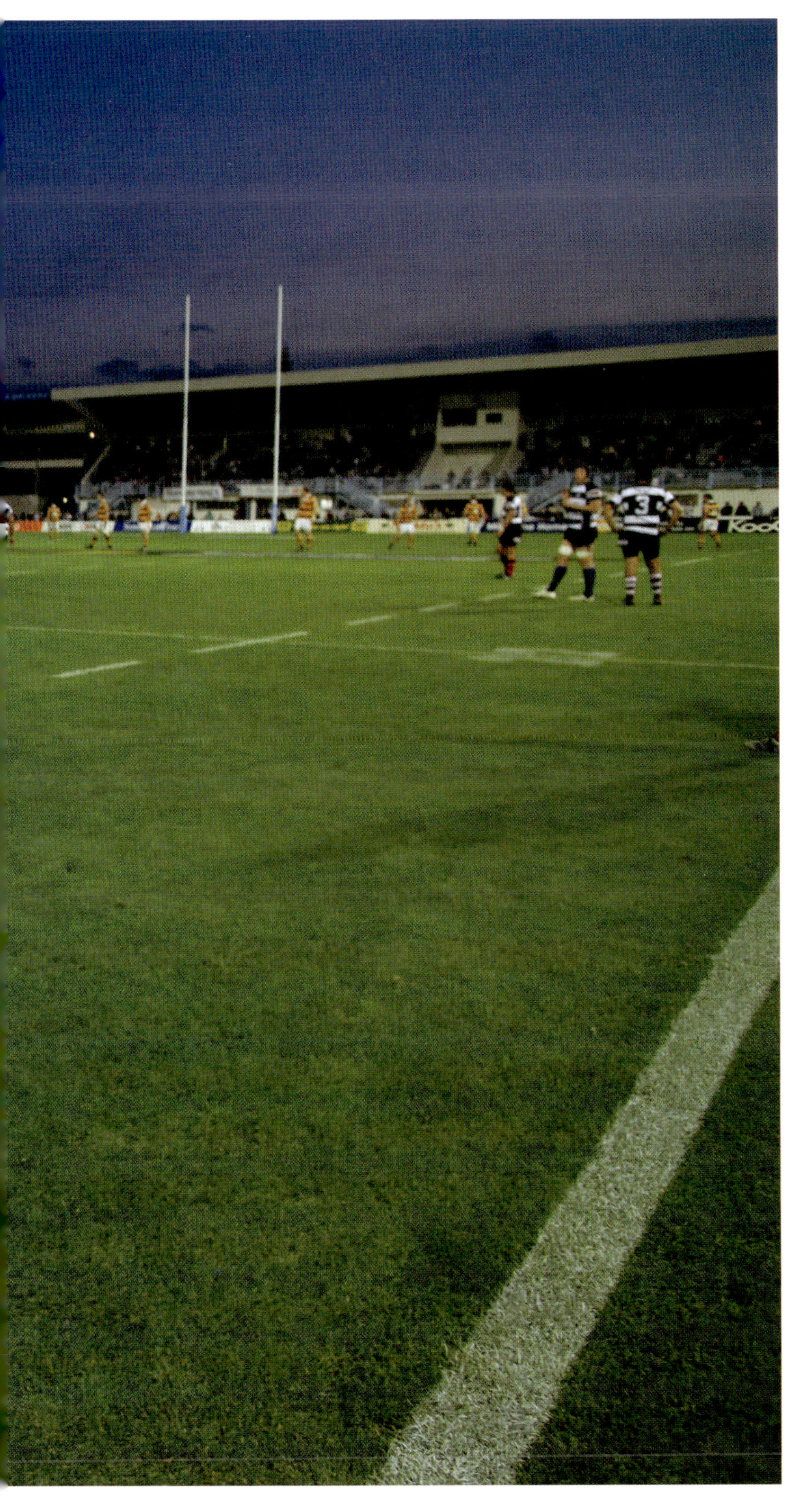

SINCERE THANKS TO OUR SPONSORS

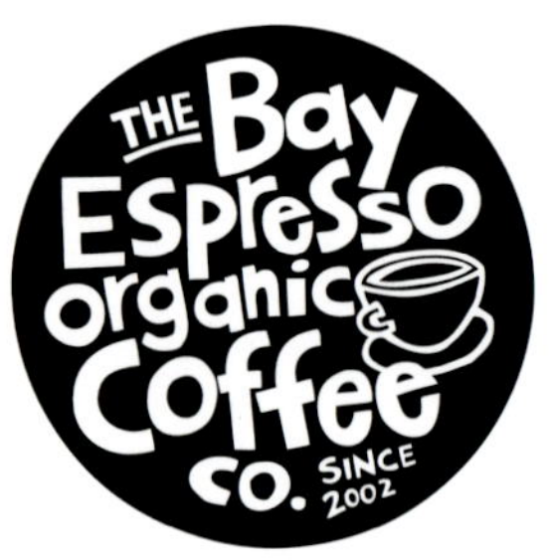

Wow! What an amazing book to be a part of. The creators of this book came to us looking for support from 'iconic' Hawke's Bay businesses. We didn't know we had made it to iconic, but it is something we set out to be nine years ago. We bought a run down café and a fledgling coffee roasting company, with a tiny custom-built coffee roaster. It was our vision to create a brand of coffee and a café for the people of Hawke's Bay. We wanted a place that reflected who our locals were and where they wanted to go. And now, with eight cafes in our group and our third upgrade of coffee roasters, we might have done it.

Thank you so much to the people of Hawke's Bay for your ongoing support and coffee drinking. We wouldn't be here without you! We hope you continue to love our organic coffee and the locations we create to drink it in. And thank you to Cranford Hospice for their support of our community in our times of need. This is a great initiative and well done to everyone involved. Hawke's Bay is such a beautiful place to live and a place where dreams still can come true, it is definitely a place worth celebrating!

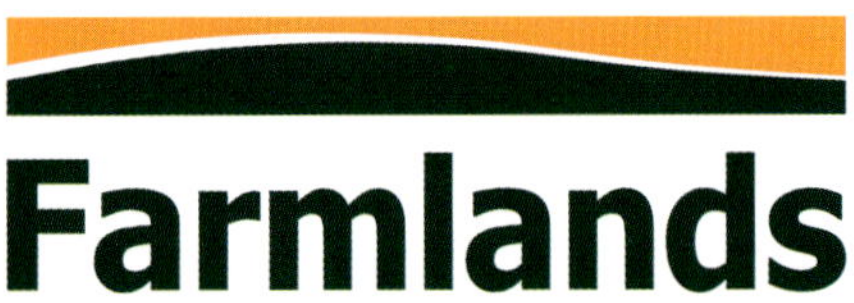

Farmlands Co-operative Society Limited was formed in Hawke's Bay more than 50 years ago by farmers, for farmers. Originally a way for farmers to avoid a rural trader monopoly, today Farmlands is one of New Zealand's most trusted companies. The Co-operative has diversified into everything from finance to fuel, across nine divisions, giving its rural shareholders unprecedented coverage in its quest to ensure the best prices.

Farmlands prides itself on being part of the local community it operates in and we feel honoured to be involved with such a deserving community institution as Cranford Hospice.

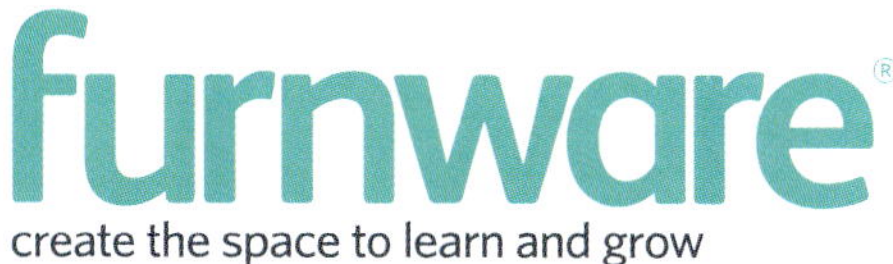

Furnware Ltd is proud and excited to be playing a part in making this book possible, celebrating Hawke's Bay and supporting the important work of Cranford Hospice.

We started out in humble beginnings in 1934 and over time have grown to become the biggest supplier of school furniture to New Zealand schools. The relationships we now have both here in Hawke's Bay and throughout the world have allowed us to become a world class research and development company.

We value Richard Brimer as a leading Hawke's Bay photographer whose relationship with Furnware includes Richard's late father managing Furnware for ten years during its early days. Our connection to Richard, Cranford and our community encapsulates our motivation to be involved in this project.

Like Cranford, we also have a long history with Hawke's Bay and aspire to be an authentic and passionate part of this community. We are committed to investing back to help make this region an even better place to live and work. Hawke's Bay offers a vibrant, multi-cultural lifestyle that is globally recognised, largely due to the spirit and passion of the people that choose to live here.

Cranford Hospice makes such a huge contribution to this community and we are proud to be involved in this project supporting such a valued organisation.

SINCERE THANKS TO OUR SPONSORS

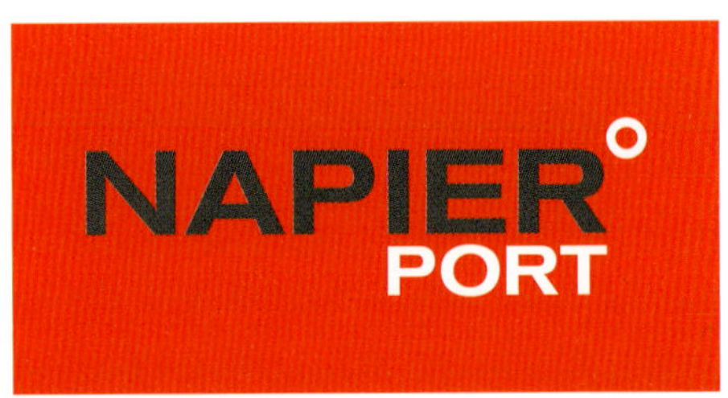

Richard's commercial photography skills are well documented, having worked with Napier Port for some time. When the motivation for 'Hawke's Bay — Portrait of a Province' was explained to us, it was an easy decision to support the project, particularly as the beneficiary is Cranford Hospice. When one thinks of Cranford and their important role in the community there can be few organisations that are more deserving of our collective assistance. We wish all involved every success.

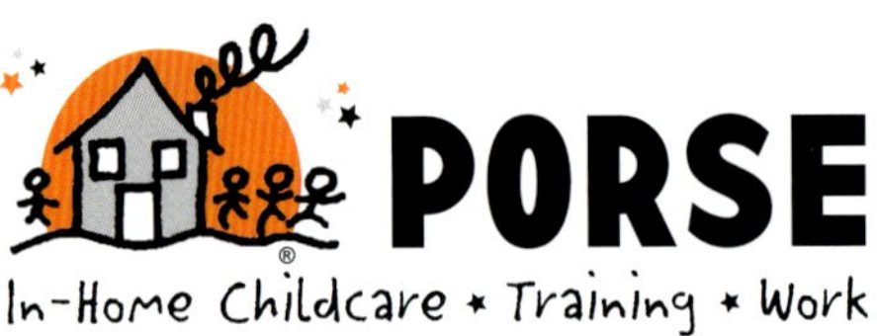

PORSE is honoured to be supporting Cranford Hospice and photographer Richard Brimer who has captured his intimate appreciation of life and living in Hawke's Bay through his camera lens.

We all live with the expectation of maintaining good health. It's not until our health is challenged that life can change in a heartbeat and living can become a moment-by-moment marathon. PORSE is forever inspired by people who choose to help others during vulnerable times in life. Understanding Richard's personal story makes this book even more poignant for the people of Hawke's Bay who find comfort in Cranford Hospice, a place where loving relationships and support matter the most.

Close relationships with love, trust and respect are so important in times of need when life becomes a daily, hour-by-hour challenge. We discover that connections with people and our environment are vital.

PORSE works closely with communities throughout New Zealand focusing on wellbeing and nurturing relationships between little people and big people in our journey to expand the hearts and minds of a nation.

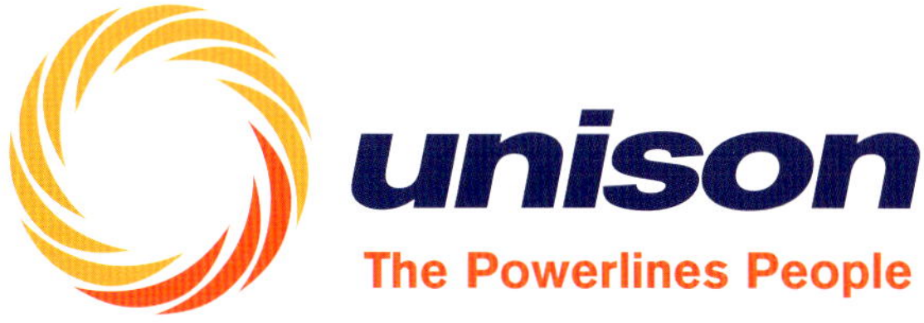

Unison has been part of the Hawke's Bay community for over 80 years, through supplying electricity to thousands of homes and businesses.

Cranford Hospice is an integral part of our community and Unison, as an essential service provider, plays an important role in supporting Cranford and its patients.

Unison is proud and humbled to be associated with such an organisation, which directly benefits the lives of so many – from those directly affected, to their families and friends.

'Hawke's Bay – Portrait of a Province' is an excellent vehicle for generating support for Cranford, whilst showcasing many of the reasons we all love living and working in Hawke's Bay.

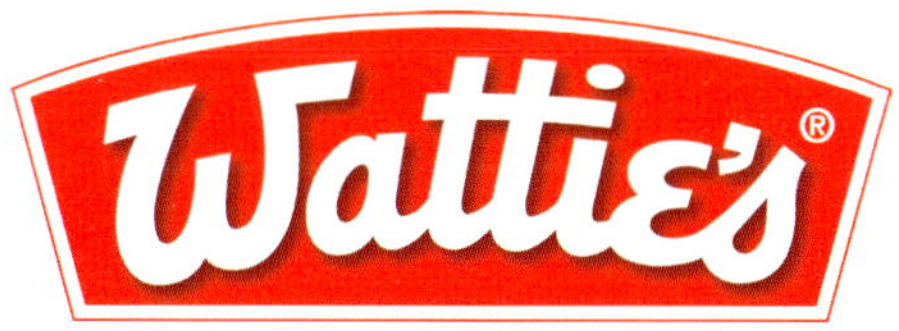

Wattie's is proud to be one of the sponsors of the 'Hawkes Bay — Portrait of a Province' book project for Cranford Hospice.

As a Hawke's Bay business who has been around since 1934 we have been a big part of the local community for a long time. Cranford Hospice has touched the lives of so many Watties' employees and their families over the years and we are in admiration of the part they play in our community.

We wish the book every success, as it so rightly deserves.

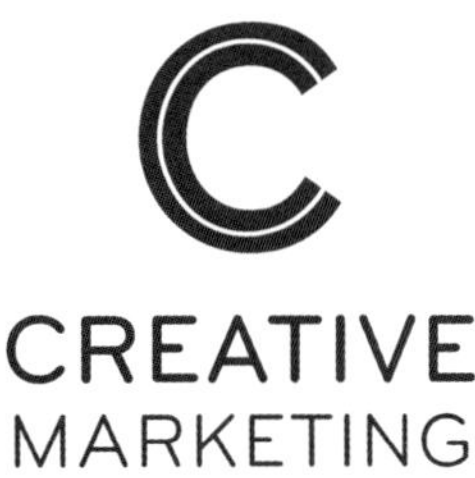

Creative Marketing is extremely proud to have initiated and project managed this fundraising opportunity for Cranford Hospice, from concept to printed publication.

Our huge gratitude goes to:

Our sponsor family who've made this project possible - you've been amazing to work with!
Richard Brimer for your photographic inspiration and your heartfelt commitment to this project.
Cranford Hospice for supporting the people of Hawke's Bay in their hour of need.
Hawke's Bay for being such a stunning region in every way.

And finally a sincere thank you to you. By purchasing this book you have supported Cranford Hospice.